Sermons and Battle Hymns
Protestant Popular Culture in Modern Scotland

Sermons and Battle Hymns

Protestant Popular Culture in Modern
Scotland

edited by
Graham Walker and Tom Gallagher

EDINBURGH UNIVERSITY PRESS

© Edinburgh University Press, 1990
22 George Square, Edinburgh

Distributed in North America
by Columbia University Press
New York

Set in Linotron Plantin
by Koinonia Ltd, Bury and
Printed in Great Britain by
The Alden Press Ltd, Oxford

British Library Cataloguing
  in Publication Data
Sermons and Battle Hymns.
    1. Scotland. Protestantism, history
    I. Walker, Graham II. Gallagher, Tom
    280.409411

ISBN 0 7486 0217 8

Contents

Notes on contributors

TOM GALLAGHER is Reader in Peace Studies at the University of Bradford. Among his books are 'Glasgow: the Uneasy Peace' (Manchester University Press) and 'Edinburgh Divided' (Polygon).

GRAHAM WALKER is Lecturer in History at the University of Sussex. He is the author of 'The Politics of Frustration: Harry Midgley and the Failure of Labour in Northern Ireland' and 'Thomas Johnston' (Manchester University Press)

CHRIS HARVIE is Professor of British and Irish Studies at the University of Tübingen in Germany. Among his books are 'Scotland and Nationalism' (Allen and Unwin) and 'No Gods and Precious Few Heroes' (Edward Arnold).

JOHN MACKENZIE is Reader in History at the University of Lancaster. He has written widely on British Imperialism and his books include 'Propaganda and Empire' and 'Imperialism and Popular Culture' (Manchester University Press).

ALLAN MACINNES is Senior Lecturer in Scottish History at the University of Glasgow and author of 'Charles I and the making of the Covenanting Movement, 1625 - 41' (John Donald).

CALLUM BROWN is Lecturer in History at the University of Strathclyde and author of 'A Social History of Religion in Scotland, 1700–1980' (Methuen).

IAN WOOD is Lecturer in History at Napier Polytechnic and author of 'John Wheatley' (Manchester University Press).

GERRY FINN lectures in the Division of Education and Psychology at Jordanhill College. He is engaged in a study of freemasonry and Scottish sport.

KAY CARMICHAEL is a former Sociology lecturer who is now a freelance writer. She has written widely on women's issues and on social policy.

STEVE BRUCE is Professor of Sociology at the University of Aberdeen. Among his books are 'God Save Ulster! The Religion and Politics of Paisleyism' (Clarendon Press) and 'No Pope of Rome! Militant Protestantism in Modern Scotland'(Mainstream).

1
Introduction

There is widespread and understandable wariness about anything with a religious label in contemporary Scotland. Prevalent in the consciousness of many people are the ugliness of sectarian bigotry, the proximity of strife-torn Ulster, and pejorative notions of Calvinist joylessness, papal authoritarianism, and evangelical gimmickry and charlatanism. Secularism holds sway and has done so since around the First World War. Long gone are the days when Presbyterianism defined the Scots to each other and indeed to an international audience. But its decline in importance has been a gradual one accompanied by surprisingly little anti-clericalism even from those radical political quarters where such reaction might have been anticipated. As Presbyterianism has had to cede much of its influence to Freud, Marx and the apostles of latter-day consumerism, it is clear that a religion that exercised a powerful sway over national life for an unbroken three hundred years still commands considerable residual influence. The centrality of Protestantism to Scotland's historical development and its significance as a determinant of identity in modern Scottish life can easily be downgraded because difficulties many have faced in coming to terms with this legacy have not made it a topic of debate or systematic enquiry. Too ready an acceptance at face value of religious decline can result in the forfeiting of an important conceptual tool in the task of dissecting the Scottish state of mind and the nation's social, cultural and political preoccupations and complexities.

Five years ago Angus Calder, in a review essay on the state of Scottish history,[1] stated: 'Dialectically, our religious heritage accounts for all distinctiveness in our culture: Hume and Burns, reacting thoroughly against Calvinism, may tower over orthodox contemporaries, but who can read Byron, or Carlyle or Stevenson or MacDiarmid or Grassic Gibbon without perceiving their various assaults on orthodoxy as fresh modulations within Knox's tradition?' Calder called on historians of Scotland to get to grips with 'Covenanting Calvinism, 'Missionary Scotland' and the extraordinary native cult of inner-directed 'independence' and 'self-help"; he argued that it was possible to deplore anti-Catholic bigotry while appreciating the powerful energising and motivating role of Scotland's Protestant tradition in the lives of outstanding men and women. More recently, in a tendentious attack on Scotland's intelligentsia from a cultural nationalist standpoint,[2] there has come a defence of a philosophic or 'secular' Calvinism which has highlighted, just as clearly, the need to understand Protestantism's part in the shaping of what is distinctively Scottish. Sean Damer, in a review of the work of one of this volume's editors,[3] has lamented the lack of a searching academic study of the Protestant working class in Central Scotland and of the 'epiphenomena' of Scottish Protestantism, namely the Orange Order, freemasonry, and Rangers FC.

This volume does not pretend to meet all these requirements; it provides, at most, a starting point for further research into the whole field of religious traditions and popular culture in Scotland. It does not, moreover, advance a neat definition of its title concept, the meaningfulness of which is certainly open to question. The concept is offered as an objective, as well as a subjective, term since it is conceded that in many cases people would not use it to define themselves or their way of life. Examination of avowedly Protestant organisations like the Orange Order, of Protestantism in relation to the educational curriculum and its values, or of a popular institution like the *Sunday Post* newspaper which has long cherished a church-going readership, may have more obviously lent substance to the idea of a Protestant popular culture: such topics cry out to be explored in depth.[4] The Lowland, west of Scotland geographical bias also has to be frankly acknowledged, although Allan MacInnes's contribution indicates quite clearly the cultural power of fundamentalist Protestantism in the Highlands.

In a positive vein, the book is intended as an attempt to transcend the stereotypes and the prejudices associated with the subject of religion. Its contributors address themselves critically to themes which relate to Protestantism either as a religious tradition or as a label of popular cultural identity. The topics chosen all have a bearing on the understanding of ourselves, whether in a historical or contemporary sense. In this respect they fall loosely under our conceptual heading.

The book as a whole is neither a celebration nor a denunciation of Protestant popular culture. It is a collection of very diverse interpretations and points of view. Kay Carmichael, for instance, is astringently critical of the Protestant cultural burden placed on women; Chris Harvie shows that the Covenanting mythology has influenced a disparate range of Scottish political and cultural forces; Callum Brown argues that the Protestant churches' relationship with the working class was closer, and lasted longer, than has often been suggested; while Steve Bruce, among other things, focuses our attention on the question of whether most contemporary activity which might be classed as Protestant popular culture revolves overwhelmingly around secular activities which are simply given a crude religious label.

The book is intended to stimulate debate on theoretical perspectives on religion and popular culture. The times seem to call for such discussion. Scotland's divergent political behaviour from that of England and Wales in the Thatcher years has been fuelled by a new national consciousness which in turn has revived the quest for evidence of Scottish distinctiveness. It is almost a common place now to hear of the Scottish people's well-developed sense of community and egalitarian fairness. The religious impulse behind communal values has been stressed by contemporary churchmen, and divines such as Thomas Chalmers have been plucked from history to represent an imperishable tradition of Christian communal idealism.[5] Calvinist notions of a moral community, promulgated by Carlyle in Victorian times, still have a cultural resonance. Protestant popular culture has to be related to this issue: isn't the Orange Order, for example, a bastion of traditional community values, whatever might be said about its culpability for religious friction? Football, too, can be viewed as a socially cohesive force for all the sectarian rivalry it may generate or reflect in Scotland. Folk memory and mythology are essential to Scots' perceptions of themselves; it is thus important to look at Protestant instances of such phenomena, both of a militant and moderate character. Covenanters and missionaries are not just historical artifacts; they are symbols of certain enduring expressions of national pride.

However, such symbols are not unambiguous, and there is perhaps a strong case for arguing that expressions of Protestant popular culture such as are discussed here indicate more tellingly a people at odds with themselves and unsure about the nationalism invoked in their name. Neal Ascherson has identified a contradiction between the self-assertion and the self-distrust of the Scots.[6] Protestantism bears down powerfully on the form this takes over the question of national identity. A prominent theme in this collection is the extent to which Protestant symbols, images and myths can do service for both Scottish nationalism and British loyalism. Scottish national feeling and anti-English sentiment are often expressed within institutions, such as army regiments or newspapers like the *Scottish Daily Express*, whose ultimate allegiance is British. The Covenanters inspire both the Scottish National Party and the Orange Order which is a traditional defender of the British crown and constitution. The Church of Scotland has witnessed a persistent tug-of-war between those generally content for a self-governing kirk to have a privileged role in a non-Scottish state and those who argue with growing boldness that parliament's abdication of sovereignty in Scottish church matters should be extended to the entire governance of Scotland.

It has been argued persuasively that religion gave rise to a surrogate nationalism in Scotland (and Wales) in the nineteenth century while also contributing to the fostering of an overall British identity.[7] The empire was central to this: it provided a context within which Scottish Protestantism, confident and assertive, could promote at once a Scottish patriotic and an internationalist vision. Bernard Aspinwall has shown how influential Scottish religious attitudes were in the USA as well as the empire in the late nineteenth and early twentieth centuries.[8] Protestantism, at this time, took up the 'civic gospel' of social reform in the city and preached a 'progressive' outward-looking Christianity; its influence was profound on the ethical socialism of the day and on the shaping of a Scottish consciousness around a belief in the Scot as an adaptable and productive 'citizen of the world'. Moreover, religion was the major source, and something of a lightning conductor, of much popular cultural activity in Scotland – both urban and rural – in the 1850-1914 period.[9]

There was, however, a negative side to this. The importance of anti-Catholicism in popular culture can be stressed with equal force. Fears of being overrun by large numbers of Irish Catholic immigrants were acute in nineteenth-century Scotland and exercised many Protestant clergymen and mob orators. The perceived Catholic threat was a powerful force in the growth of the idea of a common British identity as a bulwark against popery.[10] Anti-Catholicism has fuelled both British and Scottish national sentiment. There has been a long tradition of popular Protestant sentiment in Scotland which considers English religious traditions and practices too sympathetic to Roman Catholicism;[11] yet symbols of Britishness, especially the monarchy, have won the overriding loyalty of many Scots on account of the Protestant principles they purport to uphold. The extent to which popular Protestantism has belonged to the dual-loyalty culture of 'tartanry' since the late nineteenth century would be worth investigating. Work might be done on such expressions of this as the *Sunday Post*, popular entertainers, the Burns cult and St Andrew's societies, and it might take up points raised in Tom Nairn's seminal work[12] and subject them to less polemical scrutiny.[13]

Anti-Catholicism is a contemporary as well as a historical phenomenon. The way Catholics and their religion are often perceived in Scotland testifies to the tenacity and durability of religion-based social and cultural reflexes. Carlyle's view of Knox and the Reformation as having transformed Scotland into a believing and achieving nation from a state of 'rudeness' comparable to that of Ireland [14] is still widely subscribed to. There is still great sensitivity in contemporary Scotland in relation to the idea of mixed marriages (and the way children are brought up in them) and to education.[15] These issues raise more controversy in Scotland than in any other part of the United Kingdom including Northern Ireland where the former are much rarer,[16] and the latter's significance is subsumed in the wider religious and national conflict. Gerry Finn's chapter on freemasonry sheds light on the vexed question of anti-Catholic discrimination in employment as the product of a culture of vigilant Protestantism which seeks to defend its privileges and positions of power and control.

The contributions to this volume, taken together, provide evidence of the variety of social, cultural and political phenomena which have a peculiarly Protestant dimension. Protestantism has certainly never been monolithic in Scotland, notwithstanding the daunting rigidity of Calvinist doctrine. Virtually from the Reformation, Protestantism has been marked by a tendency towards fissure and diversity. In relation to this it may be hypothesised that the vigour of some aspects of popular Protestation has been, and is, the expression of a desire for a show of unity. As fears have mounted about the baleful effects of denominational splits and doctrinal wrangles, so the motivation to be part of an apparently united show of strength at an Orange march, at Ibrox Park or in support of Ulster has perhaps increased, particularly among the unchurched. For some, displays of popular Protestantism may supply the colour, the excitement, the emotional involvement and the commitment which they have failed to find in organised religion. Thus, as church attendances decline, alternative religious-flavoured but basically secular activities, particularly football, strengthen their hold on the imagination. Equally, there have been those for whom devout religious belief has gone hand-in-hand with militant displays of Protestant loyalism; the one has complemented and reinforced the

other. In more recent years many of the people in this category have
tended to belong to small evangelical churches rather than the main
Protestant denominations in Scotland.[17]

Another, and probably much larger, category of Protestant religious adherents has, by contrast, shunned the expressions of popular Protestantism which are of a militant, uncompromising, and
sectarian character. The current symbolism of the political events
taking place between 1688 and 1690 which helped assure the
Presbyterian character of the established Scottish church mean that
the Church of Scotland has refrained from commemorating them.
Yet those who fall into this category have by no means been
indifferent to notions of Presbyterian virtue and Protestant achievement, so long woven into Scottish cultural life in areas such as
Scottish history, education, science and philosophy, the Scottish
economy, and in relation to less easily defined phenomena such as
the Scottish 'character' or 'temperament'. Most people of a Protestant background and upbringing in Scotland have been, and are,
familiar with a cultural pride in practical achievement, rigorous
intellectual and theoretical argument, a disposition to self-examina-
tion, and a concern for moral issues.[18] The effects of the pervasive-
ness of Protestantism in this wider cultural sense require assessment.

It is hard not to reflect on times, particularly at the beginning and
the end of the nineteenth century, when Scottish engagement with
the major political, economic and philosophical issues of the day was
profound, and to reach the conclusion that the distinctive religious
atmosphere and impulse in Scotland was the crucial determining
factor. Even at a time of secular cultural dominance it is still
tempting to agree with a recent *Times Higher Education Supplement*
editorial that the Church of Scotland's role in a re-emerging nationalism is 'pivotal'.[19] As the most 'national' of Scotland's institutions,
a positive contribution from it to the current debate may help
considerably the process of transcending social and cultural phenomena into the realm of political and economic power. However,
the church has a huge job to do in reinterpreting its Calvinist
doctrines, tenets, and values and in redefining its philosophy and
theology to meet the challenges of the 1990s and the new century.[20]

NOTES

1 *Cencrastus*, No. 21 (Summer 1985).
2 C. Beveridge and R. Turnbull, *The Eclipse of Scottish Culture* (Edinburgh, 1989).
3 'A Billy or a Dan', *Cencrastus*, No. 32 (New Year, 1989).
4 But see Elaine McFarland, 'The Orange Order in Scotland, 1790-

1900' (Glasgow University Ph.D., 1987) for Orangeism; and A. McPherson, 'An Angle on the Geist', in W. Humes and H. M. Paterson (eds.), *Scottish Culture and Scottish Education 1800-1980* (Edinburgh, 1983) for education.

5 Revd. W. Storrar 'Scotland's Social Identity: A Christian Vision', a paper presented to the conference on Christianity and Social Vision in Scotland at New College, Edinburgh, 24 February 1990 and kindly made available in draft form by the author.

6 N. Ascherson, 'Scottish Contradictions', in his *Games With Shadows* (London, 1988).

7 D. W. Bebbington, 'Religion and National Identity in Nineteen Century Scotland and Wales', in *Studies In Church History*, Vol. 18 (1982).

8 B. Aspinwall, 'The Scottish Religious Identity in the Atlantic World', in *Studies In Church History*, Vol. 18 (1982)

9 See C. Harvie and G. Walker, 'Culture and Community, 1850-1914', in W. H. Fraser and R. J. Morris (eds.), *People and Society in Scotland* Vol. 2 (Edinburgh, 1990).

10 Bebbington, op. cit.

11 See B. Aspinwall, 'Popery in Scotland: Image and Reality 1820-1920', in *Scottish Church History Society Records*, vol. 22 (1986).

12 T. Nairn, *The Break-up of Britain* (London 1981).

13 See Beveridge and Turnbull, op. cit., pp. 12-14.

14 T. Carlyle, *On Heroes and Hero Worship* (London, Everyman edition, with *Sartor Resartus*, 1908), p. 374.

15 On educational controversies see articles by Bob Crampsey, *Glasgow Herald*, 2 June 1988, and Jack McLean, *Glasgow Herald*, 2 November 1989.

16 See Steve Bruce's chapter in this volume.

17 See the example of Danny Houston whose views are noted in the chapters in this book on politics and Rangers FC.

18 See Beveridge and Turnbull, op. cit., pp. 10, 97. Also interview with Professor Norman Stone in the *Glasgow Herald*, 16 February 1989.

19 *THES*, 19 May 1989.

20 See Stewart Lamont's article in the *Glasgow Herald*, 23 March 1989.

2

The Covenanting tradition

CHRISTOPHER HARVIE

I

In the book of the Scottish people the Covenanters are a shadowy
chapter – like the Culdees, the Bonnymuir rebels or John MacLean's
Scottish Labour College – which still retains its political potency,
unimpaired by myth-debunking. Burns, whose own appearances in
the Kirk had their moments, was reverential:

> The Solemn League and Covenant,
> Now brings a smile, now brings a tear;
> But sacred freedom too was theirs,
> If thou'rt a slave, indulge thy sneer.

They figured prominently in Galt, Hogg and Scott, and were the
subject of Stevenson's and Buchan's first published writings. The
National Covenant was spectacularly revived in the cause of home
rule by John MacCormick in the late 1940s, and a whiff of moorland
resolution hangs around the project of the Scottish Constitutional
Convention, the title of whose inaugurating instrument, 'A Claim of
Right for Scotland', recalls 1689 (MacCormick, 1955, 130). Lewis
Grassic Gibbon made the young Communist Ewan Tavendale, in
Grey Granite, commemorate them as 'the advance guard of the
common folk of these days, their God and their Covenant just
formulae they hid the social rebellion in', but Ewan only followed his
mother 'Chris Caledonia' Guthrie, who had identified with them
when she visited their prison at Dunnottar Castle in *Sunset Song*:

> There the Covenanting folk had screamed and died while the
> gentry dined and danced in their lithe, warm halls. Chris stared
> at the places, sick and angry and sad for those folk she could
> never help now, that hatred of rulers and gentry a flame in her
> heart, John Guthrie's hate. Her folk and his they had been,
> those whose names stand graved in tragedy... (Gibbon, 1932-
> 4, 464, 123; Brotherstone, 1989, 1.)

The cry of the south-western men – 'Whiggam! Whiggam!' – as they descended on Edinburgh in 1647 to protest at a backsliding Scottish parliament, created a party name which endured for over two centuries (Calder, 1981, 221). Even the fact that the League of Nations, when it was set up in 1919, was founded on a Covenant, probably had something to do with the fact that two of its main architects, James Viscount Bryce and Woodrow Wilson, were of Covenanting stock, the latter a kinsman on his mother's side of Robert Wodrow, who recorded the martyrdom of the 'Society Men' in his *Sufferings of the Church in Scotland, 1660 to 1688)* (1721-2) (Ions, 1968, 19, 266ff.) So all these Woodies – Allen, Hermann, Guthrie, Woodpecker – owe their names to the memory of sectarian endurance in the moors of Ayr and Galloway...

There is another side. While the names of individual Covenanters – Prophet Peden and Richard Cameron, Donald Cargill and James Renwick – no longer retain a national significance in Scotland, they still figure in print and on tape in the rhetoric of The Revd Ian Paisley, provoking echoes remote from liberal internationalism or any progressive ideal. The Ulster poet and critic Tom Paulin writes:

> In a published sermon, 'Richard Cameron: The Lion of the Covenant', there is a stark and savoured quotation from the sentence of hanging and disembowelling which the 'Council of Blood' passed on one of the Covenanters. Here Paisley appears as a Scottish Nationalist laying the 'tribute wreath' of his sermon on the memorial to a protestant martyr (his mother was 'born into a Scots Covenanting home', and he makes much of his Scottish inheritance). This is apparent in two cassette sermons on the Covenanters which are awash with cries of 'blood' and whose delivery at times resembles the intonation necessary to a reading of the closing lines of Yeats's 'Easter 1916'... These almost forgotten historical figures are invested with a vocal halo by the preacher and so are changed into transcendent heroes. This is a Protestantism which is pushing deep into the territory of mystery and mythology; it is a celebration of chthonic forces and a rejection of secular and utilitarian values. (Paulin, 1984, 170.)

Paisley is not simply a provincial politician of guile and manoeuvrability, as well adapted to his Ulster Protestant constituency as Franz Josef Strauss was to black Catholic Bavaria. He also represents a type of tribal nationalist leader common enough in the ebb-tide of 'scientific materialism'. Paulin goes on to show how Bunyan and Carlyle, potent transcendental 'sages' of 'pre-class' politics, once omnipresent in radical nonconformist discourse and now exiled by a superficial rationalism to academic theses, stud Paisley's appeal. The implication for Scotland must be that, granted certain conditions, the intellectual and emotional material for a cognate revival of expertly-led Protestant sectarianism may still be inflammable.

II

The Covenanting fixation may also help explain why the radicalism of the Red Clyde failed to sustain itself after its remarkable breakthrough in 1922. Iain McLean, in *The Legend of Red Clydeside,* pointed out how even secular left-wingers in the Glasgow area adopted the paradigm of the persecuted Israel of the Covenanters' favourite Psalm 124:

> ... *If that the Lord had not our cause maintained,*
> *When cruel men against us furiously*
> *Rose up in wrath, to make of us their prey ...*

This conformed to the Scottish radical tradition, but had little to say to the Irish voters who had contributed so much to their victory (McLean, 1983, 97-9). Scots who returned to an undogmatic, ecumenical religion, such as Edwin Muir, active in the Clydeside socialist movement in the first decades of the century, found the Covenanting legacy wholly negative. In that bleak poem 'Scotland, 1941', he depicted a country cribbed in a joyless puritanism and oblivious of its history, at its centre:

> *Hoodiecraw Peden in the stubble field,*
> *Pecks with his iron beak the naked haulms.*
> *Out of that desolation we were born.*

Even in 1990 a Catholic layman, supporting the Constitutional Convention, confessed that the resonances of 'A Claim of Right for Scotland' meant nothing to his religious community, however much it stirred Protestant memories. One of the problems of sorting out the attic of the Scottish past in order to find 'not traditions – precedents!' for contemporary politics is that obnoxious old sectarian skeletons are likely to fall on you.

But the problem may be more complicated yet. Victor Kiernan, a Marxist of great subtlety and almost incomparable range has – in his two essays 'The Covenanters: a Problem of Creed and Class' and 'A Banner with a Strange Device' – found religious militancy in Scotland an almost insoluble conundrum: an ideology usually associated with capitalist advance which ended up becoming the talisman of fanatical primitives on remote moors:

> a rare example of a class near the bottom of society holding

grimly to a creed constructed by intellectuals of higher ranks, when most of the propertied were turning away from it. These Galloway rustics learned to reason acutely, but only within the limits of a world bounded by the Shorter Catechism. They could only float up into the clouds of theology, or sink into doctrinal quicksands deeper than their bogs. (Kiernan, 1989, 45.)

Kiernan echoes a discord on the left, even the Protestant left, about the Covenanters and the religious dispensation that they represented. Theological modernism, secularism and collectivist politics combined to change their image, in Ian Cowan's words, from 'excessive adulation to denigration and oblivion' (Cowan, 1976, 12). In the 1880s the influential Scottish Liberal and secularist J. M. Robertson even-handedly castigated Episcopalian and Presbyterian alike in the *Perversion of Scotland* (1885) and Tom Johnston's extensively documented *History of the Working Classes in Scotland* (1921), while admitting that 'round the Wild Whigs, Wanderers, Faithful Remnants, Hillmen, Cameronians and Macmillanites, tradition has woven a story which one would not willingly let die' (Johnston, 1921, 94), also stressed that in their own period of hegemony in the 1640s the Covenanters had been 'narrow, bigoted, cruel, stupid and barbarously bloodthirsty'. They got little support from the Scottish peasantry for this reason, and contributed to the witch-hunting for which Scotland was so notorious (ibid., 88, 92). On the other hand, Johnston also claimed for them a greater degree of sophistication than Kiernan would credit: 'the revolutionary theological tradition and the evangelistic fervour which has come down to us is distinctly of mercantile and bourgeois origin' (ibid., 98). If it is all too easy to see the Covenanters – as Lecky and Buckle did – as throwbacks, this claim is a valuable corrective, but it is still very difficult to conceive them as progressive in any modern, and essentially collective, sense of the term.

III

This may stem from the central problem that, in the late sixteenth and early seventeenth centuries, Covenant theology and Covenant politics coincide chronologically and influence one another, but this influence is metaphorical rather than in any strict sense theological or metaphysical. The basis of Covenant theology or 'federal Calvinism' was that God had contracted with man for his salvation at the creation – the 'Covenant of Works' – but that Adam's sin had rendered the contract void; God revived the offer by sending his son Jesus to earth – the 'Covenant of Grace' – but that this grace was not restricted to the elect. This could either lead to a strict predestinarian position, with the end of the world assumed to be in the offing; or it could, with metaphorical input, emerge as a sort of special covenant between God and the Scots as his 'chosen people (Stevenson, 1988, 30). Arthur Williamson has argued that this tension produced theological politics of a very high order, as thinkers such as George Buchanan in *De Iure Regni apud Scotos* (1579) and Samuel Rutherford in *Lex Rex* (1644) put forward contractual theories of government which married Calvinism to the 'civic humanist' tradition of the Italian Renaissance. While English Calvinism gravitated towards either millenarianism or the imperialism of the 'Protestant Nation', its Scottish counterpart was much more oriented towards the problems of a smaller provincial *polis* (Williamson, 1983, p. 42). Taken with the studies of Williamson's teacher, J. G. A. Pocock, this suggests a continuum between the Scots Reformation and the political theory of the Scottish Enlightenment, carrying forward to Andrew Fletcher and Adam Ferguson (Pocock, 1975, pp. 426, 449-501). However wild the Cameronians' Queensferry manifesto of 1650 sounded, with its call for tyrannicide and the creation of a Scottish republic, it was not eccentric but securely within a tradition of Scottish constitutional thought.

The problem about this tradition was that while it put a strong emphasis on community involvement, it was weak on toleration, which was in England stressed culturally and philosophically by Milton and later by Locke, and practically by Cromwell. The 'independent' tradition of English dissent, with congregations making their own decisions as to liturgy and formulae, is not well represented in Scotland, where 'dissent' has generally tended to take the form – recognisable to anyone having to do with left-wing sectarianism – of *groupuscules* each claiming to be the legatee of the 'true Kirk', prepared to make the point by persecuting everyone else if they get the chance and meanwhile maintaining rigid discipline within their own ranks. The road from the south-western moors did not lead to a Nonconformist Enlightenment, as was the case in late-eighteenth-century Wales, but into the apparent absurdity of the Auld Licht Anti-Burgers (Williams 1985, p. 158). When opposition to the prevailing Moderatism of the Kirk re-emerged as a potent political force at the end of the eighteenth century, it seemed intent on undoing the work of the Scottish Enlightenment, to the extent that H. T. Buckle could claim in 1859 that

> in no civilised country is toleration so little understood, and
> that in none is the spirit of bigotry and of persecution so
> extensively diffused... The churches are as crowded as they

were in the Middle Ages, and are filled with devout and ignorant worshippers, who flock together to listen to opinions of which the Middle Ages alone were worthy. (Buckle, 1861, 470.)

But could such a society have produced Carlyle or Clerk Maxwell, Patrick Geddes or MacDiarmid? J. M. Barrie described the Auld Lichts' 'three degrees of damnation – auld kirk, play-acting, chapel', the last being the Episcopalian church, considered as reprehensible as Rome, yet he still observed that the Auld Lichters were to the fore in the capture of meal carts in the hungry times of the 1840s, and in the open fighting which followed between weavers and the local farmers (Barrie, 1888, 19, 126-9). Christopher Grieve's father, the Langholm postman, was a United Free Kirk elder who would not have Burns' poems in the house, but opposed the Boer War, supported trade unionism and moved towards the infant Labour Party (Bold, 1988, 24-5). Carlyle's tribute to the Presbyterian peasantry in his essay on Scott is fulsome but neither misplaced nor conservative: 'A country where the entire people is, or even once has been, laid hold of, filled to the heart with an infinite religious idea, has "made a step from which it cannot retrograde". Thought, conscience, the sense that man is denizen of a Universe, creature of an Eternity, has penetrated to the remotest cottage, to the simplest heart' (Carlyle, 1838, 71). His 'Baillie the Covenanter' of 1841 contains probably his most radical statement:

> Did a God make this land of Britain, and give it to us all, that we might live there by honest labour; or did the Squires make it, and – shut to the voice of God, open only to a Devil's voice in this matter – decide on giving it to themselves alone? This is now the sad question and 'divine right', we, in this unfortunate century, have got to settle!' (Carlyle, 1841a, 141.)

IV

As in so many other aspects of Scottish history, Carlyle, who came from the Covenanting heartland of the South-West, presents a powerful but confusing image: liberty mingled with authoritarianism and atavism, Scottish nationalism overshadowed by 'the Condition of England Question'. In *Chartism* (1839) which attracted the praise of Marx and Engels for 'sounding the social question' and – through his studies in Goethe, Schiller and Saint-Simon – 'Europeanising' the crisis of industrial society, Carlyle stigmatised the Irishman 'in his squalor and unreason, in his falsity and drunken violence ... [as] the ready-made nucleus of degradation and disorder' (Carlyle, 1839, 178). An image apparently as prejudiced as that of any Orangeman. Yet in asking, 'Has not the *Sanspotato* the same *soul* as the superfinest Lord Lieutenant?' he made himself an acceptable mentor, later in the 1840s, to the leaders of Young Ireland, (Edwards, 1969, p. 123). In the battle between radicalism and romantic Tory reaction, Carlyle knew whose side he was on (Noble, 1988, 135). His disciple James Dodds wrote his very popular *Lays of the Covenanters* to answer the Jacobite Toryism of W. E. Aytoun's *Lays of the Scottish Cavaliers*, with their emotional defence of Graham of Claverhouse. Dodds went on to write *The Fifty Years' Struggle of the Scottish Covenanters in 1860.* Its peroration reflected, however, not Scottish nationalism but the democratic patriotism of the volunteer movement against the 'paternal government' of Napoleon III and the drive to colonial settlement: 'O Britain! Continue to be the nurse of Freedom. Heaven's light points the way, and a voice from the cloud proclaims ... THE MIGHTY MOTHER OF FREE COLONIES AND OF THE FUTURE FREE EMPIRES OF THE WORLD!' (Dodds, 1860, 395).

The line between Carlyleian ambiguity and the 'scientific' anti-Irish racism which, as L. P. Curtis has noted, tended at this time largely to stem from the militantly Protestant areas of southern Scotland, is awkwardly thin (Curtis, 1968, pp. 54, 68ff). And militant Protestantism received a mighty boost by the 'Ten Years' Conflict' in the Established Kirk which climaxed in the Disruption of 1843. In the Revd Thomas Brown's *Annals of the Disruption* (1884) the first chapter is largely taken up with expounding precedents for events of the 1840s in the Covenanting period, while a later chapter deprecates the Moderates' failure to evangelise on the continent, and the closer links which the Free Church cultivated with European Protestants: 'It brings out their true brotherhood in Christ, as opposed to the external and mechanical unity of which Popery boasts.' (Brown, 1884, 558.) Certain aspects of Scottish, and in particular Edinburgh, religious-cultural life aggravated sectarian tension. The contemporary obsession with craniology seems to have been particularly strong – and was boosted by the 'pioneer' racist Robert Knox (Edwards, 1978, 135). The prevailing Anglo-Saxonism in historical writing also contributed, as did reactions to accelerating Irish immigration. Yet the separation of the Free Church from the state gave it a certain common cause with other more liberal religious denominations; and the most militant anti-Catholics were usually to be found in the Established Church, or among Free Churchmen who held by fundamentalism and the established principle.

A notable example was the Revd James Begg. Begg's origins were partly Cameronian, and he was already anti-Catholic at the time of the emancipation crisis of 1828, long before his foundation of the Scottish Reformation Society in 1851 (Smith, 1885, 2-3, 75). Later that decade he figured in the nationalist Association for the Vindication of Scottish Rights, as a radical Liberal, but as a result of Gladstone's disestablishment of the Irish Church he aligned himself completely with the Conservative Party (Gallagher, 1987, 12-13; Crapster, 1957, p. 355). He may in fact be the source of that peculiar interest in Scottish affairs that Disraeli evinced in *Lothair* (1870) with the argument that the formation of the anti-establishment United Presbyterian Church (1847) had been the result of a Jesuit plot (Disraeli, 1870, p. 32). But although Begg, also an active social reformer, in some ways fits the frame of the collectivist and racialistic nationalism which was increasingly significant in late-nineteenth-century urban Europe – Pastor Adolf Stoecker in 1870s Berlin, Mayor Karl Lueger in 1880s Vienna – within the Free Church his constituency was the highlands, an area where the Covenanting tradition had never applied (Carswell, 1927, 54-120; Roberts, 1967, 67, 197-8; Masur, 1971 ,108ff.).

The alignments of religion and politics in nineteenth-century Scotland were by no means straightforward. W. E. Gladstone, for example, became a devout Scottish Episcopalian with strong Jacobite connections through his mother's family, the Robertsons of Dingwall, but his family's earlier evangelicalism gave them links to Thomas Chalmers, and through him to the revival of the seventeenth-century ideal of the 'Godly Commonwealth' at parochial level (Brown, 1982, chs. 1, 5). Gladstone's endorsement of the religious commitment of the Free Church in his pamphlet *On the Functions of Laymen in the Church* (1851) acts in many ways as a prelude to his own later alliance with the Free Church over the issue of disestablishment in the mid-1880s (Harvie, 1990, 66). On the other hand, his well-publicised opposition to ultramontanism in *The Vatican Decrees* (1874) fuelled Presbyterian distrust of the deference of Catholic parishioners, although this was reversed by his policy of Home Rule in 1885, and the 'union of hearts' which followed.

But at a cost. Scottish liberals in the nineteenth century declared for causes like Italian unity which were almost calculated to provoke an Irish Catholic community whose loyalties were either very localised or totally confessional – in other words ultramontane. This was in itself a form of anti-clericalism recognisable in continental Europe, but while the Catholic church in France or Germany was a privileged component of the old order, Scottish Catholics were as poor and threatened a minority as the Covenanters of the 1680s had been (Gallagher, 1987b, 42-85).

V

Two factors, however, contributed to mitigate the militant Protestant threat. The first was that it was organised on party political rather than on 'movement' lines. 'Spontaneous' anti-Catholicism was in the 1860s overtaken by the importation into Scotland of Ulster Orangeism and its deployment *as policy* by the fading Scottish Conservative Party. This strategy was much closer to that employed by English provincial Tory leaders like Alderman Salvidge of Liverpool than to the native product. For the Orange Grand Master George MacLeod to claim in 1876 that 'every sound Orangeman was a Conservative and if there were any radicals in their ranks they were as rare as black swans', rules out the sort of 'opening to the left' which Chamberlainite radical unionism might later have supplied, while the mindless boisterousness of the Orangemen struck Glasgow establishment Conservatives such as Henry Craik as 'a disgrace both to our city and to our party' (Hutchison, 1986, 122-5).

The other factor was provided by the 'Celtic' issues of land reform and home rule, coupled with a religious revivalism which was ecumenical rather than fundamentalist in tone. The downturn in agricultural prices after 1873 was something common to the surviving peasant communities on the British western seaboard, and land reform was a policy which could be activated by urban radicals both to check further immigration, from the highlands and from Ireland and to mobilise anti-landlord feeling. This could be seen in the influence of the Land League's founder Michael Davitt on the land agitation and in the outpourings of the romantic nationalist Professor John Stuart Blackie both on the Covenanters and on the cause of the highlanders. Anti-English nationalism, something Scots and Irish workers had in common, obviously acted as a catalyst which enabled a cleaned-up Covenant ethos to be ingested into the Scots Labour tradition (Paton 1935; Welsh, 1920, pp. 112-3). Alan Campbell has commented on the strong nationalism of miners' organisations, particularly in areas of Lanarkshire like Larkhall; this seems to have involved some degree of militant Protestantism, but also to have been distinct from the Orangeism of Coatbridge, which was specifically organised against the substantial Irish labour-force recruited into the large-scale mines of the area (Campbell, 1979, 44, 279). A figure like Keir Hardie retained the nationalism, but (I imagine as a result of the Moody and Sankey revival of 1873-4) added to it an undogmatic evangelicalism and a specific commitment to home rule, Scots and Irish (Morgan, 1975, 27ff.).

Granted the theological opposition of Covenant and Catholicism there were still enough ideological and behavioural similarities to make some sort of dialogue possible. In Scotland both were puritan creeds, emphasising the family, temperance, the Sabbath, the role of worship in society. Both regarded the establishment with intense suspicion. The devout Catholic would be as censorious of his co-religionists whose observances were minimal and who hung around the other institution of Irish socialising, the pub, as a Presbyterian radical would be of the Orangemen. The ideological parallel is more circuitous but exists in the historic Catholic suspicion of the nation-state, and yearning for a restored Christendom. In Gladstone's concept of 'international public right' and, more systematically, in the hands of thinkers like James Bryce this ideal, realised in the Middle Ages through a conciliar church and the 'imperium' of the Holy Roman Empire, could be made to blend with the Presbyterian Buchananite doctrine of limited sovereignty (Kleinknecht, 1985, pp. 72-114; Aspinwall 1980, pp. 57-73). In comparison with this dense and ramifying thicket of political theory, the reinvoking of the Covenant by the Ulster Unionists in 1912 seems oddly slapdash – a publicity stunt, thought up in a London club, rather than any radical outburst against the abuse of parliamentary sovereignty (Colvin 1936, 137-51). Its staging replicated the images of 1638 – 1000 Ulstermen signed it on the same tombstone in Greyfriars Kirkyard that the men of 1638 had used – but there was no theological underpinning to an act which was supposed to unify Ascendancy society and to *cement* the connection with England, not call it in question.

Ulster Protestants, writes Steve Bruce in his study of Paisleyism, seem closer to Victorian Britons than to their twentieth-century descendants. Anyone who reads quantities of Orange and loyalist publications cannot help but be struck by the datedness of the image of Britain there presented. Ulster loyalists want to be part of that British Empire whose world domination was displayed in school wall-maps with huge areas of red. They sing more than one verse of the national anthem and mean it. They are the most fervent admirers of the British monarchy ... Ulster Protestants are British in the way in which Kipling was British. (Bruce, 1986, 252.)

The Ulster Presbyterian tradition had initially been radical, and in the 1790s Peden's prophecies of liberation achieved through the intervention of the French fitted into the cosmology of the United Irishmen. The wholehearted Unionism of the Presbyterians a century later can, however, be attributed to their co-option into the establishment after 1796 by bountiful state funding, so that the evangelical revival which led in Scotland to the non-intrusion move-

ment and thus to the Free Church, led in Ulster in the opposite
direction, a tendency ultimately confirmed by the revival of 1859
(Homes 1989, 176-87). The Ulster Covenant had elements of
'settler radicalism' adhering to it, but overall fitted into this deferential world-view, in which Tory politicians – Lord Randolph Church-
ill, Sir Edward Carson, F. E. Smith – who used Ulster for their own
purposes were – and still are – granted incredible indulgence.
Scottish Presbyterianism presented parallels in some respects – the
'frontiersman' ideology, the imperially-oriented Kailyard, the Scottish regiments (including the Covenanting Cameronians) – but not
in others. On balance radical Presbyterianism still seems in a state of
disaffection, overlaid perhaps by later secular dissent – Chartists,
militant crofters, Clydesiders – but still consonant with it.

VI

The outcome seems so close-run that the role of specific individuals
in 'reclaiming' the Covenanters for the unsectarian left must have
been important, perhaps critical. A case in point is that of the Revd
James Barr, who in the course of a long and active political life – he
was born in 1862 and died in 1949 – lectured 'more than any living
man' on the Covenanters, and in 1946 published the frankly
hagiographical *The Scottish Covenanters* (Barr, 1948 ,129). Tom
Johnston's eulogy of him pressed every button on the Scottish
radical keyboard:

> Born over eight decades ago amid the whaups crying over the
> graves and among memories of the Men of the Covenant on
> the Fenwick moors, and nurtured on the poetry and traditions
> of Robert Burns, his life was given a set and a direction from
> which it never deviated ... He is the type whom James VI
> castigated in his *Basilikon Doron* as 'the proud Puritane'.
> (Ibid., 3.)

The important thing about Barr was that he was a theological as well
as a political liberal. He was trained at Glasgow University under
James Veitch – the last great representative of the Common Sense
school – and Edward Caird, the friend and disciple of T. H. Green,
and was deeply influenced at the Free Church College by Henry
Drummond, who had helped organise the Moody and Sankey
mission to Scotland and whose *Natural Law in the Spiritual World*
attempted to mediate between scientific advance and religious
belief. In the 1900s he was a radical Liberal and member of the
quasi-nationalist Young Scots Society, which had its origins as a
pro-Boer group, and supported the United Free Church's relative
openness to collectivist change, something which led to his appoint-

ment to the Royal Commission on Scottish Housing in 1913. In World War I his pacifism led him to support the Union of Democratic Control and like so many of its members he joined the ILP in 1920 (Knox, 1984, 61ff.).

Barr moved in 1926 the second bill for Scottish home rule to be advanced by Labour members, a drastic measure which demanded dominion status and the removal of Scottish MPs from Westminster. It was talked out and, following this failure, several ILP activists, including Christopher Grieve, Roland Muirhead and John MacCormick, quit to found the National Party of Scotland. Barr remained a nationalist within the Labour Party, chairing in the 1930s the London Scots Self-Government Committee, although he was also one of the sponsors of the SNP-inspired Scottish Convention of 1939, which might, had it taken place, have gestated an earlier version of the Covenant of 1949.

Barr's interpretation of the later Covenanters took for granted the radical line of Alexander Shields's *A Hind Let Loose* (1678) and the Queensferry paper of 1680, with its demand to: 'Overthrow the kingdom of darkness, popery, prelacy and superstition; to reject the royal family and set up a republican government; and to separate from indulged ministers and from all those who hold communion with them.' (Barr, 1946, 51.) As a politician who had supported the Catholic Relief Bill of 1927 and attacked Orangeism, and a churchman whose membership of the United Free Church (Continuing) after 1929 distanced him from the organised anti-Catholicism of the reunited Kirk, Barr was untypical of many Presbyterians, but unquestionably influential in making the Covenanting tradition more palatable to the Labour movement. With our present interest in constitutional reform, and the role in it of ecumenically-minded clergy, Barr provides a useful bridge to the constitutional concerns of the Renaissance and Reformation in Scotland.

VII

In England and in Ulster, 1688-9 are celebrated as the triumph of 'our freedom, religion and laws'. The Whig nobility got for themselves what the Scottish aristocrats had signed the National Covenant for in 1638: the sovereignty of parliament; their own undisputed local authority. Ulster Protestantism acquired that definitive sense of being a civilisation superior to the native population. Its memories are of military success – the Boyne and the Siege of Londonderry – contending with outbreaks of savage and uncontrolled 'native' violence. This has, as A. T. Q. Stewart has forcibly pointed out, a strong Scottish and Presbyterian component, but is

essentially a 'settler' memory, comparable with that of the Boers in
South Africa or Jews in contemporary Israel, part of a mentality
shared with other Ulster Protestants, whether Church of Ireland,
Baptist or Methodist, and – at least until very recently – deferential
to the aristocratic elite of the province (Stewart, 1977, 34ff.).

The Scottish experience was far less straightforward, and the
'killing time', followed by the Darien disaster and the Union of
1707, were reminders of its ambiguity. The Covenanting episode
itself became a palimpsest, over which later writers wrote accounts
which, usually, contributed to a 'common' Scottish identity. Scott
meanwhile – in 1816 in an optimistic and assimilationist frame of
mind – deprecated in *Old Mortality* the 'extremism' of a former
Scotland which had now been 'improved' out of all recognition. Later
moderates, coping with a more fractured history, in which fanaticism and revolution were more salient, had to take the dialogue
more seriously. John Buchan, in *Witch Wood* (1928) condemned the
solipsism of the extremists, but put in the mouth of the Marquess of
Montrose a pluralistic theory of politics equally far from the abso-
lutism of parliamentary sovereignty (Buchan, 1928, 41-2).

Buchan also unmasked the Janus face of Presbyterian enthusiasm
in introducing the subject of witches, on whose persecution by the
Covenanting elite of the 1840s apologetic writers were almost
uniformly silent. Christina Larner has pointed out that although 'the
central position of the Old Testament concept of the covenanted
people in Scottish political thought gave the inversion of a covenant
with Satan a power and an intensity which it may not have had under
other regimes' (Larner, 1981, 201) the Presbyterians had no mo-
nopoly of the role of persecutors, and the gentry were more active
than the clergy. In certain respects witches and Covenanters behaved in similar ways – taking to the moors, prophesying and cursing
– in areas 'which had a history of confusing witchcraft and heresy',
and it is surely significant that the 'killing time' of the 1680s is also
the lowest decade of the century for witchcraft processes (ibid., 94,
61).

The fate of the later Covenanters – the period which enjoyed most
literary reworking – was made to exemplify the theme of persecution
of natives by an alien and 'absolute' authority. The men of Rullion
Green and Bothwell Brig, and the Cameronians, were plebeian; they
were political radicals, however archaic their religious beliefs; they
were nationalist enough to protest the Union of 1707, and half a
century later their descendants in America were still at it, when the
Revd Alexander Craighead renewed the Covenant in Pennsylvania,
an act which in due course led to the revolt in 1771 of the

'Mecklenburg Convention' (Hanna, 1902, II, 41). This repackaging seems to have come during and after the Napoleonic wars. Although John Brims has shown that moderate reformers fought shy of Cameronian republicanism and sectarianism of the 1790s in the interests of a 'popular front', later attempts to tidy this awkward squad into the dustbin of history provoked the opposite (Brims, 1989, 58). Scott's treatment of Claverhouse and his opponents was seen as whitewashing the former, and was criticised at great length by the great religious historian Thomas McCrie, while Hogg in his *Brownie of Bodsbeck* (1817) did the same, from the point of view of the oral tradition in Ettrick. In the latter story a well-doing sheep farmer, Walter Laidlaw, is arrested by Claverhouse on suspicion of succouring Covenanters, and made to witness his operations. Hogg called himself a Tory, and no-one exposed the schizoid qualities of extreme Calvinism more effectively than in his *Justified Sinner*, but his picture is one of arbitrary force unfairly exerted on religious steadfastness. Moreover, set against his portrait of Claverhouse, whose name was 'held in at least as great detestation as that of the arch-fiend himself', Hogg introduces a fictional highland trooper, Daniel Roy MacPherson, a brave, humane and honourable figure who will die at Killiekrankie. Like Scott, Hogg 'composes' history, in Georg Lukacs' sense, into ideology but this composition creates a common – and useful – theme of persecution borne by lowland Protestant and highland Catholic alike (Hogg, 1815, p. 150).

Most nineteenth- century radicals would have let Carlyle have the last word:

> many men in the van do always, like Russian soldiers, march into the ditch at Schweidnitz, and fill it up with their dead bodies, that the rear may pass over them dry-shod, and gain the honour ... How many earnest rugged Cromwells, Knoxes, poor Peasant Covenanters, wrestling, battling for very life, in rough miry places, have to struggle, and suffer, and fall, greatly censured, bemired, before a beautiful Revolution of Eighteight can step over them in official pumps and silk-stockings, with universal three-times-three! (Carlyle, 1841, p. 146.)

A Paisley favourite, I believe, but I don't see why the Doctor should have all the best tunes.

REFERENCES

ASPINWALL, Bernard (1980) Robert Monteith and David Urquhart. In *The Innes Review*, Vol. 31 pp. 57-70
BARR, Revd James (1946) *The Scottish Covenanters*, Glasgow: Smith.
BARR, J. (1948) *Lang Syne*, Glasgow: Maclellan.
BARRIE, J. M. (1888) *Auld Licht Idylls*, London: Hodder and Stoughton.

BOLD, Alan (1988) *Hugh MacDiarmid*, London: John Murray.

BRIMS, John (1989), The Covenanting Tradition and Scottish Radicalism in the 1790s. In Brotherstone, coll. cit.

BROTHERSTONE, Terry (ed.) (1989) *Covenant, Charter and Party:
Traditions of Revolt and Protest in Modern Scottish History*, Aberdeen:
Aberdeen University Press.

BROWN, Stewart Jay (1982), *Thomas Chalmers and the Godly Commonwealth in Scotland*, Oxford, Oxford University Press.

BROWN, Revd Thomas (1884) *Annals of the Disruption*, Edinburgh:
MacLaren and MacNiven.

BRUCE, Steve (1986) *God Save Ulster!* Oxford: Oxford UP.

BUCHAN, John (1928) *Witch Wood*, new edition with an introduction by
the present writer, Edinburgh: Canongate, 1988.

BUCKLE, H. T. (1871) *History of Civilization in England*, Vol. III, London: Longman.

CALDER, Angus (1981) *Revolutionary Empire*, London: Cape.

CAMPBELL, Alan (1979), *The Lanarkshire Miners* Edinburgh: John
Donald.

CARLYLE, Thomas (1838) Lockhart's Life of Scott. In *Edinburgh Review*, reprinted in *Scottish and Other Miscellanies*, London: Dent, n.d.

CARLYLE, Thomas (1839) Chartism. In *Edinburgh Review*, reprinted in
Christopher Harvie Graham Martin and Aaron Scharf, eds., *Industrialisation and Culture*, London: Macmillan, 1970

CARLYLE, Thomas (1841a) 'Baillie the Covenanter'. In *London and
Westminster Review*, reprinted in *Scottish and Other Miscellanies* (London: Dent n.d.)

CARLYLE, Thomas (1841b) *Heroes and Hero-Worship*, London:
Chapman and Hall.

CARSWELL, Donald (1927), Smith o' Aiberdeen. In *Brother Scots*,
London: Constable.

COLVIN, Ian (1936) *The Life of Lord Carson*, Vol. II, London: Gollancz.

COWAN, I. B. (1976) *The Scottish Covenanters*, Gollancz: London.

CRAPSTER, Basis (1957) Scotland and the Conservative Party in 1876,
The Journal of Modern History, Vol. xxix.

CURTIS, L. P. Jnr (1968) *Anglo-Saxons and Celts*, Bridgeport, University
of Bridgeport Press.

DISRAELI, Benjamin (1870) *Lothair*, Oxford: Oxford UP.

DODDS, James (1860) *The Scottish Covenanters*, Edinburgh: Oliphant.

EDWARDS, Owen Dudley (1969), Ireland. In *Celtic Nationalism*, London: Routledge.

EDWARDS, O. D. (1978) *Burke and Hare*, London: Polygon.

GALLAGHER, Tom (1987a) *Edinburgh Divided*, Edinburgh: Polygon.

GALLAGHER, T. (1987b) *The Uneasy Peace*, Manchester: Manchester
University Press.

GIBBON, Lewis Grassic (1986) *A Scots Quair*, Harmondsworth: Penguin.

HANNA, Charles A. (1902) *The Scotch-Irish*, Vol. II, New York: Putnam.

HARVIE, Christopher (1990) Gladstonianism, the Provinces, and Popular Political Culture. In Richard Bellamy (ed.), *Victorian Liberalism*,
London: Routledge.

HOGG, James (1815) The Brownie of Bodsbeck. In *Tales and Legends of
the Scottish Borders*, London: Sands, n.d., pp. 5-80.

HOLMES, R. F. G. (1989) 'United Irishmen and Unionists: Irish
Presbyterians, 1791 and 1886'. In W. J. Sheils and Diana Wood, *The
Churches, Ireland and the Irish*, Oxford: Ecclesiastical History Society:
Blackwell.

HUTCHINSON, Iain (1986) *A Political History of Scotland, 1832-1924*, Edinburgh: John Donald.

IONS, Edmund (1968) *James Bryce and American Democracy*, London: Macmillan.

JOHNSTON, Thomas (1921) *History of the Working Classes in Scotland*, Glasgow: Forward.

KIERNAN (1989) 'A Banner with a Strange Device'. In Brotherstone, coll. cit.

KIERNAN, Victor, (1988) 'The Covenanters: a Problem of Creed and Class'. In Terence Ranger, *History from Below: Studies in Popular Protest and Popular Ideology in Honour of George Rude*, Oxford: Oxford UP, 1988.

KLEINKNECHT, Thomas (1985) *Imperiale und International Ordnung: Eine Untersuchung zum anglo-amerikanischen Gelehrtenliberalismus am Beispiel von James Bryce*, Bayreuth: Vandenhoek und Ruprecht.

KNOX, William, (1984) *Scottish Labour Leaders*, Edinburgh: Mainstream.

LARNER, Christina, (1981) *Enemies of God: the Witch-Hunt in Scotland*, London: Chatto and Windus.

McCRIE, Thomas, (1817) Vindication of the Covenanters. In the *Christian Instructor*, Edinburgh: Whyte, 4th ed., 1845.

McLEAN, Iain (1983) *The Legend of Red Clydeside*, Edinburgh: John Donald.

MacCORMICK, John (1955) *The Flag in the Wind*, London: Gollancz.

MASUR, Gerhard (1971) *Imperial Berlin*, London: Routledge.

MORGAN, Kenneth O. (1975) *Keir Hardie: Radical and Socialist*, London: Weidenfeld and Nicolson.

NOBLE, Andrew (1988) Christopher North and the Tory Reaction. In Douglas Gifford (ed.), *The Literary History of Scotland: Vol. III, Nineteenth Century*, Aberdeen: Aberdeen UP.

PATON, John (1935) *Proletarian Pilgrimage*, London: Jarrold.

PAULIN, Tom (1984) 'Paisley's Progress'. In *Ireland and the English Crisis*, Newcastle: Bloodaxe.

POCOCK, J. G. A. (1975) *The Machiavellian Moment*, Cambridge Mass.: Harvard University Press.

ROBERTS, John (1967) *Europe 1880-1945*, London: Longman.

ROBERTSON, J. M. (1885) *The Perversion of Scotland*, London: Rationalist Press Association.

SMITH, Revd Thomas (1885) *Memoirs of Dr James Begg*, Edinburgh: Gemell.

STEVENSON, David (1988) *The Covenanters*, Edinburgh: Saltire Society.

STEWART, A. T. Q. (1989) *The Narrow Ground*, London: Faber, 1989.

WELSH, James (1920) The Underworld, London: Herbert Jenkins.

WILLIAMS, Gwyn A. (1985) When Was Wales? Harmondsworth: Penguin.

WILLIAMSON, Arthur (1983) *Scottish National Consciousness in the Age of James VI*, Edinburgh: John Donald.

3

David Livingstone: the construction of the myth

JOHN M. MACKENZIE

David Livingstone was the quintessential Victorian hero. Born in the ranks of the 'respectable poor' and educated in Glasgow through his efforts as a piecer in the cotton mill at Blantyre, he became one of the most celebrated figures of the third quarter of the nineteenth century. For his contemporaries, he represented an extraordinary conjunction of talents which reflected the concerns and values of the age: the heroic explorer, geographer, medical man and natural scientist who endowed all his activities not only with his missionary status, but also with the moral grandeur of what was perceived to be a strikingly elevated character. Moreover, he was a propagandist for some of the key ideas of the age, the abolition of slavery, free trade, white emigration, and commerce associated with a liberating and redemptive technology, all borne upon missionary endeavour to expand Christendom into the 'darker' regions of the globe. Thus he was both polymath and synoptic thinker, offering a programme that was practical and moral, an economic order embedded in Christian values.

In his own lifetime his reputation passed through three phases: celebrity as explorer, writer and propagandist after his return in 1856 from the first great journey to the interior of Central Africa; disillusion, and from some observers and associates even vilification, after the failure of his Zambezi expedition of 1858-63 and the disasters that befell the first mission established at his behest; and a renewal of his heroic stature in his final seven-year journey in search of the sources of the Nile. For some of this last period his name was kept before the public, partly through the mystery of his whereabouts and the mistaken stories of his death, partly because of the expeditions (numbering as many as eight) sent to search for him, partly as a result of the assiduous attentions of his admirers in the scientific, commercial, and missionary worlds, and partly because of H. M. Stanley's great 'scoop' in finding him in 1871 (Hall 1974;

McLynn. 1989). He received maximum publicity in the last year of his life as a result of the letters, dispatches and articles brought out by Stanley, together with Stanley's own efforts to publicise himself (Jeal, 1985, 337-53).

But if the Livingstone legend was already well-formed while he still wandered in Central Africa, it was amply confirmed and transformed into mythic status by accounts of his death at Chitambo's, the transport of his body to the coast by his followers, the intense mourning of the Victorian public, the grieving pomp of his funeral in Westminster Abbey, and above all by the careful editing and slanting of his copious last journals for publication (Waller, 1875). His posthumous reputation made him an archetype for his age, a public property displayed and used through countless biographies, heroic hagiographies, and other publications. He became a Protestant saint whose cult operated at a variety of different levels, imperial, British, and Scottish. Like all cults it was bent to suit the requirements of its age. This chapter is concerned with the development, progressive transformation and functioning of the myth of Livingstone. It moves from the general to the particular, from the role of heroic myths in an imperial age to the position of Livingstone in a didactic popular culture in Scotland, particularly the repatriation of his cult in the twentieth century.

THE IMPERIAL HERO

Hero myths are universal and have been much discussed as a psychological phenomenon. The hero is often an ancestor figure who performs striking feats, as a hunter for example, or vanquishes evil, liberating his people from destruction and death. (Jung, 1978) He is celebrated in ceremonies which exalt the participants to identification with his moral and physical virtues. He is a positive stereotype, a glorified image, even a model for control (Gilman 1985). The heroes of nineteenth-century Europe were contemporary figures who tended to be associated either with national self-awareness and the struggles for nationhood arising out of old imperial systems or with the translation of national power through modern imperialism to the wider world. British heroes of the period can perhaps be divided into three categories. The first was the hero of national defence against foreign tyranny, of whom Nelson is the prime exemplar (Hamilton, 1980). The second was the hero who involved himself in foreign nationalist struggles, expanding the incidence of free nationhood. The romantic hero Byron is the classic case, and Cochrane would also qualify. The third was the hero of empire, who expanded the moral order through the defeat of 'barbarism', the extension of Christendom, free trade and the rule of western law. The imperial hero vanquished evil overseas. Instead of being located in the past he was located in the exotic present. The remoteness of geography rather than of time served to enhance his moral stature (MacKenzie, 1990).

The imperial hero shared many of the characteristics of the romantic prototype (Calder, 1977). He was seen to push human action beyond the normal bounds, to be a wanderer who became an energising force through refusing to conform with the normal patterns of life. He was fearless, decisive and committed unto death, taking on forces, natural or human, that called forth the exercise of an indomitable will, superhuman physical stamina, and an almost miraculous courage. Following the Christian paradigm, he secured his ultimate conquest through martyrdom. Indeed, he was invariably an uncompromising Christian whose vices became his virtues, whose human frailties lent immediacy to his heroic stature (Anderson, 1971). These characteristics were exemplified by Sir Henry Havelock, who became a notable folk hero, David Livingstone and General Gordon.

These figures developed major instrumental power, particularly in an age of popular journalism and cheap publications for both adults and juveniles. They served to explain and justify the rise of the imperial state, personify national greatness, and offer examples of self-sacrificing service to a current generation. They were used as the embodiment of the collective will, stereotypes of a shared culture, and promoters of unity in the face of potential fragmentation. They also provided warnings for the future to an elite fearful of decline and acted as the instrument of pressure groups and interests in the formulation of policy. Their popular potency could be used to whip up agitations to influence government or justify the actions of administrations once decisions had been taken. They were both the producers of controversy and its anodyne. They became symbolic markers in the debates between party and interest group, government and public as represented by church and press, industry, commerce, and the military, elite and popular societies. They were also state mascots, honoured by the monarch, celebrated in monument and statuary, the source of much invented tradition.

The major myths were not self-generating. They required a mediator figure, a disciple who laboured to mould the material of the master's life into an appropriate form. They were greatly helped by an icon, generally the death scene which operated powerfully on the Victorian consciousness, liberating a range of ideas and emotions associated with the life, the cause, and the temporal and spiritual hereafter. Each promoted and fed upon major publishing and artistic endeavours. Diaries, journals and letters, usually carefully edited, deriving a peculiar fascination from the manner of their author's death, were swiftly published. These were soon accompanied by a plethora of biographies, parts of biographical series, and chapters in books of heroes. The illustrated journals carried engravings of scenes from the life, the death, the funeral, and the monumental commemorations. Publications for juveniles were illustrated by simplified versions of these engravings. Occasionally there was a major painting. Sculptors worked on busts and statues, often larger than life both literally and metaphorically. Sometimes there were theatrical presentations of the drama of the hero's life and martyrdom, with that distinctive Victorian form, the tableau vivant, acting as the climactic scene. Imperial heroes became an inseparable part of the popular culture of the late nineteenth and early twentieth centuries (MacKenzie, 1984; 1986).

Such myths could not of course be manufactured out of men of straw. Their subjects were unquestionably remarkable figures. The very complexities of their personalities, which have left them open to the debunking process in the twentieth century, were an essential aspect of their extraordinary characters. Courage, perseverance, manic energy, powers of observation, qualities of leadership, stubborn application, extremes of exaltation and depression, all developed to such a pitch as to be 'close to the dangerous edge of things' marked these individuals from the common run. But once engendered by the extraordinary capacities of the subject, the events of his life and death, the propaganda of the myth-making machine and the willingness of the public to be caught up in an emotional outburst, the myth became self-supporting because to knock it down was to endanger the system on which it fed. The successful heroic myth is by nature structurally important. It upheld the dominant ideology and value systems and impinged upon the interests (social and intellectual as much as economic) of many members of the elite. To sustain it was to sustain their own role as well as justify state action. But it is not static: the major myth is infinitely flexible fulfilling the needs of the moment or the needs of specific groups.

THE LIVINGSTONE HEROIC MYTH

The myth associated with the name of David Livingstone fulfilled all these criteria while adding additional complexities. Livingstone was inescapably a working-class Scot, who energised Englishmen and impacted on British governments. He acquired influence through moral power, not birth or schooling. He therefore appealed to a

number of levels of the Victorian consciousness: he represented
working-class advancement through spiritual stature, the application of national character from a *volkisch* tradition to state power and
imperial enterprise. His sufferings, last moments, and death had an
almost messianic quality, open to any amount of allegorical use and
iconographic representation.

One of the prime promoters of the Livingstone legend was
Horace Waller, the editor the *Last Journals*. Waller was an Anglican
cleric strikingly different in background and tastes from Livingstone. He was the son of a stockbroker, brought up in Tavistock
Square and at a country house in Leyton, Essex. In some respects he
became the classic country gentleman with a love of hunting, shooting and fishing. In 1859, however, he underwent a religious experience and followed Livingstone's call into the Universities Mission
to Central Africa. He went to that mission's first station in the
modern Malawi in 1860 and, although the mission notoriously
failed, he retained his admiration for Livingstone. He subsequently
acquired over 5000 acres of land in Malawi. After some jockeying,
he succeeded in securing the commission of the publisher John
Murray to edit the Livingstone journals. He more than edited them;
he carefully selected from them, and in some instances rewrote
them.

He did this in a number of ways. He sought to highlight
Livingstone's anti-slavery activities and played down the geographical obsessions, which might be deemed to have produced nothing
but failure. He bowdlerised Livingstone's references to natural
functions and sexual diseases; he excised all references to Muslims
and Islam which might be construed as favourable; he cut all
criticisms of public figures and other explorers; and he omitted
Livingstone's descriptions of his own rages and despairs, his physical
chastisement of his followers, and his threats to shoot those who
crossed him. He ensured that it was the saintly figure that emerged
from the journals rather than the weary traveller with very human
foibles. As Dorothy Helly (1987) has put it in her examination of the
Waller editing tactics, Livingstone was rewritten into a simple, great
man with a single high-minded objective rather than a disappointed,
flawed and complicated figure convinced of his own failure.

But Waller went further. He transformed Livingstone's followers,
Susi and Chuma, into devoted and faithful disciples, mini-heroes
transporting the great man's body to the coast. The fact that this
undoubtedly extraordinary exploit was accomplished by a larger
caravan, including the Christian and literate Jacob Wainwright, was
played down in order to develop public sympathy for the two central

characters (one of whom was a Muslim). Above all, through his careful and leading questioning of Susi and Chuma, he succeeded in creating the remarkable icon of Livingstone's death, that he had been found kneeling by his bedside, his face buried in his hands, as though in prayer (Waller, 1875, vol. 2 308-9).

Reviewers treated Waller's version of the journals as authentic. Waller became, in effect, a missionary and anti-slavery consultant closely implicated in the various pressure groups concerned with empire and Livingstone's moral and economic agenda. He wrote no fewer than eighty-five letters to *The Times* to keep Livingstone's name alive, and he sought out a successor to assume the Livingstone mantle. Inevitably, his eye fell on Charles Gordon. Attempting to create a heroic apostolic succession through the relic, he sent Gordon a strand of Livingstone's hair (Helly, 1987, 106). Once martyred in turn, Gordon was himself to be the subject of the myth-making machine with an equally striking icon to promote it (Johnson, 1982). Later, Waller looked to the very different figure of Frederick Lugard to continue the Livingstone tradition.

Waller was not of course alone in promoting the myth. While the journals were being edited and published, Henry Morton Stanley was pursuing his second expedition (1873-7) across Africa, portraying himself as setting about the completion of the great man's geographical labours. There can be no doubt at all that Stanley, the pathological liar and almost psychopathic killer, as different a figure from Livingstone as could be found, regarded Livingstone with genuine awe. His life was transformed by his encounter with Livingstone, and during the few months they spent together in 1871, his character was transformed too, though that transformation was to be of brief duration. For the illegitimate Stanley, Livingstone was the ideal father figure (McLynn, 1989). He was also to become Stanley's route to respectability, the name that unlocked the finance for future expeditions. The fact that the celebrated phrase, 'Dr Livingstone, I presume,' became a society and music hall joke did nothing to detract from the fame of both figures.

Stanley's book *How I Found Livingstone* (1872) was famously described by Florence Nightingale as 'the very worst book on the very best subject I ever saw in my life', but that did nothing to hinder its sales (McLynn, 224). It was first published in November 1872. It went through three editions by Christmas and continued in print, a favourite school prize, for decades to come. Stanley's next major work *Through the Dark Continent* (1878) opened with the news of Livingstone's death, reaching him on his way back to Britain after the Asante campaign of 1874. 'The effect this news was to have upon

me, after the first shock had passed away, was to fire me with a
resolution to complete his work, to be, if God willed it, the next
martyr to geographical science…' (Stanley, 1878,1). However
flawed and relatively unsuccessful Livingstone's geographical work
had been, he was to be the lodestar of future exploration.

Such invocations of Livingstone's work were to become conven-
tional in the many publications associated with missionary endeavour in East and Central Africa which appeared in the late nineteenth
and early twentieth centuries. It is difficult to find a missionary of the
period who did not proclaim himself as called and inspired by the
Livingstone story (*inter alia* Elmslie, 1899; Hetherwick, 1932, Laws,
1934). In the secular field, the celebrated pioneer and hunter F. C.
Selous was drawn to Africa, while still in his teens, through reading
the works of Livingstone (Taylor, 1989, 4, 8-9). The name of
Livingstone had talismanic power in commercial as well as inspirational ways. It frequently appeared in the titles of works. F. L. M.
Moir, one of the Edinburgh brothers who founded the African Lakes
Company as a practical expression of Livingstone's programme of
Christianity and Commerce, called his memoirs *After Livingstone:
an African Trade Romance* (1923). *My Link With Living-stone* and *In
the Footsteps of Livingstone* were other titles (Crawford, 1922; Dolman, 1924). Even Sir Harry Johnston, the first mildly debunking
biographer, was concerned to set his own travels and activities in the
partition of Africa into the Livingstone framework (Johnston, 1891).
The Blantyre and Livingstonia missions in Malawi were, of course,
founded to honour the name (McCracken, 1977), as was the town
of Livingstone in Zambia, the capital of that territory until the
founding of Lusaka in the 1930s. These names have survived in
independent Africa. It may be, as John McCracken has argued, that
Livingstone's memory was more inspirational than practical, since
his specific programme was seldom followed (David Livingstone
Seminar, 1973), but the principal power of myth lies in its taking
such inspirational forms. The myth is consensual; the practical
enters the realm of controversy.

The works of Waller and Stanley were soon followed by the
publication of extraordinary numbers of popular biographies. Many
of these were no more than summaries of each other or of the more
major works, such as that of Blaikie (1880). Yet most of them
remained in print for long periods, selling in large numbers (as they
often proudly proclaimed on the title pages), and authors and
publishers seem to have had no compunction about adding to them
at frequent intervals. For publishers, the Livingstone market was to
remain buoyant for decades. Myths gain their power from repetition

and demonstrate their strength through their continuing accept-
ability.

Their popular influence is also secured through an iconography
of simple, but potent visual references to the main themes and
messages of the story. This is particularly true of Livingstone. The
biographies abound in the icons: the simple cotton worker reading at
his loom, the missionary attacked by a lion, the emancipator of
slaves, the meeting with Stanley – pregnant with significance for the
future of Africa - the final indomitable journey through the swamps
of Bangweulu, the death scene, Susi and Chuma carrying the body
to the coast, the national funeral in the Abbey. These are almost
universally standard in any number of different engraved versions.
Sometimes they were supplemented by images of him preaching
from a wagon, 'discovering' the Victoria Falls, launching a steamer
on the Zambezi, writing up his journals, dealing sympathetically
with Africans.

Interestingly Livingstone, unlike many other nineteenth-century
heroes, seldom if ever made an appearance in the 'faction' of the
period. R. M. Ballantyne used Livingstone's works (and footnoted
them) in *Black Ivory*, his story of the East African slave trade, but
Livingstone himself did not appear (Ballantyne, 1873). Henty and
his successors never touched him. No play was written about him,
whereas there were several on General Gordon, three of them
performed in London by the end of 1885, the year of his death
(MacKenzie 1984). There are a number of reasons for this.
Livingstone's solitary habits did not lend themselves to the standard
formula of intruding a fictional companion into his activities. His
journeys were not susceptible to plotting. Only the Zambezi expedition, the exploit that reflected least well on Livingstone, had both a
cast of white characters and a plot. Moreover, he was too complex a
figure, at the same time too well and too little known, to be available
for factional treatment. To a certain extent, Livingstone's failure to
appear in topical fiction so typical of the age was a tribute to the
power of the myth, the saint-like character of the subject.

THE DEVELOPMENT AND TRANSFORMATION OF THE LIVINGSTONE MYTH

The Livingstone myth operated at a variety of different levels. It was
a religious myth: Livingstone was a Protestant saint who attracted
(almost uniquely) the language of sainthood, as we shall see. The
fact that he was a Congregationalist meant that he was virtually a
Christian without a denomination. He could be, and was, appropriated by any church – Scottish, Nonconformist, Anglican, even,
through the efforts of Cardinal Lavigerie, Roman Catholic. It was a

class myth, for Livingstone represented the supreme example of self-help. He was depicted as the epitome of the working-class auto-didact whose route from 'rags to fame', from the cotton mill to Westminster Abbey, was carved out through sheer application and moral worth. His achievements were a notable example to his fellow-workers and a consolation to the bourgeoisie. Working-class advancement could be secured by means other than political protest or trade union agitation.

It was an imperial myth, since the Livingstone agenda, with its stress upon the opening up of Africa through knowledge of its geography and natural resources, on cotton-growing and other raw material production, white emigration, the creation of infrastructures and the application of new technology, and the placing of Africans in a position of tutelage, was essentially imperial in character. It is significant that in a conversation with Stanley he proclaimed himself an admirer of Disraeli rather than Gladstone (McLynn 1989, 162). Yet as a religious figure his appeal clearly spanned all political divides. It was a British myth because Livingstone illustrated the manner in which empire permitted a marginal man to become the true Briton working for an English missionary society, for institutions like the Royal Geographical Society, for the Foreign Office itself, and could unite public, monarch and elite in honouring him, burying him among national heroes in Westminster Abbey.

But in the twentieth century he also came to represent a myth of Scottish nationhood, to personify a Scottish cultural awakening. Much was to be made of his Scottishness. His ancestral heritage, his character traits and spiritual qualities were used to render him the typical Scot, whose example might fuel a Scottish renaissance. He became not only the patron saint of missionaries and anti-slavers, of free-traders and emigrants, of geographers, doctors and natural scientists, but also of Scots cultural syncretism and improvement. Churches, educational institutions, museums, exhibitions and publishers promoted him as a central figure for an improving Scottish popular culture. This was to be the twentieth-century modification of the myth, and it was possibly through that development that he achieved his final apotheosis as the patron of both League of Nations trusteeship and African nationalism, the one nineteenth-century imperial figure to be honoured in independent African states. The complexities of Livingstone's achievement were therefore able to embrace both the expansion and consolidation of the imperial state and the rise of nationalism at home and overseas.

Analysis of the many popular biographies of Livingstone (over fifty have been examined for this study) reveals the extent to which the myth accommodated itself, or was manipulated to fit, the particular requirements of the age. No doubt this was one reason why there was a constant renewal process in the Livingstone biographical industry. It was a central aspect of the transmission of the myth that Livingstone was a prophet. Indeed, the titles of the popular biographies reflect the extent to which the Livingstone life reached out beyond its own span:*David Livingstone, the Explorer and the Prophet, Livingstone the Pathfinder, Livingstone the Liberator, David Livingstone: his Labours and his Legacy* are but a few that illustrate the point (Finger, 1927; Mathews,1913; Macnair,1929a; Montefiore-Brice, 1889). Rapid developments in Africa ensured that each biography had a tendency to obsolescence. They required new prefaces and postscripts or were superseded by new versions. It is possible to identify at least five periods in the production of Livingstone biographies.

The early examples of the genre were concerned with the campaign against the slave trade and continuing geographical explorations. Some of these were published during his final journey and acted as propaganda for appropriate recognition of his work and for official concern as to his welfare and safety (Adams, 1868; Roberts, 1874; Donald, 1875). It is an interesting characteristic of this early period of the Livingstone biographies that they often devote a large amount of attention to the animals of Africa, sugaring the pill of heroic action with zoological thrills and excitements, a powerful fascination of the Victorians (Adams, 1868; Roberts, 1874; MacKenzie, 1988; Merrill, 1989). From the later 1880s the biographies depict Livingstone as the harbinger and patron of the partition of Africa (Johnston, 1891; Charles, 1895). He is viewed as the prophet of European rule and of the importance that the lakes and rivers of the continent would play in the process of the scramble.

In the early years of the twentieth century the writers become concerned with the balance sheet of empire, thus illustrating the extent to which the Livingstone programme had been achieved. These works invariably end with listings of the numbers of missionaries, mission stations, and converts in Africa, the imports and exports of the territories through which Livingstone passed, and the successful creation of of the infrastructure of railways, roads and steamers which Livingstone had predicted (Hughes, 1906, 195-9; Elliott, 1908, 95; Gregory, 1913; Horne, 1912). They. set out to demonstrate how different Africa had become a mere thirty or forty years after Livingstone's death, celebrating progress through a vision of peaceful toil, comfortable tourist travel and missionary education. As one put it, the history of Africa brightened as it unfolded, its progress proving that all things were possible, all hopes reasonable (Maclachlan, 1901). In the 1920s the biographies begin to portray Livingstone as the precursor of ideas of trusteeship, the patron saint of the internationalism of the League of Nations (Campbell, 1929). Lugard, now a peer and the British representative at the Mandates Commission of the League, is again heralded as the inheritor of the Livingstone mantle. In the same period Livingstone is reappropriated for the Scottish cultural revival. The biographies begin to portray him as the typical Scot, combining in his personality the classic Scottish virtues and in the diversity of his interests and extent of his mental and practical abilities the Scottish intellectual tradition of openness – capable of spanning the disciplines and appealing to all classes, professions and religious persuasions.

Livingstone had himself referred to his mixed Highland and Lowland ancestry in his brief autobiographical introduction to *Missionary Travels and Researches* (1857), his first great best-seller. His paternal ancestors were Highlanders, Gaelic-speaking, and Jacobites. His great-grandfather had fought at Culloden. His maternal progenitors, the Hunters, were Lowlanders and Covenanters. This was picked up by many of the popular biographies, but in the 1920s it came to be highlighted as a matter of faith . In *Livingstone the Liberator*, James I. Macnair, who was the prime mover in founding the Scottish National Memorial to Livingstone at Blantyre, devoted several pages in turn to the Highland strain and the Lowland strain in Livingstone's parentage (1929a, 25-31). These twin streams, even dubbed a 'fusion of the races', were seen as providing Livingstone with a mix of contrasting and complementary virtues, virtues which made him particularly sympathetic to African peoples and which rendered him accessible to people of any temperament.

The Celtic gave Livingstone his impulsive generosity, imagination and fire, while his Lowland ancestry contributed determination and tenacity, a hatred of oppression, a self-reliant practical temper and a sense of humour; from both together he acquired his marvellous powers of endurance. In a brief penny biography, Macnair put it slightly differently: in him were joined the fire, chivalry, and mysticism of the North with the dour grit, practical forethought, and hatred of oppression of the South (1929b). Another biographer of the same period went further: R. J. Campbell attempted to link Livingstone with the major cultural traditions and historical myths of Scotland. He examined the notion that Livingstone might be descended from Betan who came to Scotland as physician to St Columba, that he might be related to the barons of Bachuill of

Lismore, to the Livingstons who had rescued and buried the body of James Stewart of the glens, whose tale had been retold by R. L. Stevenson in *Kidnapped* and *Catriona* (1929, 27-35). These claims had been put forward in various Gaelic publications in the years just before the First World War. Campbell, it is true, casts some doubt on them, but only after an extended discussion which would have left the flavour of the proposed connections in the reader's mind.

More significantly, Campbell highlighted a set of cultural references to place Livingstone at the intersection of the Scottish romantic tradition. Livingstone's father was much like his counterpart in Burns's *Cotter's Saturday Night*. (This was a comparison Livingstone himself had used.) His maternal great-grandfather was like a figure from Scott's *Old Mortality*. The Livingstones and the Hunters were great storytellers who recounted to the young David tales of his Jacobite and Covenanting inheritance just as in Scott's *Tales of a Grandfather*. From reading Dr Thomas Dick, Livingstone derived his faith in the compatibility of science and religion. The Livingstone family could be linked to a wider nationalism too. Two of his uncles had allegedly fought at Waterloo. His father Neil, while staying at home, had contributed to the family's qualities as an 'intrepid, dauntless, questing breed' by working as an itinerant tea salesman, distributing religious tracts as he did so, thus combining in his own small way Christianity and commerce. For Campbell, Livingstone mixed the keen imagination and high spirit of the Highlander with the tenacious democratic traditions, stern Calvinistic faith, strength of will and perseverance of the Lowlander (Campbell, 1929, 25).

Campbell linked all this to the mutual sympathy Livingstone enjoyed with Africans. He understood their oral traditions, their historic and didactic tales, their concern with ancestors and heroic exploits. Above all he understood the bond between Africans and their chiefs, supposedly so similar to the Scottish clan system. Accordingly, he understood the communality of the African tribe and the mutual obligations of chief and people more profoundly than many of his imperial successors. He was thus a proto-indirect ruler. Moreover, he sympathised with attitudes towards cattle raiding and lifting which were more akin to the activities of Highland and border pastoralists than anything the English comprehended. Livingstone's status as the archetypal Scot provided him with a leap of understanding to the African condition of which the English were incapable. His ancestral and familial inheritance made him at once nationalist and internationalist. It was in this context that efforts were made to repatriate the legend and make it more accessible to the Scottish working class.

THE CREATION OF THE SCOTTISH NATIONAL MEMORIAL TO LIVINGSTONE

The project to create a Scottish National Memorial to David Livingstone out of the birthplace at Blantyre was closely associated with this renewed concern with his status as the archetypal Scot. There had of course been many memorials to Livingstone already. A statue was unveiled in Princes Street Gardens, Edinburgh, in 1876, in Glasgow's George Square (later moved to Cathedral Square) in 1879. The building of a memorial church in Blantyre had begun in 1877 with a statue set into one of its walls. A Livingstone memorial library had been established by Lord Amulree. The Central African missions that bore his name or that of his birth place were conceived as a memorial, and further statues and monuments were erected at Chitambo's, Nkota Kota (on the shores of Lake Malawi), Ujiji (at the spot where Stanley had 'found' him) and later the Victoria Falls. The tembe (or Arab house) in which he and Stanley had resided in Kwihara, five miles from Tabora, became a place of pilgrimage, carefully preserved by the Tanganyika colonial authorities.

In 1911 Livingstone featured prominently in the Palace of History at the Scottish Exhibition of National History, Art and Industry in Kelvingrove Park, Glasgow (Catalogue of Exhibits, 1911). This major exhibition, the third on the site by the Kelvin, was partially devoted to the public rediscovery of Scottish arts and history and the profits from it were used to establish a chair of Scottish History at Glasgow University. In the centennial year of his birth, 1913, an exhibition devoted to his life and work was held at the Royal Scottish Museum in Edinburgh, while lectures, services and meetings were held throughout the country. The Scottish composer, Hamish MacCunn (1868-1916) composed a cantata, *Livingstone the Pilgrim*. Memorial and thanksgiving services were held not only throughout Scotland, but also in the Royal Albert Hall, St Paul's Cathedral, Westminster Abbey and many of the cathedrals of England. The Royal Albert Hall event was presided over by the Archbishop of Canterbury; Lord Balfour of Burleigh addressed the assembled throng and a message from the Prime Minister was read out. There were memorial lectures at the universities and the geographical societies. The ex-Viceroy Curzon addressed the Royal Geographical Society in May 1913:

> As a missionary Livingstone was the sincere and zealous servant of God. As an explorer, he was the indefatigable servant of science. As a denouncer of the slave trade, he was the fiery servant of humanity. Born with no social advantages, possessing no prospects, backed by no powerful influence, this

invincible Scotsman hewed his way through the world and carved his name deep in the history of mankind.

These events were extensively reported with much pride in the Scottish press, but in the same year Shuttle Row, the Livingstone birthplace, had been condemned. An old woman looked after the room in which Livingstone had been born and made a small income from the visitors who came to view it, but the surroundings had become thoroughly disreputable. The Free Church missionary Donald Fraser attempted to do something to save the building, but decided that dereliction had gone too far. Demolition was, however, held up by the war, and in 1925 James Macnair, president of the Congregational Union of Scotland, visited the building and decided to try to save it as a memorial. He established a public appeal at an exceptionally inauspicious time, the year of the General Strike, and was surprised at its remarkable success. It had originally been thought that the funds would be forthcoming from better-off Scots, from the English, and from overseas. But, he recorded, the General Strike made the rich very uncertain about the future. Nine-tenths of the finance came from Scotland, mainly from small donations from Sunday Schools and Bible classes (Macnair, 1945).

Macnair was in no doubt of Livingstone's status as a Protestant saint. The memorial was designed to be a 'place of pilgrimage, a shrine' where pilgrims would 'fire to the thrill of his story and respond to the inspiration of his noble example'. In his account of the project, Macnair entitled one of his chapters 'the gathering of the relics', Macnair, 1945, 29-32). The memorial, consisting of Shuttle Row, the adjacent building and some forty acres of land, later to accommodate the world fountain and the Africa Pavilion, was opened by the Duchess of York (later Queen Elizabeth the Queen Mother) before a crowd of 10000 people. Many of the most celebrated names of missionary work in Africa were present and the speeches were replete with the language of sainthood. The Livingstone cult had found its centre, and in a set of sculptural tableaux created for the Memorial by C. d'O. Pilkington Jackson, its icons.

The conversion of a condemned slum into a shrine had a particularly powerful resonance in the 1920s. Moreover, through this act of social and architectural redemption, the Scots had reclaimed the Livingstone legend for popular consumption at home, as part of a Scottish cultural revival. There was extensive press coverage of the development and opening of the memorial, not just in Scotland, but in the dominions and African territories where Scots were settled or worked. Fired by this enterprise, the Caledonian societies of Central

Africa paid for a statue of Livingstone to be erected by the Devil's
Cataract of the Victoria Falls. It was sculpted by Sir W. R. Dick, RA
and was unveiled in 1934. Attendance at the Blantyre memorial
swiftly exceeded expectation. Visitor figures of 90000 per annum
were soon being recorded, remarkable for the period. On summer
Saturday afternoons, there were often as many as 3000 children on
Sunday school excursions visiting the building and using the playing
fields. By 1945 the memorial had received one million visitors.

POPULAR REACTIONS TO THE LIVINGSTONE MYTH

That middle-class and clerical Scots were eager to use the
Livingstone myth for a Scottish cultural and spiritual renewal
cannot be gainsaid, but, as always, it is difficult to gauge the full
extent of its reception at the imperialist, nationalist and didactic end
of Scottish popular culture. In 1872 H. M. Stanley carried his
lecture tour into Scotland and found himself rapturously received
wherever he went (McLynn, 1989, 222-3). This was in striking
contrast to some of his experiences in England where he had often
faced distrust and disbelief. Scottish audiences seemed to be eager
to hear any news of the missionary hero, even if from the lips of a
publicity-seeking journalist, an illegitimate Welsh American. After
Livingstone's funeral Susi and Chuma built a replica at Wemyss Bay
of the hut in which Livingstone had died. It was much visited and
later in the century postcards of it were available for use by visitors.
There can be no doubt that the biographies, many in very cheap
editions, secured large sales in Scotland and became a basic staple of
the prize and present market, dished out by the thousand in schools,
Sunday schools and, from 1883, Boy's Brigade companies. In both
1889 and 1892-3 there were genuinely popular agitations in Scotland relating to the Portuguese treaty (which would have given up
the Shiré highlands of Malawi to Portugal) and to the possibility that
Uganda might be abandoned after the collapse of Sir William
Mackinnon's Imperial East Africa Company. In each of these the
name of Livingstone was repeatedly reinvoked. In 1902 a lecture
given at Glasgow University was published as a cheap pamphlet,
supposedly by popular demand. 'It argues well for our working-
men, at whose special desire this pamphlet sees the light, that they
are eager to read the story of his life and labours.' (Pryde, 1902.)

The 1913 centennial celebrations cannot have failed to touch
large numbers of people since they seem to have had almost universal expression in churches, societies, schools and public bodies, with
extensive press coverage. In the 1920s a series of remarkably cheap
publications were issued, including the penny biography by Macnair

and a pamphlet 'autobiography' (in fact the introduction to *Missionary Travels* together with Curzon's tribute at the Royal Geographical Society (Livingstone, 'Autobiography', *Missionary Travels*). In 1925 Livingstone appeared on film in a lengthy documentary feature made by M. A. Wetherell who also played the leading role (Rapp and Weber, 1989). The film was made on location in Africa in the course of a major expedition led by Wetherell and funded from a variety of sources. It was designed to lift the marvels of the cinema to the higher level (and overcome the distorted view of British achievements given in American films) and, as always, inspire the young. It was long and had the character of a travelogue (with extensive shots of African wildlife) as well as a hagiography. It was well received and extensively shown in cinemas as well as church and public halls. Both its making and its showing were newsworthy and received a good deal of press comment. It was alleged to have made a triumphal progress round the country and continued to be available for rent until at least the Second World War. As a morally earnest educational and religious film it certainly had no chance of weaning audiences away from the joys of the Hollywood product, but it was presumably viewed as a different sort of experience.

Hollywood itself joined in with *Stanley and Livingstone* in 1939, but this film had only a tenuous grip on authenticity and projected Stanley (played by the amiable and very un-Stanleyish Spencer Tracy) as the real hero, with Livingstone (in the guise of a rather straight-backed English gentleman played by Cedric Hardwicke) as a slightly depersonalised spiritual 'controller'. To a certain extent it carried the message of joint British and American endeavour in civilising the world, a message which some no doubt regarded as timely in 1939.

Still, the Livingstone myth, at least in the quantity and variety of its outward manifestations, was a remarkably durable one. Although attendance at the Blantyre memorial went into steep decline in the 1960s, 70s, and 80s, Livingstone had by that time become a patron saint of African nationalism. No fewer than six African countries issued memorial stamps on the centenary of his death in 1973 (Westwood, 1986). There were special publications in African countries (Waller, 1973) and even lectures given by nationalist politicians (Livingstone Seminar, 1973, 184). The power of the myth declined at home because with the end of empire the Livingstone story became more specialised. In the nineteenth century Livingstone was a hero of empire, his influence as much secular as religious. In the twentieth he became a hero of Scots endeavour. But by the time his name was being honoured in a decolonised

Africa, at home he had become primarily a religious figure. The popular biographies continued to be issued as prizes at Sunday schools and Boy's Brigades until the 1960s, but they had little chance of helping to initiate a religious revival, and the era of the debunking biography was at hand (Jeal, 1973; Listowel,1974). The age of the national hero had passed. The myth figures of the late twentieth century have become a curious mixture of rebels, nonconformists, members of the royal family and stars of soaps.

ACKNOWLEDGEMENTS

I am grateful to William Cunningham, John Moore and the staff of the Scottish National Memorial to David Livingstone for making available the many popular biographies, ephemera and press cuttings in the archive at Blantyre. Mr Cunningham also kindly supplied visitor figures for every year from the opening of the Memorial to 1989. The references below contain only a few of the popular biographies examined for this study and do not list the ephemera and press cuttings consulted. I also acknowledge the help of Terry Barringer and her staff at the Royal Commonwealth Society Library in London for making available popular material on Livingstone.

REFERENCES

ADAMS, H. G. (1868) *The Life and Adventures of Dr. Livingston* [sic] *in the interior of South Africa*, London: Blackwood.

ANDERSON, Olive (1971) The growth of Christian militarism in mid-Victorian Britain, *English Historical Review*, LXXXVI, 46-72.

BALLANTYNE, R. M. (1873) *Black Ivory*, London: J. Nisbet and Co.

BLAIKIE, W. G. (1880) *The Personal Life of Dr. Livingstone*, London: John Murray.

CALDER, Jenni (1977) *Heroes from Byron to Guevara*, London: Hamish Hamilton.

CAMPBELL, R. J. (1929) *Livingstone*, London: Ernest Benn.

Catalogue of Exhibits (1911), *Scottish Exhibition of National History, Art and Industry, Palace of History*, Glasgow: Dalross, 2 vols.

CHARLES, Mrs Rundle (1895) *Three Martyrs of the Nineteenth Century*, London: SPCK.

CRAWFORD, Dan (1922) *Back to the Long Grass: My Link with Livingstone*, London: Hodder and Stoughton.

DOLMAN, Alfred (1924) *In the Footsteps of Livingstone*, London: John Lane.

DONALD, James (1875) *David Livingstone: His Life and Travels in Africa*, Newcastle on Tyne: John Christie.

ELLIOTT, W. A. (1908) *Nyaka the Doctor: the Story of David Livingstone*, London: London Missionary Society.

ELMSLIE, W. A. (1899) *Among the Wild Ngoni*, Edinburgh: Oliphant.

FINGER, Charles J. (1927) *David Livingstone, the Explorer and The Prophet*, New York: Doubleday.

GILMAN, Sander L. (1985) *Difference and Pathology*, Ithaca and London: Cornell University Press.

GREGORY, J. W. (1913) *Livingstone as an Explorer: an Appreciation*, Glasgow: University of Glasgow.

HALL, Richard (1974) *Stanley: an Adventurer Explored*, London: Collins.

HAMILTON, C. I. (1980) Naval hagiography and the Victorian hero, *Historical Journal*, XXIII, 381-98.

HELLY, Dorothy O. (1987) *Livingstone's Legacy: Horace Waller and Victorian Mythmaking*, Columbus: Ohio University Press.

HETHERWICK, Alexander (1932) *The Romance of Blantyre*, London: J. Clarke.

HORNE, C. Silvester (1912) *David Livingstone*, London: Macmillan

HUGHES, Thomas (1906) *David Livingstone*, London: Macmillan.

JEAL, Tim (1985) *Livingstone*, Harmondsworth: Penguin (first published 1973).

JOHNSON, Douglas (1982) The Death of Gordon: a Victorian myth, *Journal of Imperial and Commonwealth History*, X, 285-310.

JOHNSTON, Sir H. H. (1891) *Livingstone and the Exploration of Central Africa*, London: George Philip.

JUNG, Carl (1978) *Man and His Symbols*, London: Picader.

LAWS, Robert (1934) *Reminiscences of Livingstonia*, Edinburgh: Oliver Boyd.

LISTOWEL, Judith (1974) *The Other Livingstone*, Lewes: Julian Friedmann.

LIVINGSTONE, David (1857) *Missionary Travels and Researches*, London: John Murray.

LIVINGSTONE SEMINAR (1973) *David Livingstone and Africa: Proceedings of a Seminar held on the occasion of the centenary of the death of David Livingstone*, Centre of African Studies, University of Edinburgh, Edinburgh: Edinburgh University.

McCRACKEN, John (1977) *Politics and Christianity in Malawi, 1875-1940*, Cambridge: Cambridge University Press.

MACKENZIE, John M. (1984) *Progaganda and Empire*, Manchester: Manchester University Press.

MACKENZIE, John M. (ed.) (1986) *Imperialism and Popular Culture* Manchester: Manchester University Press.

MACKENZIE, John M. (1988) *The Empire of Nature*, Manchester: Manchester University Press.

MACKENZIE, John M. (1990) T. E. Lawrence, the Myth and the Message. In Robert Giddings (ed.) *Imperialism and Literature*, London: Macmillan.

MACLACHLAN, T. Banks (1901) *David Livingstone*, Edinburgh: Oliphant, Anderson and Ferrier.

McLYNN, Frank (1989) *Stanley: the Making of an Explorer* London: Constable.

MACNAIR, James I. (1929a) *Livingstone the Liberator*, Glasgow: Collins.

MACNAIR, James I. (1929b) *David Livingstone: the Story in Brief*, Blantyre: the David Livingstone Memorial.

MATHEWS, Basil (1913) *Livingstone the Pathfinder* London: Oxford University Press.

MERRILL, Lynn L. (1989) *The Romance of Victorian Natural History*, Oxford: Oxford University Press.

MOIR, F. L. M. (1923) *After Livingstone: an African Trade Romance*, London: Hodder and Stoughton.

MONTEFIORE-BRICE, A. (1889) *David Livingstone: his Labours and his Legacy*, London: S. W. Partridge.

PACHAI, Bridgial (ed.) (1973) *Livingstone: Man of Africa, Memorial Essays (1873-1973)*, London: Longman.

PRYDE, John Marshall (1902) *Livingstone and the Slave Trade or the Opening up of Central Africa*, Glasgow: Openheim and Longman.

RAPP, Dean and WEBER, Charles W. (1989) British Film, Empire and Society in the Twenties: the 'Livingstone' film, 1923–25. *Historical Journal of Film, Radio and Television*, 9, 1, 3-17.

ROBERTS, John S. (1874) *The Life and Explorations of David Livingstone, complete so far as known*, London: Adam.

STANLEY, Henry M. (1872) *How I Found Livingstone,*, London: Sampson Low.

STANLEY, Henry M. (1878) *In Darkest Africa*, London: George Newnes.

TAYLOR, Stephen (1989) *The Mighty Nimrod, a Life of Frederick Courteney Selous, African Hunter and Adventurer, 1851-1917*, London: Collins.

WALLER, Horace (1875) *The Last Journals of David Livingstone*, London: John Murray.

WALLER, Horace (1973) *The Death of Dr Livingstone*, Lusaka: Historical Association of Zambia.

WESTWOOD, Peter J. (1986) *David Livingstone: his life and work as told through the media of postage stamps and allied material*, Edinburgh: Holmes McDougall.

4

Evangelical Protestantism in the nineteenth-century Highlands

ALLAN I. MACINNES

Public perceptions of evangelical Protestantism in the Highlands tend to conform to an agenda set by Hebridean ayatollahs, austere Calvinists dedicated to ecclesiastical legalism, uncompromising Sabbatarianism and spiritual elitism. Notwithstanding the self-parodying efforts of clerics and their acolytes, evangelical Protestantism in the Highlands should not be entirely written off as an isolated, introverted and unenlightened brand of Presbyterianism deep in faith, long in hope but short in charity.[1] Certainly, evangelical Protestantism in the nineteenth-century Highlands was directed, contained and ultimately institutionalised by the clergy in the wake of the Disruption of 1843, a trend given added sectarian bitterness by the split of the Free Presbyterians from the Free Church in 1893 as by the refusal of a minority of the latter denomination (the 'Wee Frees') to join with the overwhelmingly Lowland, United Presbyterians in the United Free Church from 1900. Nonetheless, evangelical Protestantism was not a Gaelic anachronism but an integral part of the reformed tradition which remained resistant to rationalist and scientific reappraisals of doctrine during the nineteenth century.[2]

The brand of Protestantism that stamped its distinctive mark on nineteenth-century Scottish Gaeldom was uncompromisingly Presbyterian. However, the brand of Protestantism favoured in much of the Highlands prior to 1750 was Episcopalianism, more explicitly the non-juring variety, which adhered to Jacobitism. Despite being subject to debilitating persecution verging on genocide by the Whig establishment in Church and State, Episcopalianism retained a significant presence in northern Argyll, Lochaber and the eastern Highlands in the early nineteenth century. Presbyterianism, moreover, was markedly more evangelical in the northern and north-western than in the central and southern Highlands, a situation that tended to conform to the national divide between the Moderate and

Evangelical or Popular parties in the Established Church.[3]

Faced with major problems of communications – both geographic and linguistic – of large parishes with rising populations in dispersed Gaelic-speaking communities, general assemblies of the Established Church had favoured an arid institutional approach to inculcate Presbyterianism in the Highlands during the eighteenth century. At an institutional level, the intrusion of Presbyterianism was part of an officially sponsored programme of 'civilising'. The royal bounty scheme conceded by George I in 1724 afforded an annuity of £1 000 to create and sustain missionary districts within large parishes served by itinerant preachers and catechists. After twenty years of lobbying by the general assembly, the royal bounty was increased by George IV to £2 000 from 1830, a sum which served to finance around thirty-five missionaries and catechists.[4]

Particularly favoured in the drive to 'civilise' the Highlands were the shock-troops of Presbyterianism, the Society for Propagating Christian Knowledge (the SPCK appositely rendered in Gaelic as CCCP). Established in Edinburgh in 1701, incorporated in 1709 and financed by public subscription, the SPCK earned deserved notoriety for its unstinting endeavours to stamp out Gaelic in the first half of the eighteenth century through its discriminatory missionary and educational policies which remained regressively intent on social containment. With the political threat of Jacobitism extinguished and the Highlander being rehabilitated as military cannon-fodder for the British Empire, the SPCK did change tack allowing Gaelic to be used as a medium of instruction from 1766. In the following year, the SPCK was responsible for the publication of the first Scottish Gaelic version of the New Testament and, subsequently, of the first Scottish Gaelic Bible in 1801. The SPCK have accordingly won deserved commendation as the major publisher of Gaelic religious texts in the nineteenth century, an achievement which certainly promoted the cultural association of religion, education and language. Nonetheless, its missionary and educational policies remained markedly denominational. Operating within a budget of £4–5 000, the SPCK managed to maintain around ten missionaries, 33 catechists and 261 teachers (including 105 women engaged in 105 female schools of industry) during the 1830s by keeping salaries low.[5] Albeit its funds were extremely limited in relation to the magnitude of its religious operations in the Highlands, the SPCK remained notably deficient and grudging in its educational provision, pulling out of communities faced with Clearance and dismissing catechists and missionaries openly critical of the Moderate ascendancy within the Established Church. Effectively marginalised by the Disruption of 1843, the SPCK remained distinctly sectarian in outlook.[6]

Prior to the Disruption, the SPCK did play a valuable role as a religious lobby, both locally and nationally. Landlords, especially absentees, were reminded of their legal duties to support schooling. Congregations were exhorted to match the salaries (from £7–10/– to £15) paid to catechists. The political and religious establishment was continuously advised on the need to create new parishes for sacramental purposes in the Highlands. Thus, the Reverend Daniel Dewar of College Church, Aberdeen, when delivering the annual sermon to the Corresponding Board of the SPCK in the Gaelic Chapel at Hatton Gardens, London in 1814, preached about religious deprivation. Such was the size of Ardnamurchan parish that although the minister had three assistants, there were some parts which remained for weeks without a sermon. In the adjoining parish of Lismore and Appin, the inhabitants of the district of Kingairloch only heard four sermons a year. The adjacent district of Corran and Mammore, which was scarcely ever visited by a pastor of the Established Church and was but briefly served by a missionary from Fort William, 'has not received a sermon above once in six weeks since the Reformation'?[7]

Such lobbying, however, served to confirm the Established Church's institutional approach to religious provision in the Highlands without challenging the spiritual complacency of the Moderate ascendancy in the early nineteenth century. Although chapels of ease were licensed by general assemblies from the late eighteenth century to serve populous parishes, their missionary impact in the Highlands was marginal, a situation recognised by the creation of parliamentary churches from 1824. By tapping into the engineering expertise of Thomas Telford and other surveyors engaged in the road and canal building programme, state intervention sought to provide around forty churches in the Highlands and Islands. No more than £1 500 was to be expended in each parish to build a church sufficient to hold a congregation of 400 and provide the resident minister with a manse and a glebe. The supervision of this building programme was devolved to a commission which submitted its first report to the general assembly in 1825. The commissioners identified sixty districts in fifty four parishes where parliamentary churches might be erected.[8] Lacking first-hand experience of parochial provision in the Highlands, the commissioners were too reliant on maps and surveyors' reports. Nor was the commissioners' work aided by the inaccurate and inadequate provision of information by landlords about suitable sites and existing parochial churches. Incoming landlords in Argyll, Ross, Sutherland and Caithness were among the most receptive to the building programme, agreeing not only to provide sites but to accept responsibility for repairs. Traditional landed families tended to view the parliamentary initiative as a means of getting rid of unwanted responsibilities. Thus, Alexander Norman MacLeod of Harris offered to sell the ancient kirk at Rhodel to the commission, omitting to mention that he had allowed his factor to turn the church into a barn for thrashing corn and a workshop for cartwrights after extensive clearances in South Harris in the previous decade [9]

Albeit priority was accorded to the western and northern Highlands, the commission was receptive to providing additional money for manses in all districts where support for missionaries was well attested. However, the rules for expenditure and building dimensions were rigidly adhered to. Landlords were expected to bear any additional costs incurred in building churches to accommodate congregations larger than 400. In the event, only thirty-one sites were assigned for churches and another ten for manses. Building had commenced in only four districts in 1826, though the building programme was given a further boost in 1833 with the decision of the general assembly that the districts served by parliamentary churches be constituted sacramental parishes. Perhaps the most enduring architectural legacy of the parliamentary churches, constructed to a fixed design of 60 feet by 30 feet, were the narrow windows which set standards for the subsequent narrowing of vision for Free Church and Free Presbyterian Churches in the nineteenth-century Highlands.[10]

In the interim, Principal George Baird of Edinburgh University, founder and first convener of the Established Church's Highlands and Islands committee in 1824, had submitted a report to the general assembly of his visit to the parliamentary churches in Argyll and the Isles in the summer of 1827. This visit, accomplished in a yacht placed at his disposal by revenue officials, carried the hallmarks of spiritual complacency. His primary concern was to scrutinise the ongoing building programme. Landlords were commended for their benevolence in providing church sites, manses and glebes. No comment was passed on the religious and social welfare of Highland congregations. In Lewis he did not even visit the sites of the parliamentary churches at Uig and Barvas, preferring to accept the verbatim report of Mrs Stewart-Mackenzie of Seaforth whose hospitality he enjoyed in Stornoway. He did point out, however, that the building programme was responding to, but by no means meeting, religious demand on the island. The population of

Carloway amounted to about 2,500. The parish church serving the district was situated at Lochs, twenty-four miles distant, which could only be reached by crossing a ferry twelve miles broad and travelling overland without benefit of a regular road.[11]

Establishment complacency was also in evidence in the fourth report of the Commissioners of Religious Instruction, Scotland, published in 1837 and covering seventy-four parishes within the western and northern Highlands. The commissioners, whose remit was to form a general view of opportunities for public worship, religious instruction and pastoral superintendence, were particularly given to self-congratulation. Though they had rarely felt obliged to visit the parishes, they had received evidence 'intended to disprove the allegations that any deficiency exists, or to show that it is to a smaller extent than imagined'. Eleven categories of alleged deficiencies were identified; but no parish had more than five stated deficiencies.

The principal deficiencies were overwhelmingly geographic the territorial extent of and difficulties of communication within parishes (sixty-one instances each). The inadequate size of parish churches featured in twenty-eight instances, but population pressure in only ten instances. While the inconvenient division of parishes also featured in ten instances, the inconvenient situation of parish churches was only cited five times, likewise their poor condition. That ministers had to officiate in more than one church earned twelve citations. Want of endowments were cited on only three occasions, as also the unequal allotment of sittings. Seat rents was deemed a grievance in only four parishes. However, the commissioners did admit that seat rents, even though low, were regarded as oppressive because they were not usually exacted in most Highland churches on account of the poverty of the congregations. As an afterthought, the commissioners reported that communion was only celebrated in some missionary districts. The inhabitants of most missionary districts were obliged to travel extensive distances to their parish church for the sacrament, an inconvenience that was glossed over in their bland observation that parishes of great territorial extent 'are altogether or nearly uninhabited, the population being situated on the sea-shore or along the banks of rivers'. The removal and relocation of large segments of the Highland population resulting from Clearance could thus be portrayed as enhancing spiritual welfare.[12]

However, the spiritual complacency of the Moderate ascendancy towards the Highlands must not be accepted uncritically or simply reiterated on the strength of Evangelical Party propaganda.[13] Certainly, Moderates stand accused of emptying rather than filling churches in the Highlands; of tending more to their sheep than their spiritual flock; of resisting incursions into the Highlands by dissenters and other itinerant preachers. Yet the Moderates also stand accused for their lack of hostility to popular culture – or countenancing dancing by both sexes; for encouraging violins and bagpipes at marriages; and for tolerating drinking, feasting and fighting at wakes and funerals.[14] The ministry as a whole have a poor record in defending the congregations against removal and relocation. Their contributions to the *Old Statistical Account* of the 1790s as to the *New Statistical Account* of the 1830s and 1840s tend to comment on rather than criticise Clearance.[15] The Evangelicals who stood out against Clearance tended to minister in missionary districts or sacramental parishes, like Alexander MacLeod who faced withdrawal of funding from the royal bounty for criticising the oppressive conduct of Donald Stewart, the factor who cleared Luskintyre and Scarista in South Harris from 1811.[16] Conversely, the people of Glencalive in Strathconnon, whose three years' sporadic protests against Clearance attracted national publicity, had their opposition emasculated by evangelical preaching. Those obliged to take refuge in the kirk of Croick in 1845 etched pathetically on the windowsills that their imminent removal was divine retribution for a wicked generation.[17]

Moderates no less than Evangelical ministers tended to publicise the predicament of Highland communities by incidental testimony to educational and bible societies established by public subscription mainly in the Lowlands or London. Highland communities facing destitution with the collapse of the main props of the crofting economy from the 1820s were commended for their determination to maintain schools and secure bibles for family worship. Moderate ministers, however, were also prepared to provide causal testimony to agricultural journals and topical magazines on the predicament of Highland communities. Thus, Alexander MacGregor, writing from the manse of Kilmuir on Skye, not only analysed the impact of destitution in 1837, but also identified structural weaknesses within the crofting economy notably, an excess of population; early and improvident marriages; rampant subdivision of lands among cottars and squatters, and bad husbandry. At the same time, he discounted the fashionable panacea of emigration. The 459 people who recently left Skye on emigrant ships were mainly the young and able who left behind 264 dependants of whom 103 were aged if not helpless.[18]

The dynamic of Protestantism as a living faith within Highland communities owes much to its evangelical disdain for the worldly affirming Moderate ascendancy in the Established Church in the late eighteenth and early nineteenth century. Nonetheless, the

Evangelical party in the Highlands was neither universally popular nor populist despite its averred opposition to the exercise of patronage by the leading landlord in every parish. Demonstrations by congregations against the intrusion of a Moderate minister at the behest of the parish patron, like popular resistance to Clearances, were occasional rather than commonplace.[19] The reputed Highland dislike of the Moderate ascendancy was less a regional reaction to a system of church government than a local preference for evangelical preaching. Albeit propagated as an apocalyptic faith in pursuit of social justice, evangelical preaching in the Highlands was essentially conservative and elitist. Doctrinal fundamentalism stressed the merit of individual religious experience within an inspirational framework that fostered the communal pursuit of godliness. This message, which anchored social and cultural alienation as clanship gave way to Clearance, was grounded in the Calvinist orthodoxy propagated by the Covenanting Movement, particularly by the house conventiclers who refused to conform to an Erastian Established Church in the later seventeenth century.[20]

For the orthodox Calvinist, assurance of salvation rested not on man's free will nor on predestination alone, but on election tempered by grace. Reprobates who refused to participate in divine services were not necessarily beyond redemption and should be encouraged by their community to see the error of their ways that they be made receptive to grace. Those who adhered to the church visible through attendance at divine services were both receptive to and striving after grace. But their election was not assured. Only the truly repentant sinners, as members of the church invisible, were predestined for eternal salvation. Although God alone elected the truly repentant, tangible assurance for salvation was to be found in the sacrament of communion which affirmed God's covenant with the elect. In turn, communion seasons in the Highlands became biannual happenings for the godly to affirm their evangelical faith through Christian fellowship, prayer and contemplation.[21]

In pastoral terms, evangelical preaching promoted religious observance of the sabbath as a communal exercise in ecclesiastical discipline for the godly and the reprobate, reinforced by fast days for personal atonement. However, the sacraments of baptism and communion were not open to all the church visible in localities where evangelical preaching was marked by doctrinal rigidity. Thus, Roderick MacLeod was suspended as minister of Bracadale by the presbytery of Skye in 1826 for refusing baptism to children of parents deemed unworthy to receive communion. His refusal of communion to those he considered reprobate or lacking in grace knew no social barriers, being applicable to crofters and landlords and even other ministers of the Established Church. Notwithstanding the ecclesiastical censuring of the Reverend MacLeod, evangelical preaching increasingly identified the sacraments as the preserve of church membership, in effect as bestowing assurance of salvation on the elect. Those not worthy to receive the sacraments, no matter how habitual their church attendance, were merely adherents – an elitist distinction which made church membership a minority pursuit throughout the Highlands, as borne out from sample districts in 1837.

Table 4.1 Sample Church Membership, 1837[23]

Presbytery/ Parish Population	Established Kirk Numbers	Habitual Attenders	Communicants
Islay & Jura			
Kildalton	2 222	2 215	600	235
Bowmore	4 078	4 006	1 400	449
Kilchoman	3 220	3188	1 500	202
Lorn			
Kilbrandon	2 738	2 528	1 100	450
Oban	1 626	1 398	560	360
Duror	1 600	800	300	170
Skye			
Sleat	2 923	2 892	900	222
Kilmuir	3 665	3 664	700	81
Duirnish	3 956	3 227	750	350
Lewis			
Lochs	3 432	3 432	1 000	120
Stornoway	4 500	4 500	1 200	45
Barvas	1 840	1 840	450	12
Tongue			
Eddrachillis	745	745	350	70
Durness	1 150	1 150	350	70
Tongue	2 182	2 182	1 000	108

Numbers of communicants, independent of the removal and relocation of population, were noted to be falling in five parishes – Oban, Sleat, Duirnish, Durness and Tongue – as a recent result of evangelical preaching. Moreover, the veto accorded to church members over the patron's choice of minister from 1833 was hardly a popular gesture in Highland parishes where membership varied from around a third to a fortieth of habitual attenders who, in turn, rarely amounted to more than half the numbers affiliated to the

Established Church. Indeed, the parish of Daviot in the presbytery of Inverness lay vacant for over three years after six out of the ten members chose to veto successive candidates proposed by the Crown as patron and supported by the local landlords. In effect, the Veto Act passed in the general assembly of 1833 underwrote the parochial dictatorship of the putative elect in the Highlands, a dictatorship preserved after the Disruption of 1843 by the Free Church's rigid sacramental demarcation between members and adherents.[24]

Parochial dictatorship notwithstanding, the vitality of evangelical Presbyterianism in the Highlands rested not on sacramental demarcation nor on the enforcement of ecclesiastical discipline, but on three complementary cultural influences. The principal two were indigenous developments the spread of spiritual poetry in vernacular Gaelic and the leadership of an evangelical lay elite – *na daoine* (the men). Crucial to both was the household prayer meeting, the godly alternative to the *ceilidh*. The third development was extraneous, the spread of Gaelic School Societies financed by public subscription and run from Edinburgh (established 1811), Glasgow (1812) and Inverness (1818). The work of these Societies, which flagged perceptibly in the second decade of the nineteenth century, was taken on by ambulatory, bilingual schools sponsored by the general assembly from 1826 and was continued for the Free Church post-Disruption by the magisterial Ladies' Associations for the Religious and Social Improvement of the Remote Highlands and Islands.[25]

Spiritual poetry first developed an evangelical flavour in Argyll and the Perthshire Highlands. From the mid-eighteenth century, vernacular poets like Dugald Buchanan adapted the epic heroism of secular poetry into religious eulogies of Christ. The stress laid on the worth of an individual within his or her community, on the austerity of the last supper and on Christ's lamentable suffering on the cross accorded with, yet transcended, traditional clan values. Life was indeed a 'glen of tears'. But faith in redemption and divine justice emphasised the social retribution that followed on from death, especially for oppressive landlords. Further north, spiritual poets in the nineteenth century were less concerned with the communal benefits of redemption than with the need for each individual to be born-again in Christ to attain membership of the church invisible. Such introspective concern with personal salvation led to a resigned acceptance of Clearance among Highland communities that paralleled evangelical attitudes to the industrial revolution among the urban working classes.

Notwithstanding its elitist message, spiritual verse in the Highlands never abandoned its commitment to communal inspiration, nor was Gaelic used simply as an introspective preaching medium. Communal inspiration was further galvanised by the singing of psalms which had adopted the ballad metre for Gaelic praise. The singing of metrical psalms, unaccompanied musically but led by a precentor, remained a readily identifiable feature of Gaelic services in Presbyterian churches throughout the nineteenth century.[26] The reputation of venerated evangelical preachers, from James Fraser of Alness in the eighteenth century through to Dr John MacDonald of Ferintosh and Dr John Kennedy of Dingwall in the nineteenth century, was provincial rather than national. Nonetheless, these Rosshire religious worthies were conscious of their place in the evangelical Christian mainstream whose missionary bounds were not set by the British Empire.[27]

Whereas spiritual poetry and Gaelic praise was endemic throughout the Highlands, *na daoine* was a phenomenon that spread from Cromarty and Easter Ross through Skye to the Outer Hebrides in the west and through Sutherland to Caithness in the north. The central and southern Highlands and the Inner Hebrides below Skye remained relatively untouched by the emergence of the men as a spiritual lay elite. Although few of the men at the outset of the nineteenth century had received much if any formal education, their powerful minds, their intense spiritual concentration and, above all, their retentive memories gave them the role of a local religious meritocracy. As the clan tacksmen were being phased out on the break-up of traditional townships to create crofting communities as well as sheep farms and cattle ranches, the men became self-perpetuating spiritual tacksmen for the north and north-west Highlands. In keeping with the tradition of messianic peasant leaders since the Middle Ages, the men tended to be drawn from the peasant elites of small farmers and craftsmen rather than the poorest orders of cottars and squatters. Their social origins, however, were demonstrably less significant than their religious impact. The men drew on native powers of imagination and language to interpret passages of scripture. Their interpretations, particularly when speaking to set religious questions, were always graphical, usually visionary and occasionally apocalyptical. The imagery of allegorical folk tales was severely censored and adapted for religious purposes, the *dubhchainnt* (dark saying) of individual men being greatly prized. Less tied to the parochial framework than the ministry, whom they refused to respect if not of an evangelical persuasion, the men enjoyed an uneasy and uneven relationship with the Established Church prior to the Disruption.[28] Their employment as catechists was rarely more than a temporary occurrence prior to 1843. Their refusal to truck with Moderate ministers has been characterised as 'occult dissent', in encouraging people to absent themselves from public worship and hold alternative meetings to which they imparted religious instruction as lay preachers. However, in certain localities, notably Durinish in Skye and Duthil and Daviot in the central Highlands, dissent led by lay preachers was more systematic verging on separatism, a tendency not wholly contained within the Free Church, which continued well into the 1860s to have localised problems with the men in whom anti-clericalism was ingrained.[29]

The men were undoubtedly among the most signal influences that paved the way for the widespread acceptance of an evangelical ministry in the Highlands prior to the Disruption of 1843. This contention is not so much challenged as reinforced by the contribution to religious revivalism made by evangelical teachers in the Gaelic Society Schools.[30] The teachers, who also included some of the men, were certainly more orientated towards doctrinal fundamentalism than apocalyptic visions. Ambulatory school teachers were primarily responsible for the revivalist outbreaks in Skye and the Outer Hebrides which accompanied the Disruption. Yet revivalism cannot solely be tied to the advance of Gaelic literacy through the School Societies and subsequently the general assembly schools. Revivalism, an ongoing feature of evangelical Protestantism in the Highlands from the mid-eighteenth century, was associated mainly with ministers of the Evangelical Party in areas served by the men. Although ambulatory schoolteachers were to play a significant role in revivalism in the early nineteenth century and in spreading the evangelical message to the southern Highlands and Inner Hebrides, the Gaelic School Societies were notably non-denominational in their endeavours to increase literacy among Catholic as well as Protestant communities. Indeed, from statistical evidence gleaned for the Inverness Gaelic Schools Society in 1822, the correlation between evangelical commitment and school provision would seem to be in inverse rather than direct proportion. Argyll, despite its reputed Moderate degeneracy was considerably better provided than the Evangelical godly in Ross and Sutherland. Thus, 2·5 per cent of families in Argyll were distant five miles or more from the nearest school and 22 per cent of all individuals above eight years of age were illiterate. The comparative figures for Ross were 3·5 per cent disadvantaged families and 32 per cent illiteracy; for Sutherland 7·4 per cent and 39 per cent respectively.[31]

The increased pace of revivalism from the 1790s can be attributed primarily to the influence of itinerant preachers of evangelical persuasion but rarely tied to the Established Church, like the

Table 4.2 Church attendance in 1851

County	Population	Attendance EC	Attendance FC	% of Population EC	% of Population FC
Argyll	89 298	4 238	6 305	4·7	7·1
Inverness	96 500	3 790	10 583	3·9	11·0
Ross	82 707	1 411	20 237	1·7	24·5
Sutherland	25 793	255	6 723	1·0	26·1
Caithness	38 709	442	6 779	1·1	17·5

dissenter Neil Douglas in Argyll, and more especially, the brothers James and Robert Haldane. Their tours throughout the Highlands and Islands and their founding of the Society for Propagating the Gospel at Home in 1798 should be assessed less in terms of institutional developments – Congregationalism and Baptism took no more root than Secession Churches – than to the identification and inspiration of religious restlessness. However, the anchoring of this restlessness and its channelling into lasting religious commitment required the concerted endeavours of evangelical ministers, the men and ambulatory school teachers.[32] Albeit there is no definite causal connection with economic privation, in so far as local revivals rarely coincided with famines or population removal and relocation, revivalism cannot be dissociated from the social restlessness occasioned by Clearance and by rural congestion and deprivation within crofting communities. Again, ambulatory schoolteachers exerted a positive stabilising influence by their missionary endeavours on behalf of crofting communities, endeavours recognised and appreciated by the Evangelical Party leadership as being second only to evangelical preaching in carrying the Highlands for the Free Church at the Disruption of 1843.[33]

Indeed, the overwhelming support from ambulatory teachers in preaching and promoting literacy created a receptive and informed audience for the campaigning tours as for the polemical tracts and the religious journals which propagated the cause of the Evangelical Party during the Ten Years Conflict which preceded the Disruption. In the years immediately following 1843, ambulatory teachers and the men upheld community commitment to the Free Church pending the appointment of ministers to vacant parishes.[34] An indication of the critical importance of this task can be gleaned from the report to the general assembly of the Free Church in October, that there were no fewer than 150 vacant congregations and preaching stations all calling out for ministers in Gaelic-speaking districts.

Not more than thirty-one ministers were available for supply.[35]

While the commitment rather than the division of whole communities outwith the ranks of the landed and professional classes was a noted feature of Highland identification with the Free Church, the extent of this commitment must not be overplayed or distorted at a regional level. Local returns in excess of 90 per cent commitment in Lewis, Sutherland and parts of Invernesshire were not replicated throughout the Highlands.[36] Once the dust of the Disruption had settled, returns for morning services on Sunday, 30 March 1851 suggest that attendances at Free Churches (FC) in the Highlands, in contrast to those for the Established Church (EC), tended to be well above rather than below the national average. Yet, even allowing for augmentation of numbers at the less popular afternoon and evening services, church attendance as against church affiliation remained a minority pursuit in proportion to the Highland population.

Table 4.3 Church provision in 1851[37]

County	Churches		Attendance		Congregational Average	
	EC	FC	EC	FC	EC	FC
Argyle	48	39	4 238	6 305	88·2	161·7
Inverness	35	44	3 790	10 583	108·6	240·5
Ross	27	40	1 411	20 237	52·3	505·9
Sutherland	10	19	255	6 723	25·5	353·8
Caithness	4	17	442	6 779	110·5	423·7

The comparative national proportion for the Established Church was that 12·2 per cent of the population attended morning service, a figure matched in no Highland county. The comparative proportion for the Free Church of 10·1 per cent attendance was notably exceeded in every county except Argyll. Although the Established Church was decisively outperformed in every Highland county, the Free Church did not enjoy the same overwhelming superiority in the provision of churches.

Neither denomination in the Highlands was ill-provided with churches in terms of reported attendances. In terms of the standard size specified in 1824 for parliamentary churches to house a congregation of 400 at one sitting, only Free Church congregations in Ross and Caithness averaged a higher attendance figure. Albeit these figures mask the actual size of Free Church congregations, accommodation pressure within congested localities was relieved by more than one service on a Sunday. The statistics for church provision in the Highland counties in 1851 suggest that the controversy gener-

ated by the refusal of landlords to grant sites for places of worship to
the Free Church has been overstated, especially in terms of the
Disruption's battle-lines being demarcated by class conflict.[38]

The site controversy was not characterised by endemic class
conflict. The general consensus of those testifying before the parliamentary inquiry of 1847 was that localised tension along class lines
was more the product than the cause of the landlords' refusal to
grant sites, a situation analogous to the discriminatory application of
poor relief by landlords to crofting communities during the accompanying great famine of 1845-50.[39] The claim that the parliamentary
inquiry 'unreservedly condemned the landlords' conduct' is a wilful
misrepresentation of the actual findings of the select committee's
report of 5 July 1847.[40] The select committee specifically abstained
'from judging the motives which have led, either to the secession, or
the refusal of sites'. Instead, the site controversy was placed within
its localised context. The parliamentary inquiry established that the
Free Church had obtained 725 sites throughout Scotland upon
which churches were either already built or in the process of
erection. Sites refused did not exceed thirty-five, not all of which
were in the Highlands and Islands. The most numerous incidence of
refusal was the absolute denial of a site by a landlord; a secondary
category was the rejection of sites offered as inconvenient by Free
Church congregations. The select committee did note with satisfaction, however, that in many cases where sites had been refused in
1843, landlords' objections had subsequently been waived and sites
granted.[41]

An adverse national press certainly facilitated the waiving of
objections by landlords as did their reluctance to prejudice their
patriarchal position on their estates and their disinclination to interfere with the religious instruction of communities committed to the
Free Church. Landlords who refused to grant sites – albeit not themselves members of the Established Church – were undoubtedly concerned that the Disruption marked another breach in the establishment principle opened up by Catholic Emancipation in 1829 and
compounded by the passing of the first Reform Act in 1832. Thus,
Ewan Cameron of Lochiel, an Episcopalian, was not disposed to
grant the petition signed by nine-tenths of the adult male population
of Kilmallie parish for a site for a Free Church.[42] Landlords were
further concerned that issues of ecclesiastical jurisdiction were polar-
ised by Evangelical polemicists between support for God or for Queen
Victoria; concerns that were intensified by the adherence book circu-
lated within crofting districts to encourage community commitment
to the Free Church. The reputed virulence of the language used by

Evangelical polemicists was another factor influencing landlords like Sir James Riddell of Ardnamurchan to refuse sites. Much has been made of Riddell's refusal occasioning his tenantry at Strontian to establish a floating church on Loch Suinart; little has been said of his generosity in providing sites and maintaining parliamentary churches from 1825 in the most extensive parish in Scotland.[43]

The sites for churches – and schools – which were denied in the Highlands and Islands tended to be located in crofting communities in Ardnamurchan, Mull, Skye, North Uist, Strathspey and Duthil where evangelical preaching by ambulatory teachers and the men had taken a notable hold. Social snobbery as much as class vindictiveness made bailies and legal agents willing accomplices in estate management practices which discriminated against members and adherents of the Free Church. A denominational factor was introduced into the employment of servants, the eviction of crofters and the renewal of tenants' leases. Localised discrimination and intimidation was by no means one-sided. Hugh MacAskill of Mornish claimed that his wife was subject to harassment worse than Mary, Queen of Scots during his periodic absenteeism from Mull. Another landlord, MacDonald of Skeabost, who not only granted a site but joined the Free Church, was rapidly disillusioned by the sectarian intolerance which propagated the view that to remain or even to attend divine service in the Established Church was sinful. For the latter transgression in Skye, John MacLeod, the Free Church precentor in Snizort, was required to make a public confession. One landlord, Rainy of Raasay, who remained a staunch supporter of the Free Church actually refused the minister of the Established Church access to his island charge.[44] Because of the resort to violence in certain parishes within the Synod of Ross to deny ministers of the Established Church access to their charges pending the concession of sites to Free Church congregations, the Reverend Mackintosh Mackay of Dunoon intruded into his testimony of 24 April 1847 an official disclaimer on behalf of the general assembly of the Free Church.[45]

The Free Church's affirmation of non-resistance and its call to members and adherents to abstain from acts of violence were in keeping with its determination to give institutional respectability to evangelical Presbyterianism. Its principal constituency, the urban middle classes in the towns and cities of the Lowlands, were not intent on challenging the social order or threatening rights of property. Notwithstanding the anti-establishment ethos of the Disruption and the site controversy, the Free Church was not inherently opposed to landlordism. Indeed, the relationship between ministers and landlords in seeking to relieve the regional famine of 1845-50, which endured locally well into the 1850s, was marked by co-operation rather than conflict. Sir James Matheson commended the Free Church ministers in Lewis for their 'perfect co-operation' in keeping the people of the island orderly and well behaved despite their privations.[46] The *eminence gris* of the Free Church at the Disruption, the Reverend Thomas Chalmers, eulogised the benevolence of John Campbell, second marquis of Breadalbane, to the general assembly at Inverness in 1845. Having not only defended the claims of the Free Church in the House of Lords, but made over the entire stock of larch timber stored in his yards at Perth and given two million slates to the value of £4 000 from his Argyllshire quarries on the Slate Islands to advance church building, Breadalbane had aptly demonstrated that 'the high views of chiefship sit all the more severely and all the more gracefully upon him'. The schooner chartered every summer to take Gaelic-speaking ministers around the western isles to spread the Free Church gospel in the five years following the Disruption was named *The Breadalbane*. During the summer tour of 1846, the schooner made a voyage of inquiry to ascertain areas of greatest want and duly carried meal to the destitute after £15,068 was raised among Lowland congregations. To the eternal credit of the Free Church, this relief was distributed on an non-denominational basis.[47]

The special relationship of the Free Church with the Highlands, as propagated in the wake of the Disruption by the *Monthly Statement* and the *Gaelic Witness*, was formalised by two other initiatives which marked its evangelical mission as truly national. The Sustentation Fund launched in 1843 for the support of the ministry ensured that more affluent congregations subsidised those unable to meet the full cost of stipends by voluntary offerings. This fund was complemented by the home mission scheme for church extension and educational provision, work which was devolved in 1849 to a special committee for the Highlands and Islands. The Highland Committee of the Free Church, though not conceded its own budget until 1877, drew its membership from every presbytery in Scotland thereby ensuring that its 'aggressive Christian work' enjoyed full national backing. Notwithstanding its commendable endeavours to propagate Gaelic as a preaching and teaching medium, the Free Church was intent on exercising a restraining institutional influence in the Highlands.[48]

Control over the men was exercised by their employment as catechists, lay preachers and teachers. They were also encouraged to serve on kirk sessions as elders. At the same time as weekly prayer meetings were becoming more noted for ostentatious religious

expertise than plain Christian witness, discriminatory admission to
the sacraments was intensified. Strict ministerial control over the
revivalist wave of 1859-60 ensured that the spiritual restlessness and
excessive enthusiasm that had characterised religious revivals prior
to the Disruption were not replicated. This revivalist wave in turn
launched a renewed offensive against popular culture. Music and
dancing were actively discouraged at weddings. Recreational activities came under the heading 'Never on a Sunday'. Such was the
antipathy in Wester Ross to public and commercial transport on
Sundays that an evangelical demonstration in Strome Ferry, against
late Saturday night landings of fish cargoes at the railway terminus,
degenerated into a public riot in May 1883.[49]

Temperance was also foisted on whole communities, most notably on the isle of Lewis. A repressive interpretation of the licensing
laws by a judicial bench dominated by evangelical professionals –
ministers, merchants and doctors, 'the men who have the cure of
souls, the cure of fish, and the cure of ailments' – reduced licensed
premises from seventeen 1872 to only three by 1892. The two
licensed hotels outwith Stornoway were effectively converted into
temperance houses in 1877, when the Matheson family as the island
landlords refused the tenants permission to apply for a liquor
licence. The concentration of drink, drunkenness and drink-related
crime in Stornoway stepped up petitioning by evangelical congregations, in the guise of concerned ratepayers and residents, to procure
prohibition. However, the reprobate found solace by extensions
granted to the three hotels in the town in 1893, ostensibly for coffee
houses, which catered for over five hundred drinkers in each
premise. Under cover of night, bucolic use was made of the excise
licence held by passenger steamers berthed in Stornoway. Elsewhere
on the island the desire for intoxicating refreshments was met
illegally by the *bothan* or shebeen and by grocery vans. That the
restricted availability of licensed premises can be taken as an index
of evangelical dominance of Highland communities is suggested by
the provision of licenses in the administrative divisions of
Invernesshire in 1898. In the Fort William division there was one
licence for every 264 people; in the town and immediate hinterland
of Inverness, one licence for every 515 people; in the Skye division,
one for every 753; and in the Long Island (excluding Lewis) one for
every 2,175.[50]

Against this background of institutional restraint and cultural
repression, assessment can be made of the claim that evangelical
Protestantism provided a 'forward-looking critique' for crofting
agitation in the 1880s.[51] Certainly Hugh Miller from Cromarty, a

prolific journalist and lay leader of the Free Church at the Disruption was intent on translating crofting grievances into English to ensure their wider currency in the Liberal as well as the Evangelical press. But the political alliance of the Free Church with the Liberal Party served principally to embroil the crofting community in protracted debates on union with the overwhelmingly Lowland United Presbyterians as on church disestablishment. These bilingual debates, coupled to the self-confidence and organisation abilities accrued from revivalist meeting, can be held to have equipped the crofters spiritually, morally and intellectually for political struggle.[52] But the collective nature of this political struggle was not advanced by the ethos of individualism which imbued the Free Church and the Liberal Party nor by the legalistic approach to ecclesiastical procedure – tantamount to constitutional Bolshevism – perfected by Dr James Begg and supported by Dr John Kennedy of Dingwall, as leader of the 'Highland Host', to sustain minority opposition to church union and disestablishment in general assemblies from 1863.[53] The use of the biblical texts and recourse to scriptural warrant to justify opposition to landlords was an understandable but by no means uniquely Highland technique of peasant agitation. Given that land law was loaded in favour of proprietorship, what was the alternative? Recourse to the mythical golden age of clanship as advocated by secular Gaelic poets?

Evangelical Protestantism gave a sense of dignity, not dialectic, to crofting communities. Its emphasis on enduring the travails of this world – life was a 'glen of tears' – in the hope of spiritual reward in the next was non-materialist and, indeed, a barrier to crofting radicalism. Thus, Mairi Mhor nan Oran (Big Mary of the Songs alias Mary Macpherson), as a leading propagandist of land reform claimed in her poem, 'Cogadh Siobhalta' ('Civil War'), that the people of Skye had been so affected by evangelical preaching that sorrow was like wheat for them. In her poem 'Clach Ard Uige' ('The High Stone of Uig'), she condemned evangelical preachers for their manifest lack of care for the oppressive conditions under which the people laboured. Moreover, evangelical Protestantism was non-scientific, offering no politically realisable redress this side of the grave. John Smith from Iarsiadar in Lewis made one of the most penetrating condemnations of Highland landlordism in his poem 'Spiorad a' Charthannais' ('Spirit of Kindliness'). Yet, it was God, not man, who would redress the oppressions of Sir James Matheson of Lewis.[54] Evangelical Protestantism fostered a politically regressive passivity, a passivity in keeping with its cardinal purpose of spiritual awakening and individual conversion. The emotive and often cathartic process of individual conversion, known in Gaelic as taking the *curam*, had also a profound social significance in weaning men and youths from strong drink and serving as a surrogate contraceptive for unmarried women.

While a mere handful of ministers from the Established Church actively supported land reform, the attitude of Free Church ministers to crofting agitation is more problematic.[55] One of the most elegant submissions to the Napier Commission – established to examine crofting grievances in 1883 – was made by the Reverend James Cumming, Free Church minister of Melness. In calling for the resettlement of deserted glens he pointed out that between seven and eight thousand people in the Reay country of Sutherland had only about a thirteenth part allocated for their settlement, 'the rest is under sheep, under rabbits, under hares, under deer, under grouse, and other unprofitable occupants of the soil'.[56] In 1880 the Reverend John MacMillan of Lochbroom had championed crofters facing eviction from the Leckmelm estate in Wester Ross. But by 1886 he was firmly allied on the side of the landed interest.[57] Hector Cameron of Back, revered as 'the Tory Pope of Lewis', was an uncompromising opponent of land reform. During the September communion season at Barvas in 1887, he sought to debar crofting activists from the sacrament and railed at the assembled multitude that land reform was the Devil's work. Crofting activists should pay arrears of rent, meet outstanding bills to merchants and make more significant contributions to the Sustentation Fund rather than waste their money on drink.[58]

In its institutional response to the Napier Commission, the Free Church had warned about the endemic feelings of political alienation within crofting communities because 'acts of great oppression have frequently been committed with impunity, and without redress'. While calling for the expansion of crofting, tenurial reform and checks to emigration, the Free Church refrained from endorsing crofting agitation.[59] Aversion to political violence had already led to Free Church ministers persuading the Glendale crofters, involved in the celebrated 'Battle of the Braes' in Skye, to surrender to the authorities in January 1883. Free Church ministers notably refrained from criticising landlords on whose estates their churches were sited, especially those landlords who had donated both church and site. Free Church ministers used their influence to prevent the return of the crofters' candidate at the Ross and Cromarty by-election in August 1884. Again at Sutherland in the general election of November 1885, their intervention prevented the return of crofters' candidates for all five Highland counties.[60] Free Church

ministers in Edinburgh were instrumental in establishing the Highland Land Law Reform Association in December 1884, to ensure
that Lowland co-ordination of crofting agitation did not embrace
socialism, home rule and, above all, the Irish Land League Movement whose penchant for violence, like its Catholicism, was deemed
abhorrent. Although its ministers individually and collectively acted
as the moral policemen of land reform, the Free Church refrained
from affiliation to the Highland Land League until 1888, when its
official recognition sounded the sectarian death-knell of the movement.[61]

Table 4.4 Free Church commitment, 1871-91 [62]

Synod	Population			Members & Adherents			% Commitment		
	1871	1881	1891	1871	1881	1891	1871	'81	'91
Argyll	89 817	91 246	90 779	7 939	13 148	14 552	8·8	14·4	16
Glenelg	88 392	89 501	88 676	12 114	25 342	28 990	13·7	28·3	32·7
Ross	44 250	40 956	38 905	8 609	13 216	13 184	19·4	32·3	33·9
Caithness & Suther-land	64 309	62 235	59 073	14 819	17 135	18 045	23	27·5	30·5

   Political ambivalence on land reform notwithstanding, the Free
Church's evangelical mission made significant advances in the
Highlands in the later nineteenth century. Members and Gaelic
adherents continued to increase despite a falling or relatively static
population in the four Highland synods.
   The growth in commitment to the Free Church amounted to
little more than a third of the Highland population in any synod.
However, when allowance is made for the age of adherence being
fourteen years or above – as prescribed by its general assembly of
1874- the Free Church could probably count on the commitment of
an absolute majority of the Highland population in every synod
except Argyll during the 1880s.[63] Moreover, this growth would appear to have been accomplished at the expense of non-churchgoers
rather than rival denominations. The Established Church, for example, having adopted a more evangelical approach to the Highlands following the abolition of patronage, in 1874, experienced a
growth in membership of around 8 per cent between 1881 and
1891.[64] It is also worthy of passing mention that the areas of most
intense evangelical commitment in the north-west Highlands and
Islands consistently recorded the highest incidence of mental illness
throughout Scotland.[65]

The Evangelical ascendancy of the Free Church in the Highlands was breached irreparably in 1892, when its general assembly passed the Declaratory Act which made orthodox Calvinism optional. Two ministers and in excess of four thousand members and Gaelic adherents seceded to form the Free Presbyterian Church in 1893. Determined to maintain the Westminster Confession of Faith which the Covenanting Movement in 1645 had accepted as second only to the Bible in determining fundamental points of doctrine, the Free Presbyterians propagated a notably legalistic interpretation of Disruption principles. Indeed, prescribed standards not only for religious observance but for recreational activities as for dress and deportment verged on the Talmudic.[66] The overwhelming decision of the general assembly of 1900 to unite with the United Presbyterians in the United Free Church was not accepted by a 'Wee Free' rump: a decision that can be attributed to the accumulation of widespread Highland concern about the Declaratory Act, lingering antipathy to disestablishment and, not least, apprehensions that the Sustentation Fund would be subject to market forces to promote church building in the inner cities rather than mission stations in the Outer Hebrides. Prior to the implementation of union, 84·5 per cent of Highland congregations were aid-receiving from, the Sustentation Fund as against the 16·5 per cent of self-sustaining, and aid-giving congregations.[67]

In the immediate aftermath of union, the Free Church section of the United Free Church claimed 245 congregations in the Highlands as against 119 congregations for the 'Wee Frees' as the Free Church continuing. The 'Wee Frees' enjoyed majority support in only forty Highland parishes where congregations had split on the issue of union. Moreover, the United Free Church was supported by 862 Lowland congregations whereas the Free Church continuing had only nineteen Lowland congregations. Despite its limited numbers and its even more limited means, the Free Church continuing was determined to maintain its national pretensions by appealing through the civil courts to secure the landed and financial resources of the pre-union church, a course upheld by the House of Lords in August 1904. In the interim, however, members and Gaelic adherents began to fall away from both the United Free Church (UFC) and the Free Church.[68]

Although there was a slight drift in members and adherents from the United Free Church to the Free Church and, to a lesser extent, to the Free Presbyterian Church, the rival denominations were intent on increasing the number of congregations for their dwindling bands of members and Gaelic adherence. Congregations were

Table 4.5 Denominational decline, 1900-4[69]

Year	Members & Adherents		Congregations	
	UFC	FC	UFC	FC
1900	29 559	12 385	245	119
1901	26 276	9 213	221	98
1904	25 541	8 714	227	102

increased either by church building or by church seizure, the latter option being a particular feature of evangelical guerrilla activity in the Hebrides. In their stance against the United Free Church, the 'Wee Frees' tended to be supported locally by the Free Presbyterians and on rare occasions by members of the Established Church. The uproar provoked by the seizure of the church at Ness, Isle of Lewis, on behalf of the United Free Church in 1902 led to the dispatch of a gunboat by the British government. Continuing mutual recriminations led to the establishment of a royal commission in 1905 to oversee the equitable distribution of landed and financial resources between the rival denominations nationally.[70]

The Gaelic exclusivity of the Free Church was all but confirmed by the reconstitution of its Highland Committee to include only members drawn from Highland presbyteries. Its missionary endeavours were not entirely introspective. Fishing stations were maintained to service the herring fleet throughout the British Isles. In like manner, summer stations catered for tourists to the Highlands. Contacts were maintained with Highland migrants in North America. Most imaginatively, apprenticeships were established in the Greenock shipyards for Highland youths. However, priority was accorded to church building in furtherance of sectarian rivalry among Presbyterian denominations. Faced with the loss of valuable common grazing to provide sites for churches, crofting communities in Lewis, though split along sectarian lines, began to complain that the Highlands were becoming over-churched.[71]

While evangelical Protestantism could never be accused of spiritual complacency throughout the nineteenth century, the 'Wee Frees' reliance on civil jurisdiction to maintain their ecclesiastical standing rested uneasily with their espousal of Disruption principles. Indeed, the decision of the House of Lords in favour of the Free Church continuing in 1904, following on from the Crofters' Holdings Act of 1886, meant that whole communities in the Highlands were legalistically locked in to theological and social conservatism.[72] Sectarian rivalry among evangelical Protestants, manifest through church building in the decade prior to the First World War, principally if not solely benefited the corrugated iron industry.

NOTES

1 A. L. Drummond and J. Bulloch, *The Church in Victorian Scotland, 1843-1874* (Edinburgh, 1975), pp. 85, 322, 340; J.H.S. Burleigh, *A Church History of Scotland* (London, 1973) p. 303; C. G. Brown, *The Social History of Religion in Scotland since 1730* (London, 1987), p. 116.

2 J. Macleod, *Scottish Theology* (Edinburgh, 1973), pp. 329-31; A. P. F. Snell, *Defending and Declaring the Faith: Some Scottish Examples, 1860-1920* (Colorado Springs, 1987), pp.13-14

3 *Commissioners of Religious Instruction, Scotland* (Parl. Papers, 1837, IV), ix-x; *Ibid.* (P.P. 1838, V), pp. vi-ix; *Ibid.* (P.P. 1838, VI), viii-ix; *Ibid.* (P.P. 1838, VIII), ix-x;.Anon., *An Account of the Present State of Religion throughout the Highlands of Scotland* (Edinburgh, 1827), pp. 1-47; J. MacInnes. *The Evangelical Movement in the Highlands of Scotland, 1688 to 1800* (Aberdeen, 1951), pp. 79-128.

4 Principal Baird's Report as to Government Churches Visited in 1827 and Narrative of the Rise, Progress and State of the Royal Bounty with Report to General Assembly, 1831, Scottish Record Office (S.R.O.), General Assembly Papers, CH 1/5/66.

5 *Commissioners of Religious Instruction* (P.P. 1837, IV), appendix 2, 316-22; A Sermon Preached in the Gaelic Chapel, Hatton Garden, Before the Corresponding Board of the Society in Scotland for Propagating Christian Knowledge in the Highlands & Islands by Revd Daniel Dewar, College Church, Aberdeen, 1814, SRO, SSPCK Records, GD 95/13/99, fo. 42-9; V. E. Durkacz, *The Decline of the Celtic Languages* (Edinburgh, 1983), pp. 66-9.

6 *Moral Statistics of the Highlands and Islands of Scotland compiled from Returns received by the Inverness Society for the Education of the Poor in the Highlands* (Inverness 1826) pp. 16-8; *Select Committee on Sites for Churches, Scotland* (Parl. Papers, 1847), QQ. 3523-5, 3543-8, 3939-62; A Sermon preached before the Society in Scotland for Propagating Christian Knowledge by Revd Norman McLeod, minister of the Barony Parish, Glasgow, 1852, SRO, SSPCK Records, GD 95/14/32, fo. 11-22, 27-8.

7 SRO, SSPCK Records, GD 95/13/99, fos. 50-1, 66-7, 70-1.

8 Highland Churches, Copy of Minutes, 1825, SRO General Assembly Papers, CH 1/13/2.

9 Revd Alexander MacLeod, Address to the Honourable Committee for Managing his Majesty's Bounty for the Reformation of the Highlands & Islands, 1820, SRO, SSPCK Records, GD 95/13/105, fo. 29.

10 Second Report of the Commissioners for Building Churches in the Highlands & Islands of Scotland, 1826, SRO. Miscellaneous Ecclesiastical Records, CH 8/215; *Commissioners of Religious Instruction* (P.P. 1837, IV), xiv-v.

11 SRO, General Assembly Papers, CH 1/5/66.

12 *Commissioners of Religious Instruction* (P.P. 1837, IV) iii-xv.

13 Cf. J. Hunter, 'The Emergence of the Crofting Community: The Religious Contribution 1798-1843', *Scottish Studies*, 18 (1974), 95-116.

14 *Present State of Religion*, pp. 49-59, 67-71; MacInnes, *The Evangelical Movement*, pp. 50-1.

15 Cf. the removal and relocation of population was the subject of comment in thirteen of the thirty-six Argyllshire parishes in D. J. Withrington and I. R. Grant (eds.), *The Statistical Account of Scotland,*

1791-99 edited by Sir John Sinclair (reprinted Wakefield, 1983), vol. VIII (Argyll-mainland) & vol. XX (The Western Isles), pp. 255-446. Of these thirteen commentaries, six were indirectly critical and only three directly critical of estate management. Ministers in fourteen parishes commented on removal and relocation in *New Statistical Account of Argyle* (Edinburgh, 1845). Five were indirectly and three directly critical of estate management. The scatter-gun attack on the clergy in A. MacKenzie, *The History of the Highland Clearances* (reprinted 1966), pp. 21-2, is constructively modified in E. Richards, *A History of the Highland Clearances* (2 vols., London, 1982-6), II, 336.

16 SRO, SSPCK Records, GD 95/13/105, fos.. 9-13, 40, 49-50.

17 J. Barron, T*he Northern Highlands in the Nineteenth Century* (3 vols., Inverness, 1903-13), III, 73-5, 303; J. Prebble, *The Highland Clearances* (London, 1982 edn.), pp. 218-25; Richards, *Highland Clearances* I, 369-73.

18 *Moral Statistics of the Highlands and Islands*, appendix pp. i-xxxv; Barron, *Northern Highlands*, I, 192, 214-15; II, 233-34. The Revd MacGregor wrote to the Quarterly Journal of Agriculture.

19 E. Richards, 'How Tame were the Highlanders during the Clearances?', *Scottish Studies*, 17 (1973), 35-50; K. Logue, *Popular Disturbances in Scotland, 1780-1815* (Edinburgh 1979) pp. 54-74, 168-76; Brown, *Social History of Religion*, pp. 123-4.

20 *S.C. on Sites for Churches* (P.P. 1847), QQ. 3586-8, 3754-79; MacInnes, *The Evangelical Movement*, pp. 41-78.

21 Macleod, *Scottish Theology*, pp. 28-9, 85, 219; MacInnes, *The Evangelical Movement*, pp. 167-96.

22 *S.C. on Sites for Churches* (P.P. 1847), QQ. 2476-81, 4639-50, 4765 — 90, 4863- 8,4878-81,4995, 5036-44, 5154-65, 5410-19, 5476-8, 5515-1 6, 5522-5, 5565-8, 5674-6, 5887-98, 5940-5, 5956-67; *Present State of Religion*, pp. 54-5, 66-8 MacInnes, *The Evangelical Movement*, pp. 45, 190-1; Barron, *Northern Highlands*, II, 183; Drummond and Bulloch, *Victorian Scotland*, pp. 321-2.

23 Figures collated from digests in *Commissioners for Religious Instruction* (P.P. 1837, IV), appendix, 2, 6, 12, 36, 46, 72, 126, 146, 148, 174, 178, 182, 222, 230, 234. Figures for habitual attendance are estimates. Population figures are based on the 1831 census with adjustments made for subsequent migration in and out of the parishes.

24 Barron, *Northern Highlands*, III, 8-9; R. Howie, *The Churches and the Churchless in Scotland: Facts and Figures* (Glasgow, 1893), 115 note.

25 MacInnes, *Evangelical Religion*, pp.197-294; *Royal Commission of Inquiry on the Condition of Crofters* and *Cottars in the Highlands and Islands of Scotland, Report* (Parl Papers, 1884), appendix a, lxxxvii; Report of the Committee of the General Assembly for Increasing Means of Education in Scotland, particularly in the Highlands and Islands, 1839, SRO, SSPCK Records, GD 93/13/120, fo. 7; Durkacz, *Celtic Languages*, pp. 113-6

26 J MacInnes, 'Gaelic Religious Poetry, 1650-1850', Records of the Scottish Church History Society (RSCHS), X (1948), 31-49; K. D. MacDonald, 'Na Marbhrannan Soisgeulach' in *Gaelic and Scotland: Alba agus a' Ghaidhlig*, W. Gillies (ed.) (Edinburgh 1989), 175-84.

27 A. P. F. Snell, 'John Locke's Highland Critic', *RSCHS*, XXIII (1987), 65-76; Sell, *Defending the Faith*, pp. 17-38; MacInnes, *Evangelical Religion*, pp. 152-5; *Present State of Religion*, pp. 99-101.

28 J. MacInnes, 'The Origin and Early Development of the "Men" ', *RSCHS*, VIII (1942), 16-39; *Present State of Religion*, pp. 75-6;

Hunter, 'Crofting Community', 105-7; Brown, *Social History of Religion*, p. 121; K. MacDonald, *Social and Religious Life in the Highlands* (Edinburgh, 1902), pp. 104-18

29 *S.C. on Sites for Churches* (P.P. 1847) QQ. 2247-54 2262-6, 2281-5, 2297-305, 2399-406, 2450-75, 2463-75, 2548-52, 2622-4, 3571-4, 3580-1, 3759-68, 3643-89, 4016-18, 5046-78, 5102-5, 5142-53, 5234-46, 5569-81, 5677-8, 5726-37, 5906; Barron, *Northern Highlands*, II, 263; III, 8-9; MacDonald, *Life in the Highlands*, 119-27.

30 Durkacz, *Celtic Languages*, pp. 122-33.

31 MacInnes, *Evangelical Religion*, pp. 158-63; *Present State of Religion*, pp. 80-2; *Moral Statistics of the Highlands and Islands*, pp. 45-60.

32 MacInnes, *Evangelical Religion*, pp. 90-1, 128, 142-51, 164-6; Brown, *Social History of Religion*, pp. 121-2; *Present State of Religion*, pp. 59-67, 90-7.

33 *S.C. on Sites for Churches* (P.P. 1847), QQ. 2063-4, 2072-3, 3561-70, 3575, 3589-600, 5019-28, 5179-80, 5990-6609.

34 *Ibid.*, QQ. 3514-22, 5452-60, 5464-8, 5508-13, 5530-51, 5562-4, 5652-73, 5899-902, 5968-70; Barron, *Northern Highlands*, II, 263; III, 19; Durkacz, *Celtic Languages*, pp. 131-3.

35 T. Brown, *Annals of the Disruption, 1843* (Edinburgh, 1892), p. 651.

36 Brown, *Social History of Religion*, p. 125; Burleigh, *Church History*, p. 352; Hunter, 'Crofting community', pp. 109-10; A. L. Drummond and J. Bulloch, *The Church in Late Victorian Scotland, 1874-1900* (Edinburgh, 1978), pp. 149-50.

37 Both tables 4.2 and 4.3 are based on statistics extrapolated from Howie, *The Churches*, table xx, 91. D. J. Withrington, 'The 1851 Census of Religious Worship and Education', *RSCHS*, XVIIII (1973), 133-48, provides a useful critique on church accommodation nationwide.

38 Hunter, 'Crofting Community', pp. 110-1.

39 *S.C. on Sites for Churches* (P.P. 1847), *passim*; T. M. Devine, *The Great Highland Famine: Hunger, Emigration and the Scottish Highlander in the nineteenth century* (Edinburgh, 1988), pp. 83-105.

40 Hunter, 'Crofting Community', pp. 111-12.

41 *S.C. on Sites for Churches* (P.P. 1847), third report, pp. iii-iv.

42 C. Fraser-Mackintosh, *Antiquarian Notes: Historical, Genealogical and Social* (Inverness, 1897), pp. 217-19.

43 S.C. on Sites for Churches (P.P. 1847), QQ. 2052-7, 2074-8, 2398, 2409-10, 3116-71, 3193-5, 3201, 3233-68, 3294-312, 3313-407, 3414-18, 3423-36, 3509-12, 3552-4, 3601-27, 3697-741, 3747, 3782-827, 3924-37, 3971-95, 4047-78, 4148-50, 4159-82, 4228-30, 4283-93, 4386-97, 4437-9, 4479-83, 4495-9, 4516-20, 4639-723, 4750-64, 4814-20, 4833-44, 4893-9, 4929-51, 4996-8, 5005-18, 5033-5, 5154-5, 5400-9, 5431-40, 5490-3, 5903-30, 6053-79, 6092-105, 6136-51, 6211-19, 6226-42.

44 *Ibid.*, QQ. 2374-97, 2411-49, 2486-7, 2497-502, 2510-14, 3147-54, 3172-90, 3198-200, 3470-80, 3836-7, 3742-5, 4045-6, 4180-224, 4398-426, 4440-61, 4521-33, 4724-49, 4845-52, 4867-77, 4915-29, 5264-95, 5378, 5479-84, 5494-504, 5526-9, 5618-37, 6182-203, 6254-8.

45 *Ibid.*, QQ. 3605.

46 *Ibid.*, QQ. 2067-72; Baron, *Northern Highlands*, III, 133, 359.

47 Brown, *Annals*, pp. 269, 465-7, 652-3; *R.C. on the Condition of Crofters and Cottars, Report* (P.P. 1884), appendix a, lxxxvii.

48 *S.C. on Sites for Churches* (P.P. 1847), QQ. 3838-89, 4821-32; *R.C. on*

the Condition of Crofters and Cottars, Report (P.P. 1884), appendix a, lxxxvii; *Royal Commission of Churches, Scotland* (Parl. Papers, 1905, II), QQ. 1257-60.

49 MacDonald, *Life in the Highlands,* pp. 116-18, 198-9; Drummond and Bulloch, *Late Victorian Scotland,* pp. 151-2; I. M. M. MacPhail, *The Crofters' War* (Stornoway, 1989), pp. 2, 87.

50 *Royal Commission on Liquor Licensing Laws,* Scotland (Parl. Papers, 1898, VI), QQ. 47, 400-672, 51, 602-787.

51 Hunter, 'Crofting community' 108-9, 111-12.

52 MacPhail, *The Crofters' War,* pp. 2, 22; Durkacz, *Celtic Languages,* p. 128.

53 Snell, *Defending the Faith,* pp. 24-9; MacDonald, *Life in the Highlands,* pp. 137-75; Drummond and Bulloch, *Victorian Scotland,* pp. 322-6.

54 D. E. Meek (ed.), *Mairi Mhor nan Oran* (Glasgow, 1977), pp. 73-4, 97-100; D. Thomson, *An Introduction to Gaelic Poetry* (London, 1974), pp. 241-5.

55 MacPhail, *The Crofters' War.* pp. 103-6. I am deeply grateful to Dr MacPhail for his advice and assistance and, above all, for the generosity of his scholarship on this issue.

56 *R.C. on the Condition of Crofters and Cottars, Evidence* (P.P. 1884, II), QQ. 25, 256-351.

57 I. M. M. MacPhail, 'Prelude to the Crofters' War', *Transactions of the Gaelic Society of Inverness* (TGSI), XLIX, (1974-6), 159-88.

58 *Scottish Highlander,* 29 September 1887.

59 *R.C. on the Condition of Crofters and Cottars, Report* (P.P. 1884), appendix a, lxxxvii.

60 I. M. M. MacPhail, 'The Highland Elections of 1884-86', *TGSI,* L (1976-8), 368-402.

61 J. Hunter, 'The politics of highland land reform, 1873-1895', *Scottish Historical Review,* LIII (1974), 46-68.

62 Statistics extrapolated from Howie, *The Churches,* table xxxiii, 113-15.

63 *Churches (Scotland) Act Commission* (P.P. 1910, II), pp. 16-17.

64 Howie, *The Churches,* table i, 38; Burleigh, *Church History,* pp. 391-2.

65 J. P. Day, *Public Administration in the Highlands and Islands of Scotland* (London, 1918), pp.136-8.

66 MacDonald, *Life in the Highlands,* pp. 227-41; Burleigh, *Church History,* p. 361 Drummond and Bulloch, *Late Victorian Scotland,* pp. 269-73.

67 *R.C. of Churches* (P.P. 1905, II), QQ. 1196-205, 1259-77, 1285-6, 1739; appendices, pp. 117-21; Drummond and Bulloch, *Late Victorian Scotland* pp. 312-20.

68 *R.C. of Churches* (P.P. 1905), QQ. 1864-84; 1986-2029.

69 Statistics extrapolated from *R.C. of Churches* (P.P. 1905, II), appendices, p. 135. Returns include statistics for the synod of Moray and four Arran congregations as well as the synods of Argyll, Glenelg, Ross and Caithness & Sutherland.

70 *R.C. of Churches* (P.P. 1905, II), abstracts, pp. 186, 193, 195, 197, 201, 220, 231; MacDonald, *Life in the Highlands,* pp. 291-2; MacPhail, *The Crofters' War,* pp. 223-4.

71 Highland & Islands Committee Minutes, 1907-11, SRO, Free Church Papers, CH 3/983/5-6; Crofters' Commission Report (Parl. Papers, 1905-6) pp. xx-xxi; *Ibid.,* (P.P. 1906-7), xvii-xix.

72 Brown, *Social History of Religion,* pp. 127-8; A. I. Macinnes, 'The Crofters' Holdings Act of 1886: A Hundred Years Sentence?', *Radical Scotland* (February/March 1987), 24-6.

5

'Each take off their several way'?
The Protestant churches and the working classes in Scotland

CALLUM G. BROWN

I

In 1893, Keir Hardie entered a debate in *The Thinker* with two leading Church of Scotland ministers on the churches' relations with labour. The 'Social Question' had erupted within the churches after the 1889 London Dock Strike, which propelled the righteousness of trade-unionism and industrial action to the forefront of theological debate, thereby challenging the evangelical agenda of moral-led social improvement. The Revd Professor W. G. Blaikie wrote that though he had supported Scottish railway workers in a strike over shorter hours, and though 'the Church has something to do with social problems', yet he asserted 'that the churches, for the most part, are *not competent to decide* when a strike is warranted and when it is not, and that it would be very unwise for them to commit themselves to one side under a vague impression of what is right'. Objectives like the eight-hour day, the redistribution of land and fair rents might be right, but the churches should do no more than give 'cheer and encouragement' to the labourer (Blaikie, 1893, 9, 13, 15; Lang, 1893).

In a spirited reply, the Member for West Ham laid out a simple thesis:

> But for the apathy of the Church, there would be no social question to discuss ... I do not claim any monopoly of virtue for the working classes. They are, as others are, what they have been made by their surroundings and life conditions. But I do protest emphatically against the assumption that they stand in special need of having the surplus graces of the intellectual classes bestowed on them. It is this insulting spirit of patronage, overt or covert, which makes the clergyman stand in the mind's eye of so many of the workers as the type of all that is canting and unreal... The poor worker is having his revenge. If he cannot voice his resentment, he can enter his dumb protest,

and this he does by not attending Church. (Hardie 1893, 105-8.)

This division between church and labour has long been regarded as the foundation for the decline of the Protestant churches; a loss of the working classes induced by the failure of organised religion to support the proletarian cause. It used to be taken for granted that the industrial revolution of 1760-1850 had first breached the ties between common people and religion. (Reviews of the literature are given in McLeod, 1984 and Brown, 1988a.) However, recent research has shown that church membership per capita in Scotland, as in England and Wales, continued to grow until the turn of the century. Moreover, research has demonstrated that even after popular religiosity started to decline in Scotland in 1906 the working-class contribution to Protestant church membership stayed remarkably constant; we shall examine the evidence shortly. But despite the buoyancy of the working-class contribution to church membership, the very fact of declining adherence from 1906 is suggestive of an important connection with the rise of the Labour Movement after 1890. Even during periods of relative success in church recruitment in the twentieth century, the rise of militant and apparently atheistical Labour in the 1910s, 1920s and 1930s introduced an ideological confrontation with the churches more fierce than that experienced by Hardie. As he suggested in 1893, it was when it became heterodoxy 'to literally apply the words of Jesus to the worldly affairs of to-day' that 'the Church and the Labour movement "each take off their several way"' (Hardie, 1893, 106).

Yet underlying the issue of ideological struggle between church and labour is the irony of the religiosity of the Labour Movement and the majority of labour supporters. In this respect, Keir Hardie was not the exception but the rule: a staunch churchgoer and a senior lay member of the Evangelical Union, one of the plethora of dissenting churches to have emerged from Scottish Presbyterianism. Like the membership of his Church as a whole, Hardie was a teetotaller, a Sabbatarian, and an advocate of all those moral virtues which his protagonists felt that labour was usurping to itself. It was not that the worker was becoming immoral, but that his search for social advance changed direction from religion to Labour. As a United Presbyterian minister from Dumbarton said of the dock strikers: 'Who were the spokesmen of these miserable dockmen in making a righteous demand? Not the ministers of Jesus Christ; not the magnates of the religious world; but a few socialists who, amid the starving multitudes, kept themselves and the sufferers in such moderation and self-control as to be the admiration of the world'. (Matheson, 1890, 176-7.)

In short, to approach the relationship between the Scottish working classes and Protestant churches on the premise that the former stopped attending the latter at some point in the last one or two hundred years is to get that relationship very wrong. The issue is manifestly more complex than even Hardie's comments allow.

II

One of the most striking features of popular Protestant culture in contemporary Scotland is how the weakness of formal church adherence has eroded both popular and academic awareness of the country's church and religious history. There are few issues in Scottish history about which so much ignorance prevails. The reasons for this lie in the history itself – and especially in the changing relationship between the working classes and the Presbyterian churches.

Scottish Protestantism has since the Union of 1707 meant essentially Presbyterianism. Today it is dominated by the Church of Scotland which developed out of the Scottish Reformation of the 1560s 'by law established' as the only church which could lawfully exist. In the seventeenth century, this 'one and universal kirk' was riven by fierce and often violent disputes between, on the one hand, Episcopalianism, encouraged by the English-based Stuart monarchs James I, Charles I, Charles II and James II who favoured an English-style bishop-controlled church, and on the other hand Presbyterianism, based on government by a hierarchy of church courts stretching from the parish kirk session up to the national general assembly. In the seventeenth and early eighteenth centuries, the social and regional differences in the support of these two ecclesiastical camps were complex, but Presbyterianism obtained its staunchest early support in Lowland urban districts from craft guilds and the commercial classes. But the Presbyterian 'Godly Commonwealth' spread out into the countryside, acquiring there a more rustic peasant character. Episcopalianism enjoyed popular support in some rural districts (especially the north-east, the Highlands and the south-west), but it became more generally associated with monarchy and many large landowners. In this way, Presbyterian government became associated in Scottish popular culture and mythology with popular custom and rights, whilst episcopacy became increasingly associated with the landed classes (Brown, 1987 23-8).

This entered Scottish consciousness especially through the Covenanters, who were the staunch Lowland upholders of a strict Presbyterian religion and culture. Their position, in modern parlance, was 'extreme', holding out through violent rebellion against the episcopal regime of the 1660-88 period, and thereafter objecting to the unworthy form of the Church of Scotland created under the final Presbyterian triumph in the Revolution Settlement of 1688-90. The numbers of Covenanters (known by a variety of names such as Cameronians, Hebronites and McMillanites) who held out is uncertain, but the idea of a separate 'covenanting' church – in the mould of English dissent – is perhaps inappropriate. It was a culture of the 'hillmen' who met in conventicles to conduct worship, weddings and baptisms in the open countryside, initially in the seventeenth century to avoid prosecution but after 1700 to perpetuate the aura of 'a suffering remnant'. But it is important to remember that its adherents often worshipped in the Church of Scotland; theirs was an 'extreme' party which maintained links with the state church, dedicating themselves to reclaim it to 'true Presbyterianism'.

In this respect, all forms of Protestantism – episcopacy, state Presbyterianism and Covenanting Presbyterianism – formed a continuum of allegiance until at least the 1730s. Members of the different elements drifted in and out of close adherence to the Established Church, and were for the most part contained within it. But the appearance of the Associate Presbytery (or Secession Church as it became known) in 1733 initiated an era of very rapid religious pluralisation in Scotland. This pluralisation saw the growth of Presbyterian dissent – a variety of sects and denominations claiming various degrees of independence from but continuity with, the Church of Scotland. In the same way as the simultaneous Methodist movement in England started the renewed growth of Nonconformism, so in Scotland most of the new Presbyterian congregations that were formed between 1733 and 1843 proclaimed their desire to return to a purified and 'true' Presbyterian Church of Scotland (Brown, 1987, 28-44).

The most prominent of these churches were the Secession Church (which, though it split itself into many smaller portions, consumed the majority of Covenanters and the Covenanting heritage of the seventeenth century) and the Free Church formed in 1843. Dissent and establishment were distinguished in various ways. Firstly, as in England and Wales, the difference in religious terms was between an effete, gentrified 'lukewarmness' in religion and an evangelical puritanism of strict Sabbath conduct, seriousness of manner and devotional exercises. Dissent became evangelical, proselytising and anti-theological, dedicated to action in the saving of souls and the salvation of a rapidly-changing society from the evils of drink, poverty, prostitution and crime. Evangelical dissent claimed to have the answers to the disrupting effects of agricultural and industrial change. It held out the conjunction of religious individualism (expressed in salvation by individual effort and prayer) with economic individualism.

The break-up of the paternalistic commercial capitalism of merchant guildry and craft incorporations in the burghs, and the break-up of the neo-feudal rural life of the fermtouns, was mirrored by the break-up of the main agency of social cohesion – the Church of Scotland. In this context evangelical religion of Presbyterian dissent had a wide social appeal. For those forced or enticed to seek new forms of livelihood and to move to factory villages or industrial cities, the Secession or Free Churches offered a religious faith founded on denominational self-determination mirroring their own experiences, and a code of action in Sunday schools, temperance societies and religious charities which provided a response to the disintegration of social stability and moral rectitude (Mechie, 1960; Checkland, 1980; Brown, 1981; Duthie, 1984; Hillis, 1988). Evangelicalism spurned philosophicalism, ritual, and 'high culture'. Instead it demanded commitment, voluntary work, self-assurance and, above all, action.

Evangelical dissent grew with enormous speed in Scotland. In 1733 the Church of Scotland held a near-monopoly of Protestantism. By 1760, perhaps 10 per cent of the people adhered to Protestant evangelical dissenting churches. By 1800, the figure was at least a quarter and probably more. By 1830, the figure was over a third, and by 1851 it was 59 per cent. Despite some small decline, the figure stayed above 50 per cent until 1929. Bearing in mind that these figures exclude non-evangelical Protestantism (the Scottish Episcopal Church) and non-Protestant churches (primarily the Roman Catholic Church) which also grew in importance during the nineteenth century, the Church of Scotland was reduced to a rump of less than a third of Scottish church members and less than 15 per cent of the Scottish population (Brown, 1987, 57-87).

It is easy – too easy – to ascribe the social appeal of this religious schism in Scottish Protestantism to the new middle classes. It is not difficult to see why. The growth of Protestant dissent appeared to mirror the growth of modern capitalist society in both rural agriculture and urban industry. Its appeal to religious self-determination complemented the rise of social and economic self-determination – the erosion of a 'rank' social structure, and the appearance of opportunity, hard work and earned wealth as the criteria of success. Evangelical dissent seemed to be based on the rise of the *laissez-faire* values of the middle classes – the new large tenants in farming who employed labour, and the urban bourgeoisie in commerce, industry and the professions. Indeed, many historians have chronicled the importance of the urban middle classes to the dissenting Presbyterian churches of the nineteenth and early twentieth centuries. In studies on Aberdeen (MacLaren, 1974; 1983) and on Edinburgh (Gray, 1977), the successive suburbanisation of Scottish cities has been shown to have interacted with the growth of dissenting denominations and congregations whose church spires and towers proclaimed the wealth and status of the upwardly mobile of different generations. The importance of the capitalist middle classes to the rise of the modern kirk in Scotland is undeniable, and in every town in the country palatial Victorian churches still stand on prime urban land as testimony to the sources of denominational prosperity.

But it would be wrong to see in the economic transformation of Scotland in the late eighteenth and early nineteenth centuries the origins of some mass working-class alienation from the churches. The rise of evangelical dissent encompassed a complex social fragmentation which gave Scottish Protestantism a strong proletarian tradition.

This can be traced initially through the immediate causes of secession from the gentry-controlled Church of Scotland. (These are discussed in Brown, 1990a.) In the eighteenth and nineteenth centuries there was a series of issues which, at congregational level, split Scottish Presbyterians apart. Amongst these were: the abolition of 'reading the line' of psalms prior to singing (which had allowed the illiterate to join in); the teinds or church taxes which were a grievance in many agricultural and fishing parishes where the Church of Scotland ministers received around a fifth of the harvest and catches; pew-renting, introduced in parish churches between 1720 and 1820 by landowners seeking to pass on the burden of financial costs (notably for the poor fund); and shortage of church accommodation, which the rise of population occasioned in nearly every parish – urban and rural – in the country.

But the greatest issue fomenting the rise of dissent was the grievance of patronage which existed between 1712 and 1874. This was the system whereby hereditary patrons, usually large landowners of episcopal persuasion, had the right of presentation (or selection) of parish ministers, in opposition to the alternative Presbyterian principle of 'the call' in which the congregation as a whole, through popular vote, selected the minister. When patrons selected their own choice of minister for a vacant pulpit, member of the congregation objected and invariably ended up forming their own Secession Church. After 1766, a second denomination appeared for the same purpose, called the Relief Church (so called because it offered 'relief to Christians oppressed in their liberty'). Then, in 1843, many of the remaining evangelicals within the Established Church walked out because of government refusal to enforce a general assembly veto of unpopular patron-chosen ministers, and formed the Free Church of Scotland.

The patronage issue more than any other was the dividing line, the schism between light and darkness, which shaped the growth and tenor of Scottish Protestant churches. The anti-patronage movement developed as the centre of a Scottish notion of the 'common man', of individual and 'commonwealth' liberty, and, after the 1790s, of 'democracy' itself. For patronage conflicted with the 'democratic' role of the kirk session, with its supposedly popularly-elected elders, and with the hierarchy of popularly-responsive courts which stretched above it. Large landowners, be they Presbyterian, Episcopal (as perhaps two-thirds were) or even Catholic (as a small percentage were), had hitherto been forced by the Scots state to uphold the kirk by enforced provision of funds for the parish kirk and the minister, and by enforced maintenance of parish schools. But from the 1730s, the landowners found a 'party' of clergy within the Church of Scotland who shared their views on religion and church management: the so-called 'Moderates'. These were men generally opposed to religious puritanism and to evangelicalism; they were the clerical representatives of the aristocratic and anglicising 'Enlightenment' of the eighteenth century – those who, like Rousseau, wanted not to abolish man's 'chains' but to legitimate them by benevolence and philosophical reasoning. It was when a Moderate minister was selected for a parish charge in the face of congregational hostility that schism occurred, renting Scotland's parish congregations one after another from Wigton to Unst, sometimes repeatedly.

The congregational patronage dispute was by far the major occasion for the formation of dissenting churches. Not only was it the trigger for schism, but it remained well into the Victorian period a popular symbol – a symbol of 'civil rights'. The perception lingered that certain ecclesiastical rights were amongst primary 'secular' rights; the right to 'sit under' a minister of popular (i.e. congregational) choice; the right to enter a parish church and to obtain a seat in it; the right to maintain 'traditional' forms of worship – in particular the right to resist the encroachment of 'high-church' liturgy (including the 'popish' recitation of the Lord's Prayer, responses, kneeling, and celebration of Christmas and saints' days); and the right to preserve a puritanical moral and social code (including the imposition of kirk-session justice for Sabbath profanation, sexual immorality, gambling, dancing and drunkenness). These rights played an important part in focusing popular grievances during the industrial revolution in Scotland. Until the mid-nineteenth century, Protestant religion was held to be emblematic of wider rights and customs which working people were struggling to maintain in the face of economic change.

The proletarian identification with religious rights reached a high point during the 1840s, arguably the most important decade in the development of modern Scottish religion. It was the decade of the Irish famine which induced large-scale immigration to Scotland with about two-thirds of the migrants being Catholic and one-third Protestant (a mixture of Presbyterian, Episcopalian and Methodist). It was the decade of the unification of the old Presbyterian dissenters of the Secession and Relief Churches to form in 1847 the United Presbyterian Church. And it was the decade in which the Free Church of Scotland was formed.

The Disruption of 18 May 1843 took 37 per cent of Church of Scotland ministers, and between 40 and 50 per cent of its lay adherents, into the Free Church. At the root of this mass defection were powerful social forces. In the Highlands and Hebrides, the emerging crofting communities had been evangelised for decades by southern preachers and teachers, and the defection of around 95 per cent of adherents in that region reflected the social and economic schism with the landowning classes; as James Hunter has written: 'In the Highlands the Disruption was not an ecclesiastical dispute. It was class conflict.' (Hunter, 1976, 104.) In the rural Lowlands too, the emergence of the Free Church often interacted with 'agricultural improvement' and aligned the Free church with an 'oppressed' peasantry (Carter, 1979).

In urban and industrial districts, however, the working classes of the 1840s seem to have found less association with the Free Church than with other denominations and sects. The 1840s was a cathartic decade for the industrial working classes: handloom-weaving was in crisis, the Chartist movement gave hope of democratisation but crumbled; severe economic depression characterised many trades and occupations; yet, at the same time, there was the emergence of the new industries of the age of steam – shipbuilding, iron and steel industries, the railways, and all forms of engineering. In this context, it was the evangelical religion of Arminianism – of universal atonement – which found enthusiastic and revivalist support across the Scottish Lowlands.

This had started in the early 1830s with the 'heretical' popularity of Edward Irving, Robert Story and John McLeod Campbell on the Lower Clyde, leading to the formation of the Catholic Apostolic Church. This was followed by revivals in 1839-50 all over industrial Scotland: at Kilsyth, Glasgow, Dundee as well as in many smaller places. These events developed a constituency for evangelical religion amongst the Scottish working classes – a constituency that became evident during the 1840s by the appearance of new sects: the Chartist Churches, the Church of the Latter Day Saints (the Mormons) and the Morisonians (the Evangelical Union). In addition, there was tremendous growth in the popularity of other evangelical churches: the Baptists, the Congregationalists and the Methodists (though they remained small in number compared to England). The Disruption issues of congregational democracy helped to promote all forms of evangelical dissent, and overwhelmingly amongst the working classes (Brown, 1990b).

The social composition of the evangelical churches during the industrial revolution of 1770 to 1850 comes from a variety of sources. The accounts of evangelists make clear that their congregations were attracting almost exclusively working-class adherents during this period. A local comment on the revival at Kilsyth in 1839 commenced: 'The web became nothing to the weaver, nor the forge to the blacksmith, nor his bench to the carpenter, nor his furrow to the ploughman' (quoted in Hutchinson, 1986, 66). The Royal Commission on Religious Instruction noted in 1837 that the dissenting churches of Glasgow and Edinburgh were 'generally composed of the poor and the working classes' (quoted in Brown, 1987, 154). And social-class analysis of congregations stretching from 1770 to 1865 shows clearly the dominance of the working classes in congregations of the Church of Scotland, the Free Church, the Burgher Seceders, the Antiburgher Seceders, the United Presbyterian Church, the Glasites and the Mormons. In every case the working classes made up a minimum of 53 per cent of congregations, with the ratio rising as high as 79 per cent (Hillis, 1981; Murray, 1977, 83-4, 88-9; Brown, 1987, 109-111, 150; Buchanan, 1987).

Though the dominance of the working classes as members of Scottish Protestant churches did not change in the four decades after 1850 (and indeed may well have increased), the proletarian-dominated small sects of Chartist Churches and Mormons either disappeared or declined appreciably in number. At the same time, older denominations with a heritage of proletarian Presbyterianism also declined or disappeared, being absorbed by larger churches; amongst these were the Reformed Presbyterian Church and the Original Secession Church. The mid-Victorian period was characterised by a reassertion of middle-class control over Protestant churches, with adherents tending to concentrate in larger denominations. The Protestant churches and the middle classes who controlled them as elders and generally-assembly commissioners (MacLaren, 1974; Hillis, 1981) turned their efforts to evangelise the working classes, to envelop the slums of Scottish cities by massive campaigns of religious, temperance and educational proselytising (Hillis, 1988). This was a period of vigorous church growth which exceeded population rise. An increasing proportion of the population was being attached to churches, Sunday schools and religious voluntary organisations, and the mainstay of this recruitment seems to have been amongst the urban working classes (Brown, 1990a).

Proletarian involvement in the Protestant churches was thus sustained very strongly between the 1850s and 1890s, but the level of proletarian self-determination in religion was diminishing. And the century closed with the commencement of a protracted crisis for the Scottish Protestant churches in its relations with Labour.

III

The 1889 London Dock Strike marks the beginning of an important watershed in the relations between the working classes and the Protestant churches in Scotland. The strike itself was no more than the trigger. It precipitated amongst Scottish Protestant churchmen an immediate crisis of faith in the evangelical solutions to social problems. The solutions of individual Christian salvation, the teetotal pledge, thrift, the revivalist experience, hard work and family self-reliance were seen by many ministers neither as sufficient in combating problems of house overcrowding, low wages, unemployment, casual labour, ill health and high mortality, nor as socially acceptable given the growth of labour unrest, trade-unionism, Labour Parties, and piecemeal state intervention in social policy. On the other side of the coin, the Dock Strike was the trigger for a new form of working-class alienation from organised religion – not an alienation from the churches *per se*, nor from religion and religious faith, but an alienation from the political ideology which traditional churches represented (Brown, 1987, 169-207).

A variety of circumstances promoted and aggravated 'the social question' in the two-and-a-half decades before the First World War: the emergence of a new suburban lower-middle class alienated from inner-city problems with the rise of state welfarism, ecumenical reunion in Scottish Protestantism (with the formation of the United Free Church in 1900 and the immediate commencement of negotiations for reunion with, and the disestablishment of, the Church of

Scotland), and the diffusion of religious doubt through the advance
of liberal biblical criticism (called the 'Higher Criticism'). But at the
root of these developments was the emergence of Labour political
ideology with its emphasis on the righting of social injustice, and the
advanced role of the state. In this context, the ideology of evangelical
religion was tarnished with the same brush as modern capitalism:
religious individualism was the symbol of economic individualism.
Just as economic *laissez faire* was challenged by co-operativism and
collectivism, so individual religious salvation was being challenged
by social secular salvation in the form of state welfarism.

One response to this was the formation of Labour Churches in
the 1890s, with the largest concentration in Britain occurring in the
Glasgow area. However, they never competed in size with mainstream Protestantism and they had all but disappeared by the start of
the new century (Summers, 1958). More important were developments *within* the major churches. Many influential Scottish Protestant clergy tried to adapt to the new environment of the 1890s and
1900s by professing an apolitical Christian socialism which emphasised the stewardship of wealth, the promotion of social service,
municipal socialism and *rapprochement* with the Labour movement.
By 1911 the main Presbyterian churches were confirmed in a new,
anti-evangelical social theology and strategy. The Church of Scotland and the United Free Church became between 1904 and 1914
major providers of homes for the elderly, inebriate, destitute, delinquent and disabled. From the economic depression of 1908 onwards, these two churches were distributors of cash aid to unemployed members – a major breach of the evangelical code of self-
reliance. They organised congresses on social problems, ran baby
clinics and holiday homes for slum children, campaigned for improved workers' housing, for regulation of the milk trade, for the
creation of labour exchanges, for the unionism of women workers,
and some clergy were active in industrial arbitration.

The effects of this ideological transformation were twofold.
Firstly, and most importantly, the Scottish Protestant churches and
the working classes did not fulfil Keir Hardie's prophecy of 1893 of
antagonistic segregation. However much a wedge might be seen to
exist between church and labour in the Edwardian period, there was
no absolute breach in Scotland as occurred in Germany during this
period where the Social Democrats undertook very successful campaigns of mass resignation from church membership (McLeod,
1982). Leaving aside the success or otherwise of the churches'
dealings with labour, the very *attempt* in the years before 1914 diminished militant secularism in Scotland and sustained the working

classes as a numerically dominant component of Scottish Protestantism. The evidence of studies on Falkirk (Sissons, 1973) and on
Alloa (Panton, 1973) in the 1960s showed that the proportions of
working-class membership in all Protestant churches had not
changed since the Victorian period or, indeed, since the late eighteenth century. A minimum of 60 per cent of the membership of the
Church of Scotland and minor Protestant churches came from the
working classes. The evidence of working-class participation in
Protestant religion is also strong for the first half of the twentieth
century. Autobiographical and oral-history testimony (for example
in Brown, 1987, 158, 216-7; and Brown, 1990b) demonstrates the
importance of not only the mainstream churches but also 'Tent
Missions', the Faith Mission and the Salvation Army in proletarian
experience in Scottish towns and villages. Moreover, the period
1941-56 witnessed an extraordinary growth in Protestant church
membership in Scotland which at its peak in 1956 only narrowly
failed to match the level attained at the all-time peak of 1905
(Brown, 1990c).

However, this is not to say that the relationship between the
Protestant churches and the working classes has not changed since
the 1890s. Though no major and specifically working-class breach
of church connection occurred, the rise of militant socialism during
the 1910s and 1920s destroyed the apolitical Christian-socialist
movement within the Presbyterian churches, and left Church socialists as a politicised and small minority. The social-reform consensus
between the churches and the Labour movement which had been
developing in the late Victorian and Edwardian period was undermined by the successive impact of the First World War and the
General Strike of 1926. In each the churches emerged as clarions of
national unity and patriotism. They denounced industrial action
during the war and preached openly against the General Strike. Yet
the noticeable falls in church membership on these occasions were
more than matched by periods of vigorous growth in membership
during periods of economic depression (Brown, 1990c).

Whilst this tends to discount the notion of a widescale, or even a
significant, level of working-class alienation from the Protestant
churches during the inter-war period, it yet demonstrates the
marginalisation of the churches as working-class ideology was being
reshaped. The churches no longer held – or even aspired to hold –
the answers to the manifest social and economic problems of inter-
war Scotland. This became even more apparent in 1929 when the
popularly-elected County Education Authorities and the Parish
Councils, on both of which church representatives had dominated,

were abolished. In that one year, the Protestant churches' traditional close control of education and poor relief was removed, and the working classes and the poor no longer had to face a phalanx of clergy at defaulters' (truancy) meetings and when claiming parish relief. Taken together with the effective disestablishment of the Church in Scotland in 1925 (with the removal of heritors' ownership of parish churches and control of pews, amongst other measures) and the virtual demise of evangelical dissent in 1929 (when the United Free Church united with the Church of Scotland), Scottish Protestantism lost its image as the religious face of the Scottish civil establishment.

It was because the Scottish Presbyterian churches became marginalised from social-policy formation, local government and what might be called 'social prophecy', that the social significance of organised religion diminished in Scotland. Whilst membership remained very buoyant until the mid-1950s, the functions of the churches as agents of the state and of public political ideology diminished. Despite ecumenical reunion, the Protestant churches became estranged from the fulcrum of community identity. In the late 1950s and especially the 1960s, social forces were unleashed (especially amongst the young) which were to propel the Scottish Protestant churches into one of the most severe slides of church adherence yet experienced in the western world. The years 1963-5 were the watershed when all indices of religion's social significance fell with staggering sharpness; baptisms, religious weddings, Presbyterian recruitment to new membership, existing membership, and Sunday-school and bible-class enrolment (Brown, 1990c). In all of these categories the Church of Scotland, and to slightly lesser extents the Baptist, Congregational, Methodist and Episcopal Churches, experienced the first years of a transatlantic youth culture which in both its moral concerns and its behavioural characteristics deprecated 'traditional' religion and churches. By 1989 the Church of Scotland had lost more than a third of its 1956 membership and more than half of its Sunday-school pupils with no signs of a 'bottoming-out' in its decline.

IV

The secularisation of social prophecy starting in the 1890s was thus followed some seventy years later by a secularisation of society which has been sweeping aside the relevance of church connection. The end result of these developments in the post-war period in terms of the churches' relations with the working classes of Scotland has been ambiguous.

On the one hand, there is clear evidence that the churches in their publicly-stated policies were, until the 1960s at least, out of step with the political inclinations of the majority of the Scottish people – and by implication the working classes. A survey of general-assembly commissioners in the Church of Scotland in 1964 (Robertson, 1966, 366) showed that 74 per cent voted Conservative, 13 per cent voted Liberal and 13 per cent voted Labour. Even in the mid-1980s, Church of Scotland members as a whole were more likely to vote Conservative (45 per cent) and Liberal (19 per cent) than for the Labour Party (17 per cent) (survey published in *The Scotsman* 15 May 1986). In the inter-war period, the Church of Scotland's Church and Nation Committee had little constructive assistance to offer those suffering during economic recessions. It repeatedly stated its opposition to both Church involvement in policy-making and to increased state spending. It reported in 1932: 'The Church may, in a limited measure, co-operate with the State in discovering ways and means of stimulating employment; she may to a considerable extent alleviate the distress associated with unemployment ... but it is not primarily the Church's business to create or to find work for the unemployed.' (*Reports to the General Assembly of the Church of Scotland*, 1932, 504-5.)

In the late 1970s and 1980s, when high unemployment next afflicted Scotland, the Church of Scotland's response was very different. Through its general assembly committees and through hard-working parish ministers, it supported, and in many cases led, campaigns to prevent factory closures and to promote state spending on economic-development projects. A notable example was in Clydebank where Church of Scotland and Roman Catholic clergy co-operated to assist in successively the UCS work-in, the Singer's Sewing Machine campaign and the SDA Clydebank initiative (Brown, 1988b, 196-7). Moreover, the church has initiated workschemes providing employment and training for young people. Through its ecumenical work it has been a leading pressure group seeking to influence Conservative government policy on the economy and on employment in particular. Though this action probably does not enjoy a majority support of the membership (or even the eldership) of the church, the growing dominance of the clergy within the public-policy sections of the church, and their increasing politicisation, had given the impression at least of a Church much more in touch with, and sympathetic to the interests of, the Scottish working classes.

This has been apparent amongst many of the British churches in the 1970s and 1980s, and covers realms other than the economy and employment, The Church of England's *Faith in the City* reflects a general ecclesiastical concern with the alienation of the inner-city poor from the suburban and country focus of the major denominations. It must be emphasised that this is probably a *clerical* phenomenon rather than a more general change in the outlook, political and otherwise, of the church laity. An important factor here may well be changes in the recruitment pattern of church clergy. Between 1910 and 1950, the geographical origins of Church of Scotland clergy shifted markedly. In 1910 almost half were born in the Highlands and Hebrides, and three-quarters were born in rural areas generally. Forty years later four-fifths came from the Lowlands and half came from the cities (Maxwell-Arnot, 1974). It seems plausible to suggest that these trends were maintained in the post-war period, and that Church of Scotland clergy today are overwhelmingly urban in their birth and upbringing. Whilst they may not necessarily be any more working-class in their origins than their predecessors, the urban location of their upbringing, coupled with the intellectual environment of university divinity colleges they experienced in the 1960s and 1970s, may have cultivated both a greater awareness of working-class life and a greater religious and political commitment to values of social justice. The fact of, and the tenor of clerical reaction to, Mrs Thatcher's celebrated 'Sermon on the Mound' at the General Assembly of 1988 may be a reflection of a major shift in the ideological alignment of the British clergy since the inter-war period.

This does not bring much succour to the churches when they survey the declining membership and attendance figures of the 1980s. In 1984 only 17 per cent of the adult population of Scotland attended Church on an average Sunday, with the highest regional figures coming in the puritanical Hebrides and Lochalsh (53 per cent) and the strongly Catholic areas around Glasgow (where the figures ranged from 21 to 27 per cent). But *Protestant* religious enthusiasm for church-going and church membership has diminished to a marginalised level in the Lowlands – to a level identical with England and Wales (Brown, 1989, 214-15). Around 6 or 7 per cent of the non-Catholic adult population of Scotland attend Church on an average Sunday, and the figures look set to fall further. Church buildings are closing rapidly in both urban and rural areas; congregations are amalgamating not once but several times; and arrangements are made between congregations of different denominations to share buildings, Sunday schools and crèches.

Arguably, the sharp edge of this crisis of church connection has been occurring during the 1970s and 1980s within the Scottish middle classes, and the extent of working-class connection – though falling – is falling less steeply. The churches (both the Church of Scotland and the Roman Catholic Church) have through the experiences of the 1970s and 1980s developed – if not a 'liberation theology' – then at least a 'theology of the council-housing scheme'. Church of Scotland clergy are perhaps more socially aware, have more political *savoir-faire*, and have greater commitment to working-class interests than at any point in their history. In part, the decline of local-scale democracy consequent upon the reorganisation of local government in 1975 has left the clergyman or, increasingly, the clergywoman as one of the few resident community leaders. This has brought new functions and new status, especially in areas of industrial decline. Whether this will have any appreciable affect on long-term levels of Protestant working-class church connection remains to be seen.

REFERENCES

BLAIKIE, W. G. (1893) The relation of the church to social problems, *The Thinker* 3, 1-16

BROWN, C. G. (1981) The Sunday-school movement in Scotland 1780-1914, *Records of the Scottish Church History Society* 21, 3-26.

BROWN, C. G. (1987) *The Social History of Religion in Scotland since 1730*, London and New York: Methuen.

BROWN, C. G. (1988a) Did urbanization secularize Britain?, *Urban History Yearbook* 1988, 1-14.

BROWN, C. G. (1988b) Religion. In Hood, J. (ed.), *The History of Clydebank*, Carnforth, Lancs.: Parthenon.

BROWN, C. G. (1989) Religion. In Pope, R. (ed.), *Atlas of British Social and Economic History since c.1700)*, London: Routledge.

BROWN, C. G. (1990a) Protest in the pews: interpreting presbyterianism and society in fracture during the Scottish economic revolution. In Devine, T. M. (ed.) *Conflict and Protest in Scottish Society c.1750-c.1850*, Edinburgh: John Donald.

BROWN, C. G. (1990b) Religion, class and church growth. In Fraser, W. H. and Morris, R. J. (eds.) *People and Society in Scotland, v. 2. 1830-1914*, Edinburgh: John Donald.

BROWN, C. G. (1990c) Religion and secularisation. In Dickson, T. and Treble, J. (eds.) *People and Society in Scotland, v. 3. 1914 to the Present*, Edinburgh: John Donald (forthcoming).

BUCHANAN F. O. (1987) The ebb and flow of Mormonism in Scotland, 1840-1900, *Brigham Young University Studies* 27, 27-52.

CARTER, I. (1979) *Farmlife in Northeast Scotland 1840-1914: The Poor Man's Country*, Edinburgh: John Donald.

CHECKLAND, O. (1980) *Philanthropy in Victorian Scotland*, Edinburgh: John Donald.

DUTHIE, J. L. (1984) Philanthropy and evangelism among Aberdeen seamen, 1814-1924, *Scottish Historical Review* 63, 155-73.

GRAY, R. Q. (1977) Religion, culture and social class in late nineteenth and early twentieth century Edinburgh. In Crossick, G. (ed.) *The Lower Middle Class in Britain 1870-1914*, London: Croom Helm.

HARDIE, K. (1893) The Church and the Labour problem, *The Thinker* 3, 104-9.

HILLIS, P. (1981) Presbyterianism and social class in mid-nineteenth century Glasgow: a study of nine churches, *Journal of Ecclesiastical History* 32, 47-64.

HILLIS, P. (1988) Education and evangelisation: presbyterian missions in mid-nineteenth century Glasgow, *Scottish Historical Review* 66, 46-62.

HUNTER, J. (1976) *The Making of the Crofting Community*, Edinburgh: John Donald.

HUTCHINSON, J. (1986) *Weavers, Miners and the Open Book: A History of Kilsyth*, Cumbernauld: published by the author.

LANG, J. M. (1893) The Church and the Labour problem, *The Thinker* 3, 295-9.

MACLAREN, A. A. (1974) *Religion and Social Class: The Disruption Years in Aberdeen*, London and Boston: Routledge and Kegan Paul.

MACLAREN, A. A. (1983) Class formation and class fractions; the Aberdeen bourgeoisie 1830-1950. In Gordon, G. and Dicks, B. (eds.) *Scottish Urban History*, Aberdeen: Aberdeen University Press.

MCLEOD, H. (1982) Protestantism and the working class in Imperial Germany, *European Studies Review* 12, 323-44.

MCLEOD, H. (1984) *Religion and the Working Class in Nineteenth Century* Britain, London: Macmillan.

MATHESON, A. S. (1890) *The Gospel and Modern Substitutes*, Edinburgh: Oliphant, Anderson and Ferrier.

MAXWELL-ARNOT, M. (1974) Social change and the Church of Scotland. In M. Hill (ed.), *A Sociological Yearbook of Religion in Britain*, vol.7, London: SCM.

MECHIE, S. (1960) *The Church and Scottish Social Development 1780-1880*, Oxford: Oxford University Press.

MURRAY, D. B. (1977) The Social and Religious Origins of Scottish Non-Presbyterian Protestant Dissent from 1730-1800. Unpublished Ph.D. thesis, University of St Andrews.

PANTON, K. J. (1973) The Church in the community: a study of patterns of religious adherence in a Scottish burgh. In Hill, M. (ed.), *A Sociological Yearbook of Religion in Britain*, vol. 6, London: SCM.

ROBERTSON, D. R. (1966) The Relationship between Church and Social Class in Scotland. Unpublished Ph.D. thesis, University of Edinburgh.

SISSONS, P. (1973) *The Social Significance of Church Membership in the Burgh of Falkirk*, Edinburgh: Church of Scotland.

SUMMERS, D. F. (1958) The Labour Church and Allied Movements of the Late Nineteenth and Early Twentieth Centuries. Unpublished Ph.D. thesis, University of Edinburgh

6

Protestantism and Scottish politics

GRAHAM WALKER AND TOM GALLAGHER

(I)   PROTESTANTISM AND POLITICAL CULTURE 1890-1990
Graham Walker

In the late Victorian and Edwardian eras political culture in Scotland overlapped singularly with the popular culture of the time. In
urban west-central Scotland at least, empire and religion were
prominent in the common ground. This was the period and this was
the era in which Conservatism as a popular Protestant Unionist and
imperialist ideology, challenged a hitherto dominant Liberalism
which had been nourished by a rich tradition of Presbyterian radical
individualism. It was also the period and the era of the emergence of
a Labour movement which attempted to steer the same Presbyterian
radical impulse in a collectivist direction. The popular cultural
backdrop to these political struggles was one in which imperial
images dominated the press, the music hall and the youth organisations and Irish issues underscored community divisions based on
religion.

Gladstone's commitment to Irish Home Rule in 1886 created a
Liberal Unionist opposition which was to form the most influential
part of the aforementioned popular Toryism:[1] it also gave rise in
Liberal circles to ideas of 'Home Rule All Round' – separate parlia-
ments for Scotland, England, Ireland and Wales along with an
Imperial assembly – in order to strengthen the imperial unity which
the opponents of the Irish measure claimed was under attack.
Indeed, such schemes were viewed by some as a first step to a
Federation of the Empire.[2] Nobody pushed the idea of 'Home Rule
All Round' harder than the Liberal MP for Bridgeton in Glasgow
after 1906, Alexander McCallum Scott. Scott was an archetypal
Scottish Liberal of the post-Whig school; his political outlook was
shaped by his Presbyterian religious beliefs and his deep Scottish
patriotism and he took a 'progressive' line on social reform. His

voluminous papers detail the challenge he faced in his own constituency from his Unionist opponents at the time of the crisis over the third Irish Home Rule Bill in 1912-13. In Bridgeton – an overwhelmingly working-class constituency – organisations like the Junior Imperialist League were strong and, in conjunction with the Orange Order, they agitated on the Irish issue and depicted the Liberals as enemies of empire. Scott retaliated by promoting 'Home Rule All Round' as the saviour of empire unity.[3]

Home Rule, in fact, was overwhelmingly an Irish or an Imperial issue in Scotland before the First World War; only a small minority supported it as a Scottish nationalist end in itself or as a step towards complete independence. This minority was most likely to be found in small towns and in the Highlands where the burning question of landownership and a deep-rooted hostility to landlordism often fused with nationalist sentiment. Liberalism's greater strength in these places reflected the absence of a popular Toryism based, as in Glasgow and the West, on the fusion of religious and imperial appeals, and the success of the Liberal Party in tapping the democratic and culturally distinctive strands of Presbyterian tradition. However, cultural nationalism in Scotland was nowhere near as strong as the contemporaneous phenomenon in Ireland and religion was essentially a force caught up in the ambiguities of the Scottish-British-Imperial sense of national identity.

This was evident in the position of the national church – the Church of Scotland. It was probably the most distinctive of Scottish institutions and its influence on Scottish society remained profound for longer than has often been suggested.[4] It embodied a heritage which, as has been remarked, was ripe for plunder by Liberal and Labour political movements in search of historic, democratic and egalitarian credentials. However, its established status and the loss of many of its more radical elements in the Great Disruption of 1843 resulted in a more conservative, comfortable and affluent image as the century wore on; its social profile became more strikingly middle-class. On top of this there developed a special relationship between the church and the monarchy in the reign of Queen Victoria,[5] and an antagonism between the church and the Liberals over the issue of disestablishment. By the end of the nineteenth century the church was clearly bound up with popular expressions of empire such as the Boys' Brigade (founded in Glasgow in 1883) and was more notably identified with missionary work abroad than protests over social injustice at home. More clearly motivated by the latter issues were the Free Church and the United Presbyterian Church, founded in 1843 and 1847 respectively.

There were, undoubtedly, tensions between British imperialism and Scottish nationalist feelings. However, the political effects of this were marginal before 1914. It might be argued that nationalist impulses were absorbed in the competitiveness *vis-à-vis* England that many Scots seemed to evince in relation to empire; the latter was, indeed, seen as providing an opportunity for the Scots to display the qualities, skills and genius which they celebrated in a popular cultural sense quite immodestly. The Scots – urban and rural – wanted confirmation of their international importance, something which, in a genuinely popular sense, they considered to be their rightful heritage.[6] Emigration, in this respect, was not lamented; rather there was great pride taken in the creation of a Scottish diaspora.

This outward-looking attitude was most pronounced in Glasgow and the industrialised lowlands.[7] This region's identity had been shaped quite obviously by its economic character and the success of Scottish capitalism in capturing a substantial share of the imperial markets in heavy industry. It even possessed a mercantile capitalist heritage which linked it to Europe and America. Glasgow's great municipal experiments of the nineteenth century had bestowed international recognition upon her and reinforced the breadth of her civic designs. In addition, of course, Glasgow and its environs was the area of densest population concentration in Scotland with the vast bulk of Irish immigrants and their descendants. This community remained in this period unassimilated and continued to identify with its homeland. While Edinburgh functioned as the urban seat of Scottish privilege and rural Scotland continued to be weighed down by its aristocratic legacy, Glasgow stood out as a democratic city in which the self-improving ethos ran deep and a skilled working-class political culture,[8] largely liberal but also in part socialist and Unionist, claimed its place. Scottish nationalism, to these workers, seemed antiquarian and romantic.

Before the First World War, therefore, Scotland's overall worldview was, in general, empire-orientated. It fed on notions of international prestige in industry, science and education; it was proud of its regiments and missionaries; it liked the idea of 'partnership' with England and it shared with its partner a broad cultural affinity, however great the tensions and whatever the arguments about cultural 'colonisation' from the metropolitan south.[9] By contrast with Catholic Ireland at the same time, Scotland did not recoil from English 'materialism' and did not disparage 'modernism'.[10] Scotland remained profoundly different from England but its Protestantism among other things ensured that differences were not – as in Ireland – pushed to the point of conflict. Protestantism, particularly in relation to missionaries, was a central part of the Scottish 'empire-mindedness'. It was perhaps no accident that some of the intellectual voices of Scottish nationalism which would make themselves heard after the First World War were those of Roman Catholics; their world- view, moreover, bore a close resemblance to that of the prophets and ideologues of Irish nationalism such as Pearse,[11] and was of a similarly spiritual, ascetic and pious character.

Scottish political culture underwent profound change in the First World War. Faith in those who ruled received a battering from which it was never quite to recover; labour unrest over 'dilution' and rent strikes shifted the popular mood on Clydeside in an anti-government direction. Only Labour (in Scotland the ILP at this time)[12] could benefit from this; only they had clean hands in a war which brought grief and misery, shattered illusions of glory and superiority, and saw government incompetence and profiteering on a vast scale. Class consciousness and collectivist doctrines emerged from the war immeasurably stronger political forces in Scotland. The 'coupon' election of 1918 was a poor barometer of this, as of much else; Labour's breakthrough in Glasgow in 1922 – it won ten seats out of fifteen – was a truer guide to the shift in popular opinion.

Labour in Scotland, particularly the ethical socialists of the ILP, had always conveyed a religious style of appeal. Until 1918 they had directed their message to the skilled worker in an attempt to 'out-Gladstone' the Liberals. Notions of the dignity and the self-education of the skilled craftsman were often given more emphasis than those of class solidarity or class struggle. The early Labour movement in Scotland was Protestant in make-up and Protestant in its mentality.[13]

It had to modify this image after the war when the largely unskilled Irish Catholic vote became vital, and Labour's stance on Irish self-determination in this period served it well to this end. The Catholic community was also politically mollified by the Education Act of 1918 which provided for state support for its schools; Labour opportunistically pledged itself to the defence of this Act and so calmed the Catholic church's fears of socialism. The period 1918-22 was crucial in the shaping of Labour Party organisation in Scotland: it reached out to the Catholics and captured what was to be the subsequent backbone of its support in Glasgow and the West and it managed, at the same time, to retain, and in many cases gain, the allegiance of large number of Protestant workers, skilled and unskilled. It did so in spite of religious sectarianism which was rife at local level. Class cut across religious and ethnic loyalties; it tempered, but in most cases did not remove them. It was perhaps the case that the most sectarian Protestant and Catholic workers voted, respectively, Conservative and Labour out of tribal consciousness – Protestant working-class Conservative loyalties will be considered below; however, many other workers increasingly expressed their class-consciousness politically through support for Labour and left tribal matters to other spheres. It can also be added that Labour might even have benefited by Home Rule in proportion to the damage that it caused the Liberals. Working-class Unionism – the expression of both Protestant and Scottish-British national identities – was for many a temporary phenomenon in terms of support for the Tories and it was something many went on to weld – however uneasily – to support for Labour. Unionism was a gut reaction against Irish Home Rule and therefore the Liberals. Once the tradition of support for Liberalism had been broken, an anti-Tory tendency arguably steered many towards Labour. Moreover Labour, after World War I, did not officially spurn imperial designs; indeed, Scottish spokesmen such as Tom Johnston eagerly advocated empire trading schemes.[14] The Labour Party could still be considered 'safe' in relation to the Constitution and an overall sense of British loyalty. The Irish issue departed British politics in 1922 and with it much of the potential to cause sectarian strife between Protestant and Catholic workers. It might be said that a degree of the early Protestant character of the movement lingered on and served as a counterweight to the great increases in Catholic support and participation. Certainly, Labour's successes in Scotland since 1922 have rested on its ability to appeal across the religious divide.[15]

However, Labour's achievements in this respect cannot detract from the fact that there was a substantial working-class Tory vote in Scotland until the 1970s. It has been suggested that factors such as the Empire and Irish Home Rule encouraged its growth before 1914. At this time, the Orange Order, which had been transplanted from Ireland in the 1830s, was institutionally bound up with the Tories and functioned as a link between the squire and the worker; in some industrial firms, usually small-scale ones, it was instrumental in the establishment of a paternalistic employer-worker relationship.[16] Orange ideology, with its stress on the Crown and Parliament as guardians of civil and religious liberty, inspired a fundamentally British patriotism and loyalism; however, it was capable also of playing up Scotland's Covenanting history and of being suspicious about the Anglican establishment in England and its commitment to Bible Protestantism. The Order's relationship with the Tories was always an edgy one and the political allegiance of Orange Order members could not be taken for granted. The Orange

Order shared in the ambiguities of Scotland's political culture: the tensions between and within class, religious, and national loyalties.

The Irish Treaty of 1921 actually led to a split between Orangeism and Conservatism and the setting up of a short-lived Protestant Party. With the Irish issue out of British politics, attention then focused on the 1918 Education Act; complaints about 'Rome on the Rates' became the cornerstone of popular Protestant political appeals, particularly at local government level. Two movements which achieved a measure of success in this regard were the Scottish Protestant League in Glasgow in the 1931-6 period and Protestant Action in Edinburgh from 1934 till the outbreak of the Second World War. Both parties won municipal seats and took Protestant politics, often violently in the case of the Edinburgh movement, on to the street.[17] These outbreaks of militant Protestant activity were an embarrassment to the Conservatives and, thereby, to those in the Orange Order who wanted to influence party policy. While, in the inter-war period, senior Tories were sometimes leading Orangemen, it was clear that the Conservative Party was happier to see the Order concentrate on its religious and social activities. Indeed, it can be argued that with the passing of the Irish issue in 1922, the Orange Order's significance became primarily social. Accordingly, divisions opened up in politics between officers and rank-and-file members, the participation of local Orange bands in marches during the 1926 General Strike being an example.[18] In addition, a kind of rapport between Orangeism and local ILP or Labour Party branches existed in certain mining areas in Ayrshire, Lanarkshire and West Lothian.[19]

The Scottish-British dual sense of national identity seems, unsurprisingly, to have been reinforced by the experience of the Second World War. The Covenant Movement 1949-50 showed that expressions of Scottish nationalist feeling could be popular and intense and significantly Protestant in character. However, demonstrations of British patriotism could be described in the same terms, most notably the celebrations of the Queen's coronation in 1953 which were viewed as essentially Protestant displays by some Catholics.[20] The writer James Campbell has said of his Glasgow upbringing in the 1950s: 'the predominant feeling among my schoolfriends was not the force of Scottish patriotism, though that had its place, but loyalist Protestantism, which conflicts with it.'[21]

Even with the decline of empire, therefore, 'Britishness' or 'Loyalism' continued to matter. As a result the Conservatives, still called 'Unionists' in Scotland until the 1960s, held on to a strong measure of cross-class support among Protestants in west-central

Scotland. This is illustrated by Budge and Urwin's sample of voters in selected Glasgow constituencies in the 1955 and 1964 general elections and in local elections.[22] The Tories held several seats in Glasgow at local elections until the 1960s which could be classed as predominantly Protestant working-class, namely Kinning Park, Govan, Whiteinch and Govanhill.[23] Since the 1970s the Conservative grip on such seats has been broken, a result partly of demographic changes, but also of an unmistakable shift away from the party by such voters. This trend has been accentuated in the Thatcher years to the point where Conservative support in Glasgow and the west of Scotland, outside affluent middle-class constituencies, is derisory. Economic change has undoubtedly been a factor in this. Small firms have not fared well in Scotland in the last decade, particularly those which served the declining heavy industries, and it was, arguably, in such firms with paternalistic worker-employer relations that Protestant exclusivism and working-class Conservatism were strongest.[24] In the heavy industries themselves, strong trade-unionism had tended to ensure voting along class lines, whatever the sectarian views of workers. Social attitudes seem also to have changed significantly; far fewer Protestant working-class voters now take a snobbish view of Labour as the party of the badly-educated, morally defective 'lumpen' (and in this view largely Catholic) proletariat.

However, the image of Protestant working-class Tory voters still endures: Tories try to boost morale by convincing themselves that such voters can be won back and, at another level, the novelist Ian McGinnis could write this as late as 1987: 'The Orange vote was not to be moved. No Surrender! They voted Unionist, and they still do, in the guise of the Conservative Party.' That, as Conservatives know to their cost today, really is fiction.[25]

The 'Orange vote', in fact, is a highly questionable phenomenon. As has been suggested earlier, the Order cannot easily regulate the political behaviour of its membership. Teddy Taylor, the populist Tory MP who held the Glasgow seat of Cathcart from 1964 to 1979, doubts whether such a vote really existed and denies that it was of importance to his party's fortunes in the 1960s and 1970s. Moreover, he does not believe that the Ulster troubles since 1969 have had any meaningful political impact in Scotland. Taylor was more concerned with making inroads into the Catholic vote which *was* coherent and powerful, but admits that his party's 'Loyalist' and Protestant image made this immensely difficult.[26] On the other hand, Danny Houston, a trustee of the Orange Order and a Tory councillor for the Glasgow ward of Dennistoun in the mid-1970s, believes that the Tories have blundered in their cavalier treatment of the Protestant working class and their indifference to Orangeism and to issues of Protestant concern. He argues that the Labour Party has been turned into a vehicle promoting Catholic Church interests in Glasgow.[27] Houston's view is that the Protestant working class remains *Unionist*, if not Conservative, and that the Tories have suffered since they stopped calling themselves 'Unionists'.[28] This latter view is shared by Taylor who sees the past use of the labels 'Unionist' at parliamentary level and 'Progressives' at local level as beneficial tokens of the party's Scottish distinctiveness, the erosion of which, he believes, is at the root of many of the party's current problems.[29]

The Unionism of working-class Protestant voters is also a debatable claim. Brand's 1976 figures do not distinguish by class, but the strength of the Protestant vote for the Scottish National Party suggests that it embraced a not insignificant portion of the working class.[30] By-election wins for the SNP in Govan in 1973 and 1988 suggest the same, but the inability of the SNP to sustain their performance in urban working-class constituencies up until the present invites the explanation of a protest vote being cast. At the very least, however, it might be said that Protestant workers are more likely than their Catholic counterparts to register a protest vote of this nature. Both Scottish and British patriotic feelings are probably still more keenly felt by Protestant workers, although it would seem that the decline of the Conservatives has been accompanied by some measure of decline in 'Britishness' if the recent overwhelming opinion poll evidence in favour of a Scottish Parliament is any guide. The Orange Order and sundry Loyalist groups in Scotland – working-class in character[31] – continue to agitate on behalf of the Unionists in Ulster and against Irish Republican sympathisers in Scotland, but this has no real political relevance to the way most Scottish Protestants, practising or nominal, view politics, and arguably does not impinge on the current debate on nationalism in Scotland.

Scotland has had a secular political culture for some time now. It is non-sectarian (in the religious sense), still largely class-based, and British in its party structures (excepting the SNP) and points of reference. It is a culture which has generated its own loyalties, networks, values and sense of identity and it has diluted religious sectarianism as a political force in Scotland. However, over the period studied, this culture has developed in co-existence with a sectarian sub-culture in Lowland Scotland which has involved 'British' and 'Irish' loyalties being grafted on to Scottish ones. This sub-culture has primarily been a social phenomenon and has had an increasingly tangential relationship to politics, but nonetheless such interaction as there has been has given rise to several ambiguities and cases of divided loyalties, for example, Scottishness and Britishness, Scottishness and Irishness, Orangeism and Labourism, Catholic Labourism and Scottish nationalism, Conservatism and Scottish patriotism. It remains to be seen if the present upsurge in a strictly Scottish national consciousness brings about changes to the political culture which revive or diminish still further the significance of religion.

(II) SCOTTISH PROTESTANTISM AND POLITICS: THE CHURCH DIMENSION
IN THE PRESENT CENTURY
Tom Gallagher

The true character of Scottish political culture has often been obscured by membership of a larger political state system that, in large measure, rests upon the different political traditions and formative experiences contained in English history. Accordingly, the continuing relevance of certain aspects of popular religion as well as the persistent if understated role of the Church of Scotland in political life can often fall from view.

That until very recently the church may have been unaware of its own distinctive governing traditions and their contemporary relevance is a view advanced by the Very Revd Dr W. B. Johnston, a former Moderator. He points to the Kilbrandon Commission on the Constitution to which Church of Scotland representatives gave evidence in 1969. Dr Johnston noted that: 'The grounds of justification for their appearance before this enquiry was "not that the Church has any expertise in the devising of constitutions" but that it is the "national church ministering to the Scottish people in every parish, the Church of Scotland is deeply concerned for the welfare of the Scottish nation ...".'[1] Here was a different premise from that contained in the founding articles of the church which saw it as expressing the corporate faith of the nation. In its formative years the Church of Scotland had been at pains to define its relationship with the State and the Crown in terms that it would be difficult to reconcile with English perceptions even after the 1707 Act of Union. It drew on the Scottish constitutional tradition of limited sovereignty to reject political control by the state.

The Act of Union conceded that the English model of state regulation of the Established church was inappropriate for Anglicanism's Scottish counterpart. But parliamentary endorsement of lay patronage in the church broke the spirit of this compromise. Escalating church-state disagreement culminated in the 1842 Claim of Right drawn up to reassert the Kirk's right to self-regulation in matters of faith and its own order. Eventually this principle was confirmed when, in 1921, the British parliament passed the Church of Scotland Act in which, according to J. H. S., Burleigh the '"civil magistrate" for the first time since the Reformation, acknowledged in the fullest sense the freedom of the church in matters affecting its own life and work'.[2]

In the intervening eighty or so years mainstream Presbyterianism had been preoccupied with coming to terms with the seismic effects of the 1843 Disruption, or split in the Established Church, which the 1842 Claim of Right had anticipated. Long years devoted to formalising the split in angry diatribes and rival church-building schemes were followed by gradual efforts at reconciliation once the reasons for the 1843 split ceased to exercise fascination in pew and pulpit. These efforts finally came to fruition in 1929 when the bulk of the United Free Church re-entered the Church of Scotland.

Against this background of church schism and careful diplomacy to persuade Parliament implicitly to recognise that a different constitutional tradition in Scotland required the church there to be self-governing, it is not surprising that as a body it fought shy of active political involvements. Unlike Anglicanism it never enjoyed a mutually supportive relationship with any one political party, nor has it ever had corporate representatives in the House of Lords accustomed to being present at the very heart of the state's political life.

Nineteenth-century Scottish Protestantism's broad endorsement of the doctrines of *laissez-faire* individualism may also explain why its voice was relatively muted as social and economic questions increasingly overshadowed political debate with the gradual expansion of the franchise. The exercise of moral authority was confined largely to questions of the family and individual religious practice, with issues like the Highland Clearances or factory conditions inviting few Kirk pronouncements that reaffirmed the prophetic role of the Church to challenge a fallible social order. Between 1870 and 1914 the growth of a north British outlook among social groups providing the bulk of the Church's most active membership at a time when the union was an object of general satisfaction may also have inhibited it from drawing on precedent, originating in pre-union times, to comment on public affairs.

In the confident atmosphere before 1914 with Scotland virtually seen as a co-partner in empire, her economy in a buoyant state, and national prospects apparently undimmed, whenever the major Protestant churches spoke up for the nation it was in the language of certainties. A socially advanced wing attempted to persuade middle-class church members of the need to sympathise with and support – on Christian grounds – the social aspirations of the workers.[3] But when the Social Problems Committee of the United Free Church organised a Labour week in Glasgow at which addresses were delivered by Labour movement figures on social, economic, and industrial questions from a Christian standpoint, the lukewarm response from the middle-classes denoted a suspicion of Labour and its leaders.[4]

The note of prophetic criticism beginning to make itself heard in the church as social tensions overshadowed the Edwardian era was drowned by the onset of the Great War. Many churchmen blessed it as a holy war and a self-righteous crusading spirit took hold of the church for much of the 1914-18 period. Then, as the toll of death and destruction mounted, a more realistic and questioning attitude emerged in some quarters. In 1917 a Church of Scotland commission on the war warned in its report that 'self-interest has been accepted as the proper and natural basis of action in practical relations'. The church was urged to secure 'a drastic and permanent amelioration of social conditions. "Never again" must be her watchword as she contemplates the chaos of pre-war conditions.'[5]

But in the depressed and uncertain mood of post-war Scotland, the new social awakening made little headway as the narrow conservatism of the dominant social classes asserted itself within the church. The bleak outlook for Scotland's major industries and an uncertain political situation, combined with the disproportionately heavy Scottish casualty rate in the fighting, soon produced a mood of grim retrenchment; and to the dismay of the social reformers, the Church reflected rather than transcended the low morale of the Scottish middle classes and of many of the institutions and pressure groups which shaped Scottish public opinion.

At a time when national self-confidence had slumped, the church may have revealed its own diminishing importance in Scottish life by its failure to rally the nation behind goals or visions that might have helped to allay the pessimism and rancour that were increasingly noticeable in the social sphere. Instead, a policy of silence was adopted on contentious social, political and economic questions that revealed Scotland to be a bitterly divided country where class and ethnic conflicts bubbled menacingly below the surface. As initial enthusiasm for social reconstruction was quickly abandoned within mainstream Presbyterianism, the blame for rising unemployment and the miserable slum conditions to which a large proportion of the Scottish employed population was condemned was allocated, not to an unfeeling government or an irresponsible economic system, but to the unassimilated Catholic Irish immigrant population. Strongly worded attacks on the Catholic Irish presence in Scotland became a feature of the annual General Assembly of both the Church of Scotland and the United Free Church during the 1920s as senior clergymen, like the Very Revd Dr John White, perhaps the most eminent Scottish church man of the first half of the century, quietly endorsed the bitter critique of inveterate No Popery campaigners.[6]

Dr White was Moderator of the church of Scotland in 1926, the year of the General Strike and a long drawn out miners' strike. He held back from joining English church leaders in a joint effort to seek a settlement by means of a compromise and no special effort was made by the relevant church committees to alleviate the suffering of mining families facing destitution and hunger as the strike dragged on into the winter of 1926. During the fifth month of the strike the United Free Church even staged an evangelical campaign in West Fife among communities suffering from a lack of food and fuel. The two churches that were shortly to be reunited claimed to be neutral in the dispute but the temper of their leading members was shown by 'the hero's welcome' Prime Minister Baldwin received 'for his firm stand against the strike' when he made a surprise appearance at both Assemblies.[7]

The church did not ignore the mass unemployment of the 1920s and 1930s but its declarations often sounded like pious platitudes which may well have weakened its already diminishing base in many working-class communities. One church historian has commented that:

> It is difficult to read ... the assembly debates of the depression period, and to note how much more time was spent by the fathers and brethren in discussing the Maintenance of the ministry Fund than in examining the plight of the nation's unemployed, and in how gingerly a manner they handled all questions of social justice, without feeling that official Christianity had little to offer the oppressed but pious platitudes, assurances of strictly non-political sympathy, and bland exhortations to grin and bear it. This, certainly, was the way in which many of the industrial workers themselves – and not only those who with Willie Gallacher, John Maclean and John Maxton were making the reputation of 'Red Clydeside' – reacted to ecclesiastical deliverances during those bitter, destructive years.[8]

A 1932 Church and Nation Committee report on unemployment detailed the scale of the problem and offered some useful suggestions. But a motion to have the means test removed and to restore to the unemployed the cuts in benefit was defeated at that year's Assembly after speakers alluded to the fear that its removal would destroy the 'traditional spirit of independence' of the Scottish working class'.[9] During this debate, J. M. Munro, a minister who in 1924 contested the Scottish University seat as a Labour candidate, was moved to declare: 'Believe me, nothing has done the church more harm than the attitude taken up by some of the "pillars" against the drawers of the "dole".'[10]

Anti-clericalism directed at the national church did not become a feature of inter-war Scottish politics despite the Church of Scotland (finally reunited with the United Free Church in 1929) losing ground in many hard-pressed communities and revealing itself increasingly to be the church of the comfortable classes. Nearly 31 per cent of the inter-war Scottish Labour Party leadership (MPs and trade-union leaders) belonged to the Church of Scotland;[11] the attachment of most was a loose one but some were pillars of the Church, such as the Ayrshire mining MP, James Brown who was the first commoner in three hundred years to be Lord High Commissioner of the Church of Scotland during the period of the two inter-war Labour governments; Thomas Cassells, a Hamilton lawyer and MP for Dumbarton from 1936 to 1944, was another devout Christian who at public meetings, would go armed with a copy of the Bible. A surprising unity of outlook has been detected between these types of Labour politicians and the churches: 'The social gospel of the Scottish Churches, which concentrated on the need to abolish or legislate away material impediments to man reaching God, was mirrored in the desire of the Labour elite to improve morally, the Scottish working class. Each was a religious message, elitist in concept and aim.'[12]

Shorn of the facile optimism and crusading spirit of the First War, the church was better able to function as the moral guardian and spokesman of the nation in the 1939-45 conflict. In 1940 the Commission for the Interpretation of God's Will in the Present Crisis was set up to investigate the implications of the war for the life of the Church and the Nation. The reports it issued which called for a more progressive and equitable social order in which to build the peace received a favourable reception in the socially cohesive war years. The 1942 report entitled *God's Will in Our Time* connected 'the present weakness of the spiritual life of our land' to 'the failure of Christians to realise and act upon those social implications of the Gospel' for the existing industrial system.[13] It asked: how can men be drawn to a Gospel whose one practical expression is serving Christ by serving the least needy of His brethren if we preach it in abstraction from the crying needs of the poor and oppressed of our own society?[14]

The advocacy of churchmen like the academic theologian, the Revd Dr John Baillie, rather than pressure from the Church's grassroots, produced this burst of activity. *God's Will for Church and Nation* was an unusually radical document to emerge from the Church of Scotland. Not only did it insist that 'extreme inequalities in the possession of wealth are dangerous to the common interest and ... should be ... controlled' but it pointed to the 'anarchical' tendencies of capitalism embodied in its general lack of social purpose and direction. Its strongest passage declared that henceforth: 'Economic power must be made objectively responsible to the community as a whole. The possessors of economic power must be answerable for the use of that power not only to their own consciences, but to appropriate social organs.'[15] The report sold of 14000 copies but, if the 1945 general election is a useful guide, the desire for radical change which gave dozens of once-safe Tory seats in the south of England to Labour was relatively muted in middle-class and small-town Scotland.

Formed in 1920, the Church and Nation Committee took time to rise above the constraints of inter-war Scotland before pronouncing with increasing confidence on national affairs and the condition of Scotland. Detailed reports on the state of Scotland's economy and society were drawn up and from 1948 the General Assembly threw its weight behind the campaign for a Scottish Parliament to deal with Scottish affairs. Leading ministers identified with the Scottish Covenant movement which organised a national petition with two million signatures in favour of Home Rule during the early 1950s. A warning was issued in 1960 about the future when the Church and Nation Committee declared: 'The sense of hopeful neighbourhood, of a country with tradition, characteristics, and opportunities strong enough to hold its young people in their country and with a future bright enough to attract them, seem to be losing force in an ominous way.'[16]

The Church of Scotland was fulfilling its role as one of the nationally recognised institutions through which national feeling could be expressed. But it was following a lead already created by others rather than offering an example; perhaps, as one source has commented, it was too intertwined with the existing order, too much a slightly dissenting member of the establishment, to be a very active supporter of nationalism.[17] Certainly, in the wake of the secularisation of Scottish life its opinions on national political matters fell on a lot of deaf ears. But in the late 1950s its views on

Africa were listened to by government. The Church's anti-colonial stance (deriving inspiration from a large contingent of missionaries in Nyasaland) was awkward for officialdom but Ian Macleod the Colonial Secretary, attended the 1959 Assembly and the church's endorsement of self-government may well have hastened British withdrawal from this part of Africa.

The peripheral housing estates on the edge of Scotland's largest cities, into which many of the residents of run-down inner-city areas had been decanted, were in some ways as mysterious to the church as the African interior had once been. To reconstitute its links with the working class as it was substantially uprooted, the church turned the 1950s into a decade of 'mission' in the new estates. The church extension scheme, first pioneered in the 1930s, met with some success, perhaps because for the displaced people in unfamiliar surroundings the Kirk offered some continuity with a sundered past. By 1961 Church of Scotland membership stood higher than in 1931. But the church was unable to counteract the poor planning, the lack of amenities and the lack of job prospects which soon tarnished many of these new communities, or to sink permanent roots in what became marginal settlements that were an indictment of the lack of vision in much post-war planning. Housing policy is a particularly vivid illustration of governmental decisions being largely made on a utilitarian basis with politics being seen as totally divorced from an ethical basis. A church only dimly aware of Thomas Chalmers' vision of Britain as a godly commonwealth of parish communities or of the emphasis on social integration within the Christian community offered by the post-Reformation church was not well-placed to develop a moral underpinning for public policy which the welfarist, full-employment strategy of the post-war era fatally lacked.

The mass rallies, emphasising personal conversion, that began with the 'Tell Scotland' crusade of the Revd Tom Allan in 1947 and rose to a climax with the Scottish crusade of Dr Billy Graham in the winter of 1954-5, conveyed the impression of surface vigour and continuing popular appeal for Protestantism. But despite the packed rallies in Glasgow's Kelvin Hall, widely broadcast by radio and television and relayed to churches and halls throughout the country, it is difficult to see any lasting impact from this late evangelical upsurge.[18] Occasional charismatic figures were found like the Revd James Currie, who could relate strongly to the needs and concerns of the Pollok community in which he ministered from 1955 to 1972, and build up a flourishing congregation. But the middle-class orientation of what, after all, was one of the traditional Scottish professions, meant that such wholehearted identification with an ordinary working-class community was not easily arrived at;[19] the Revd Geoff Shaw, from a family of Edinburgh physicians, accomplished the transition upon choosing to channel his ministry into youth work to the end of the 1950s in the Gorbals area of Glasgow. He soon became a legend in his own lifetime and inspired future emulators in some of Glasgow's bleaker housing estates.

Away from areas of social deprivation and planning blight, the Church was able to fit into a comfortable social niche across much of Scotland well into the post-war era. Not just in rural localities but in suburban and small-town areas as well, the parish kirk and its minister could be the focal point for much community activity. Presbyterian values and related social attitudes exercise a continuing, if weakening, appeal in a country where the economic boom and the pace of social change was notably slower than in the rest of Britain (see the chapter on the press). In such close-knit communities that drew on well-established social traditions and a shared idea of community obligation, the political beneficiary was likely to be the Conservative Party. Surveys into working-class voting behaviour in Glasgow and Dundee during the 1960s found a strong correlation between church affiliation and voting patterns which indicated that churchgoing members of the national church were predisposed to vote Conservative.[20] The impact of continuing tensions over Ulster and Irish immigration from which the Tories derived particular benefit should not be discounted, but the fact that Dundee, a city traditionally free of such tensions, virtually duplicated the Glasgow result, suggests other forces were also at work.

In local government, the Progressive Party's identification with local community needs rather than national party concerns, and its stress upon public service for the common good rather than on behalf of specific class interests, was appealing to many ordinary members of the kirk. However much the Progressives fell short of their ideals in practice, this formula extended their influence beyond the political right so that the Conservatives did not feel the need to contest local government elections until the 1960s. Upon invading the local government arena and displacing the Progressives, the Tories proved unable to express the local civic patriotism that the Progressives had traded upon and any unity of outlook with the Kirk in the name of good government also faded fast.

The record of Labour's Willie Ross, a church elder and Secretary of State for Scotland from 1964 to 1970 and from 1974 to 1976, reveals that the conservative agenda and outlook of the mainstream Kirk was not just channelled through one specific party. In carrying out his role as Scotland's most influential representative in any post-war cabinet, James Kellas reckons that Ross 'reflected the Conservative wing of the Church in such matters as liquor licensing, Sunday observance, homosexuality, family planning and divorce. In all these the Church tends to Conservatism, and parliamentary legislation on the above subjects was either not forthcoming or seriously modified in its application to Scotland'.[21]

As a devotee of the immortal memory of Robert Burns, Scotland's premier bard, and as a discreet but steadfast freemason, Ross identified with two symbolic constants in Protestant popular culture. With such an archetypally Protestant figure at the Labour helm in Scotland, the passage of working-class Tories to the Labour camp was perhaps rendered easier. In cabinet he showed more understanding for the beleaguered Unionist position in Ulster than most other ministers, especially during the successful 1974 Protestant challenge to the British-backed power-sharing government.[22] But Ross was able to work in tandem with the large Scottish Catholic Labour contingent at local and, increasingly, parliamentary level. They made common cause with him against the inroads of the permissive society while he functioned as a more active custodian of homespun Protestant values than any of his post-war Tory predecessors in the Scottish secretaryship.

Ross bowed out of active politics in 1979 but not before acting as Lord High Commissioner to the Church of Scotland, the role of Queen's representative to the national church affording him much evident satisfaction. Margaret Herbison, a member of the Wilson cabinet in the mid-1960s, preceded him in this role and it is possible to point to Labour MPs on different wings of the party from Bruce Millan to Gavin Strang who identify strongly with the Kirk and often play active roles in their local church.

Perhaps a more telling sign of the closer understanding that existed between the national church and Scotland's largest party was the meteoric rise of the Revd Geoff Shaw in Labour's ranks. After years spent helping some of Glasgow's underprivileged, Shaw decided that if the scales were to be adjusted in favour of the poor, his place needed to be in the political arena striving on their behalf.[23] Within a few years of being elected for a ward which, in the 1930s, had been held by the standard-bearer of a militant Protestant party, he was, in rapid succession, appointed leader of the majority Labour group on Glasgow District council in 1973 and, in the following year, he was chosen to be head of the newly-formed Strathclyde Regional council, Britain's largest local authority. The rapid promotion of a Presbyterian minister in what was a heavily Catholic party reflected well upon the state of community relations as terrible deeds were being carried out on behalf of rival sectarian totems in nearby Ulster. Moreover, it illustrated how it was possible to harness the parallel political traditions of Catholic collectivism and Presbyterian democracy in order to shape a political culture based on mutual obligation and the defence of humanitarian ideals necessary for sustaining communities vulnerable to assault from impersonal economic forces and indeed from the actions of government.

On the eve of his untimely death in 1978, Geoff Shaw was being spoken of by colleagues and the media as Scotland's first Prime Minister in the event of the 1978 devolution bill clearing the various hurdles erected by a central parliament reluctant to cede any of its powers. True to its devolutionary instincts, the Church of Scotland endorsed this measure, but absent was an inspirational figure who could rally sentiment inside and beyond the church and give a measure of unity to a pro-devolution camp weakened by party political divisions. Instead the conservative Unionist lobby in the kirk, ably marshalled by ex-Moderator Andrew Herron, fought a successful rearguard action and managed to halt the reading from pulpits of a call to vote 'Yes'.[24] The impression was given that the Church of Scotland was neutral on the issue, which was not the case, and although in the referendum of 1 March 1979 a majority voted 'Yes', devolution fell because it failed to meet a condition laid down by parliament requiring 40 per cent or more of the *entire* electorate to back the scheme.

It is impossible to determine to what extent, if any, the muted voice of the kirk significantly determined the outcome. Although the result was a bitter anti-climax for the proponents of self-government, it was also very much a last hurrah for those who were content for the kirk to have a privileged role in a non-Scottish state whose priorities increasingly reflected those of the privileged region in which the seat of government was located.

Conservative-minded figures still enjoyed positions of influence such as the editorship of the monthly *Life and Work*, long in the experienced hands of Robert Kernohan, but they were unable to rally substantial backing for the new orthodoxy of the Thatcher government. It began its lengthy reign in May 1979 with the backing of a smaller percentage of the total electorate than Scottish devolution had received a few weeks earlier, but this did not deter the new Prime Minister from breaking with the post-war consensus policies designed to keep at bay large-scale unemployment and poverty by channelling investment into disadvantaged regions and maintaining a welfare state financed from public revenue. The new political orthodoxy rehabilitated materialist individualism and its boldest practitioners insisted that morality could only be pursued by personal rather than collective action.

The attempt to construct an ethical code to buttress the new hard-edged politics that supporters and opponents alike termed Thatcherism found the British Christian churches thrown on to the defensive. But in Scotland a more forthright defence of the post-war settlement and the moral values underlying it was forthcoming from the churches. The kirk's absorption with the rhythm of life in a country far removed from the seat of power meant that it had not become enmeshed with the secular political elite. Every Moderator automatically becomes a member of Edinburgh's prestigious New Club, but no Scottish equivalent exists of dinners in Lambeth Palace at which top civil servants are authorised to defend government policy on matters such as nuclear deterrence, speaking explicitly as committed Christians in the hope that it will influence the thinking in the church.[25] Accordingly, the Church of Scotland may not have been as disorientated as its English counterpart when the 1980s saw this establishment in part substituted by a very different one.

The growing social awareness of sections of the middle classes, especially those located in the professions, and their identification with wider community concerns and with the Scottish rather than the British political dimension, meant that enthusiastic disciples of the new secular creed were in short supply. The Church of Scotland reflected this new social awareness by its response to specific Thatcherite measures, and it turned out that a surprising number of the more effective opponents of policies aiming to weaken public provision and introduce market principles in the realm of education, health, and local government had grown up in the manse; an often peripatetic existence, spent living in different parishes and coming into contact with people from many walks of life, probably helped to reinforce a sense of the oneness of society and the sense of interdependence of those living within it.

The emergence of a more oppositional kirk was signalled in 1981 when the outgoing moderator, the Very Revd Dr W. B. Johnston described the government's monetarist policies as 'immoral and blasphemous' because they had the effect of increasing unemployment and destroying the prospects of many of those living in already precarious conditions.[26] Even more outspoken was the Iona Community (founded by the Right Revd Dr George MacLeod in 1938), whose commitment to the social gospel, as well as to a more mystical and ritualistic form of Protestantism, had led it to work in the most deprived areas of Clydeside as well as to reconstruct the medieval abbey of Iona. In 1981 *Coracle*, the journal of the community, recommended that Christians should take to the streets in non-violent action to overthrow the government's 'blasphemous monetarist policies'.[27] In 1982 the General Assembly finally took the step so long urged by George MacLeod and declared its opposition to nuclear weapons; it went back on its decision two years later before total opposition was reinstated in 1986.

In the 1980s, concern about the practical effects of government policy had been expressed on numerous occasions by the Church and Nation Committee, the single most important policy-making body in the church. Its remit enables it to comment on matters of public importance: 'to watch over developments in the nation's life in which moral and spiritual considerations especially arise and consider what actions the Church from time to time may be advised to make to further the highest interests of the people.'[28] Perhaps it is a sign of the new-found social awareness of the Scottish professional middle classes that successive convenors in the 1980s were men who, before entering the ministry, had been high-flying civil servants.

To internal critics who argue that it is no job of the Church's to pronounce on sensitive political topics, the Revd Norman Shanks, the convenor of the committee, responded in 1989 by saying that 'engagement with the issues of the day has a religious and moral dimension as well as a political dimension, and is an important part of the witness of the church'.[29] On issues like defence or the place of Scotland within the United Kingdom, Dr Andrew Herron spoke up for many in the kirk during 1989 when he argued that since a religious matter is not at stake, it should be left to those whose business it is.[30] However, when the government (in its third term) turned its crusading zeal towards education, this quietist attitude had far fewer defenders. Since education was a keystone of the Reformation in Scotland, concern about the over-emphasis on education as a marketable product, or about the retrogressive effect of schools being allowed to opt out of the state system, sprang from a well-established ecclesiastical tradition rather than from new-found radicalism.

Accordingly, by the end of the 1980s the national church and the state found themselves further apart than at any point since the dawn of political democracy in Britain. In 1989, the year that a constitutional convention met in the Edinburgh Assembly Hall of the Church of Scotland and pledged to make Scotland a self-governing political community, the General Assembly approved a report of the Church and Nation Committee on the Government of Scotland which had come out in favour of democratic control of

Scottish affairs by a Scottish Assembly made secure by constitutional guarantees that would be beyond the power of parliament to repeal. In effect parliament's abdication of sovereignty in the religious sphere would be extended to the governance of Scotland, with sovereignty and autonomy being distributed through the United Kingdom. More completely than before, here was the church unafraid to base its approach to the national question 'on biblical, constitutional, and historical insights within the Reformed tradition'.[31].

When the Prime Minister addressed the General Assembly in 1988 she spoke to a church in which influential elements were engaged in a process of historical re-examination so that the church could define its mission in the light of traditions pre-dating that of nineteenth-century individualism, asserting instead the older tradition of social integration within the Christian community. Mrs Thatcher's visit was not unrelated to the fact that she is a Prime Minister who looks for religious legitimation for her policies more ardently than any of her modern predecessors.[32] It came hard on the heels of two developments controversial even in the context of the new politics : a budget which gave £1.2 billion to those on the highest bands of tax (which were reduced from 60 to 40 per cent), and an overhaul of social security provisions which sharply reduced the ability of local services to help the needy with immediate support at a time when the level of homelessness was sharply rising. Her address to the Assembly was widely billed as a key engagement in the *kulturkampf* that she and her supporters were waging against the values running counter to her vision of a Britain where individualism would be the touchstone of the new morality. In what was quickly dubbed 'the Sermon on the Mound', Mrs Thatcher set out her own moral philosophy, extolling the virtues of personal responsibility, and the necessity for self-reliance, defending the creation of wealth as a laudable pursuit, and insisting that Christianity was about spiritual redemption, not social work. The Prime Minister was given a courteous if cool reception and nine months elapsed before a public response came from the Moderator, the Rt Revd Prof. James Whyte, again very much in line with the kirk's low-key approach. However, he took issue with her overriding emphasis on the individual and her failure to comprehend that 'the human being is a social animal. We are none of us self-made men and women.' Identifying a 'great hole' in the theology by which we are governed, he went on:

> As I listened last May to the theology of the Prime Minister in her speech to the General Assembly, and as I have heard and read speeches since, I hear much about the importance of the

individual, a little about the family, but nothing about those other communities which give us our sense of where we belong. If a government has a defective view of human nature and doesn't understand what makes us tick, then it is liable to exercise power in ways that are quite insensitive to the things that are important to us and that influence us – our sense of community, our sense of belonging.[33]

In the 'Just Sharing' report which the Moderator had presented to the Prime Minister in 1988, 'the beginnings of a renewed Christian social vision rooted in the neighbour' had been detected. This was a cause of hope for a visionary like the Revd William Storrar who, acknowledging that the decline in church membership meant that the parish model was 'no longer socially plausible in Scotland', finds in the idea of the neighbour 'a Christian social model that will allow Christians to express their unconditional sense of our common social identity'.[34]

Those who argued that it was a churchperson's duty to maintain a constant, if informed, critique of the morality and theology that underlie not just public life but specific government policies did not have it all their own way. After the Moderator's 1989 reply to the Prime Minister, a new pressure group emerged from within the church which boldly asserted that Mrs Thatcher was in effect doing God's work for Him. The Revd Roderick Campbell, chief spokesman of 'the 1988 Forum' argued that 'a right-wing philosophy gives us a more complete and wholesome understanding of God's ideology'.[35] More might be heard in future of the ideas behind this group as younger ministers imbued with a strongly evangelistic outlook begin to step into positions of influence. But Prof. Whyte's emphasis on the social gospel found general favour in the church and was warmly endorsed in the press. In the aftermath, Stewart Brown, Professor of Ecclesiastical History at New College, argued that there was nothing new in such a stance and it was wrong to imply that keeping out of politics had been a time-honoured tradition of the church;[36] since 1984 New College has been the base for a Centre for Theology and Public Issues which has arranged regular events that have thrown into sharp relief the church's continuing part in the political process.[37]

But the church's concern with the social consequences of ideologically-driven policies was occurring at a time when community-based politics seemed to be in a parlous condition even in outposts of non-Thatcherism like Scotland. A much more splintered and privatised world that was consumer and leisure-orientated with the video as its symbol was recognisable even in Scotland.[38] The church was affected in membership terms – down to around 837,000 in 1983 and showing no signs of improving – and in its ability to mobilise active citizens able to defend gospel values where they were threatened by the pace of technological or political change.

Nevertheless, the kirk's quiet but persistent influence on different aspects of corporate and social life in Scotland should not be discounted. In the event of the drive for self-government reaching a successful conclusion, it may well be that it will emerge from its limbo-like existence to play a far from negligible role in helping Scottish civil society to adapt to shouldering new responsibilities. In terms of exercising authority and exerting a mass influence, perhaps no other Scottish institution has quite such a record of unbroken continuity. Unconscious recognition of the kirk's symbolic role in articulating Scottish opinion may help to explain how two emblematic churchmen, the Revd Geoff Shaw and Canon Kenyon Wright, came to exercise such pivotal roles respectively in Strathclyde Regional Council and the Scottish Constitutional Convention. Whether others come forward to exercise the weighty responsibilities that Scots (however infrequently the majority may now choose to celebrate their faith) are surprisingly content to see devolved upon religious shoulders, could well decide if the church's ability to influence political culture and its attendant values is merely in limbo or instead has entered headlong decline.

NOTES

I. PROTESTANTISM AND POLITICAL CULTURE 1890-1990

1 M. Fry, *Patronage and Principle: a Political History of Modern Scotland* (Aberdeen, 1987), p. 109.

2 K. Robbins, 'Core and periphery in Modern British History', *Proceedings of the British Academy* Vol. LXX (1984), pp. 275-97.

3 McCallum Scott Diaries 1912-13, Glasgow University Special Collections.

4 See C. Brown, *A Social History of Religion In Scotland* (London, 1987) *passim*, and the same author's contribution to this volume.

5 J. Brand, *The National Movement In Scotland* (London, 1978), p. 128.

6 T. C. Smout, 'Core and periphery in history; with some thoughts on Scotland as a case-study', *Journal of Common Market Studies*, Vol. XVIII, No. 3 (March 1980), pp. 256-71.

7 Fry, op. cit., pp. 110-11.

8 See Joan Smith, 'Labour Tradition in Glasgow and Liverpool', *History Workshop*, no. 17 (Spring 1984); 'Class, Skill, and Sectarianism in Glasgow and Liverpool', in R. . Morris (ed.), *Class, Power and Social Structure in British Nineteenth Century Towns* (Leicester, 1986).

9 See P. Dodd, 'Englishness and National Culture', in R. Colls and P. Dodd (eds.), *Englishness* (London, 1986). See also critical commentaries on the 'kailyard' literary phenomenon, for example, C. Harvie,

'Drumtochty Revisited: The Kailyard', *Scottish Review*, Vol. 27 (1982).

10 See T. Garvin, *Nationalist Revolutionaries in Ireland 1858-1928* (Oxford 1986).

11 See, for example, articles by Compton Mackenzie in the *Scots Independent* in the early 1930s.

12 See C. Harvie 'Before the Breakthrough 1888-1922', in Harvie, I. Donnachie and I. S. Wood (eds.), *Forward! Labour Politics in Scotland 1888-1988* (Edinburgh, 1989)

13 See W. Knox's introduction to his edited volume, *Scottish Labour Leaders* (Edinburgh, 1984); Harvie, 'Before The Breakthrough'; D. Howell, *British Workers and the ILP* (Manchester, 1983), chapter 7: and the profile of Gordon McLennan in *Marxism Today* (December 1989); also N. Ascherson, 'Scottish Contradictions' in *Games With Shadows* (London, 1988).

14 See G. Walker, *Thomas Johnston* (Manchester, 1988), chapter 4.

15 See Iain McLean, *The Legend of Red Clydeside* (Edinburgh, 1983), pp. 200-1.

16 The only two detailed and informative studies of the Orange Order are Elaine McFarland, 'The Orange Order in Scotland, 1780-1900' (Ph.D. Thesis, University of Glasgow, 1987); and W. Marshall, 'The Historical Development of the Orange Order in Scotland' (unpublished dissertation located in the Glasgow Room, Mitchell Library, Glasgow).

17 See T. Gallagher, *Glasgow: The Uneasy Peace* (Manchester, 1987), chapter 4; *Edinburgh Divided* (Edinburgh, 1987), *passim*; and S. Bruce, *No Pope of Rome* (Edinburgh 1985), chapters 2 and 3.

18 See C. Harvie, *No Gods and Precious Few Heroes* (London, 1981), p. 94.

19 ILP branches used Orange halls as meeting places in the 1930s in Ayrshire towns such as Dalry and Beith – information from *Forward*. The point should also be made that 'Orange' areas such as Larkhall, in Lanarkshire and Bo'ness in West Lothian and Bridgeton in Glasgow consistently record a heavy Labour vote.

20 See Gallagher, *Glasgow*, p. 247.

21 J. Campbell, *Invisible Journey* (Oxford, 1984), p. 3.

22 I. Budge and D Urwin, *Scottish Political Behaviour* (London, 1966), pp. 60-5, 68-71.

23 Gallagher, *Glasgow*, p. 269.

24 See, for example, the report in the *Scottish Daily Express*, 12 August 1960 about anti-Catholic discrimination in a small engineering firm in Johnstone and the management's justification of the firm's all-Protestant policy.

25 Ian McGinnis, *Inner City* (Edinburgh, 1987). See also Allan Massie, 'Govan Revisited', in *The Independent Magazine*, 5 November 1988.

26 Interview with Teddy Taylor, 28 June 1989.

27 Interview with Danny Houston, 21 May 1989. On the subject of the Catholic presence in the Labour Party see M. Keating, R. Levy, J. Geekie and J. Brand, 'Labour Elites in Glasgow', *Strathclyde Papers on Government and Politics*, No. 61 (Glasgow, 1989).

28 Interview with Danny Houston.

29 Interview with Teddy Taylor.

30 Brand, op. cit., pp. 150-4.

31 See chapter by Steve Bruce in this volume.

II SCOTTISH PROTESTANTISM AND POLITICS: THE CHURCH DIMENSION
IN THE PRESENT CENTURY

1 W. B. Johnston, 'Church and State in Scotland Today', in A. Elliot
   and D. B. Forrester (eds.), *The Scottish Churches and The Political
   Process Today* (Edinburgh, 1986), p. 6.
2 J. H. S. Burleigh, *A Church History of Scotland* (Oxford, 1960), p. 402.
3 Donald c. Smith, *Passive Obedience and Prophetic Protest: Social Criticism in the Scottish Church* (New York, 1987), pp. 354-5.
4 See note 2.
5 Smith *Passive Obedience*, note 54.
6 Evidence for what amounts to a substantial reinterpretation of Dr
   White's role during his period of influence in the Church of Scotland
   has been found in his papers by J. Stewart Brown, Professor of
   Ecclesiastical History at the University of Edinburgh. The references
   to Dr White in this chapter are based on a preliminary assessment of
   his views on the immigrant and attendant social questions which
   preoccupied Scotland in the inter-war period which Professor Brown
   delivered as a paper in the Department of Sociology, University of
   Edinburgh, during February 1989.
7 See note 5.
8 A. C. Cheyne, *The Transforming of the Kirk* (Edinburgh, 1983), p. 183.
9 Smith, *Passive Obedience*, p. 370.
10 Smith, *Passive Obedience*, p. 371.
11 W. Knox, *Scottish Labour Leaders, 1918-39* (Edinburgh, 1984), p. 30.
12 Knox, *Scottish Labour Leaders*, pp. 33-4.
13 *God's Will For Church and Nation* (Edinburgh, 1942), p. 45.
14 *God's Will For Church and Nation*, p. 49.
15 *God's Will For Church and Nation*, p. 62.
16 J. Brand, *The National Movement of Scotland* (London, 1978), p. 134.
17 Brand, *National Movement*, p. 130.
18 C. Harvie, *Scotland and Nationalism* (London, 1977), p. 204.
19 W. Coffey, *God's Conman* (Glasgow, 1989).
20 Details in J. G. Kellas, *The Scottish Political System* (Cambridge, 1979
   ed.), p. 103.
21 Kellas, *Scottish Political System*, p. 156.
22 Tony Benn, *The Politics of Illusion, The Benn Diaries, 1974-1979*
   (London, 1989).
23 See Ron Ferguson, *Geoff, The Life of Geoffrey M. Shaw* (Gartocharn,
   1979).
24 J. Bochel, D. Denver and A. Macartney (eds.), *The Referendum Experience, Scotland 1979* (Aberdeen, 1981), p. 40. In a letter to *The
   Scotsman*, published on 19 March 1990, Dr Herron wrote: 'I am
   prepared to admit that I may have been wrong in my opposition to
   devolution and wrong also in my abhorrence of the involvement of the
   Church in politics.'
25 D. B. Forrester, 'Introduction', in A. Elliot and D. B. Forrester (eds.),
   The Scottish Churches and the Political Process Today (Edinburgh,
   1986), p. 2.
26 *The Scotsman*, 4 May 1989.
27 See note 26.
28 *Scotland on Sunday*, 26 February 1989.
29 *Glasgow Herald*, 27 February 1989.
30 See note 29.
31 Revd. Norman Shanks, in J. Stein (ed.), *Scottish Self-Government:
   Some Christian Viewpoints* (Edinburgh, 1989), p. 24.

32 See note 25.
33 *The Scotsman*, 18 February 1989.
34 Revd. William Storrar, 'Scotland's Social Identity: A Christian Vision', a paper presented to the conference on Christianity and Social Vision in Scotland at New College, Edinburgh, 24 February 1990 and kindly made available in draft form by the author.
35 See note 28.
36 *Edinburgh Evening News*, 3 March 1989.
37 Norman J. Shanks, 'Scotland', in M. Walsh (ed.), *Religion In Politics* (London, 1990), p. 293.
38 Adrian Hastings, *A History of English Christianity 1900-1985* (London, 1987), p. 598.

7
Protestantism and Scottish military tradition

IAN S. WOOD

On 14 May 1968 the Cameronians returned for the last time to Douglas in Lanarkshire, where the regiment had been raised nearly three centuries previously, for a final conventicle prior to being disbanded. At the open-air service held to mark this event weapons were carried by all ranks and sentries were posted as they always had been at battalion church parades around the world. This was in keeping with the regiment's Covenanting origins in the 'killing times' of the seventeenth century when any Presbyterian worship in the area had to be guarded against the reprisals of Claverhouse's dragoons. The service only commenced when the picquet officer of the day saluted the senior officiating chaplain and reported, 'Sir, the picquets are posted. There is no enemy in sight. The service may proceed.'[1]

Psalms were sung and prayers offered, a message from the Queen read, a lament and a Last Post played, and the battalion marched off parade for the last time. More than any other Scottish regiment, it still embodied a Protestant tradition for it had been raised in 1689 to defend the Revolution settlement, was named after a Covenanting hero, and was first blooded in battle against troops serving under Claverhouse, the Covenanters' most hated persecutor.

In reality, the regiment's distinctive Protestant traditions had of necessity been diluted over the years. The year before, when disbandment was announced, an officer informed the press that the practice of issuing a Bible to every man as part of his kit was no longer observed.[2] Another officer, who wrote the final volume of the regiment's history, recalls that in his time with it, the chaplain was lucky to get twenty men to attend a voluntary church service.[3] Others recall that, increasingly, the regiment was recruiting Catholics, especially from Coatbridge. One of them joined the regiment in 1964 having been brought up there in a Catholic orphanage and having played locally with a republican accordion band. As a Catholic he had trouble initially getting employment in the area, but he recalls none when he applied to join the Cameronians.

He still thinks that the Protestant tradition of the regiment mattered, though he denies that it ever resulted in any discrimination against Catholic soldiers like himself, though it was, he recalls, common for them to be given sentry duty at the conventicles held on important anniversaries. Like other ex-Cameronians he has stories of Catholics not achieving the promotion they hoped for, and it does appear to be true that the Catholics were not as a general rule picked to be either Commanding Officers or Regimental Sergeant-Majors in the regiment. He quotes the case of a Catholic Colour-Sergeant who, he claims, left the Cameronians to get made up elsewhere more quickly to the rank of Sergeant-Major.[4]

Other regiments also embodied a strongly Protestant religious tradition almost from their formation, a good case being the 93rd or Sutherland Highlanders (later amalgamated with the 91st Argyll regiment of Foot). On their passage through Plymouth in 1814 after service at the Cape in South Africa, an observer commented: 'On such occasions it was no uncommon thing for soldiers to spend in taverns and gin shops the money they had saved. In the present case the soldiers of Sutherland were seen in booksellers' shops supplying themselves with Bibles and such books and tracts as they required.'[5]

Another account from this period describes the grim ritual of execution after a deserter from the 92nd or Gordon Highlanders had been found guilty by court martial in Spain in 1813.

> The fatal cap was drawn over his eyes and the provost marshal with his party advanced from the rear to carry the sentence of the court into effect. At this awful and affecting part of the scene the whole regiment, officers and men, knelt down and on behalf of him who then stood on the verge of eternity, offered up humble supplications to the throne of mercy.[6]

Modern Scottish history and demography would indeed have made it unwise for regiments to base their recruiting policy on sectarian or denominational considerations, something that would seem to be borne out by a breakdown of recruits currently in training at the Scottish Division's depot. In November 1988, of 240 recruits there mainly drawn from the central belt of Scotland, 181 gave their religion as Protestant and 56 as Catholic.[7] At the regular passing out parades at this depot a Church of Scotland chaplain normally conducts the accompanying service jointly with a local Catholic priest.

Army spokesmen deny vigorously that religious denomination is an influence on recruitment or promotion in Scottish regiments, and point out that, in the case of the Royal Scots, the oldest line regiment in the army, the present Regimental Sergeant-Major is a Catholic, as were two Commanding Officers prior to the present one.[8] A major who was with the Royal Scots Fusiliers prior to its controversial amalgamation in 1958 with the Highland Light Infantry recalls that the first Commanding Officer he served under was a Catholic, as were the RSM and Quartermaster, key figures in the day-to-day life and discipline of any battalion. The chaplain who made the biggest impact, he also recalls, was a Catholic sent to the battalion from the brigade to which it was attached. His services were always well attended, though this was very much a product of his own strong personality.[9]

The tradition of Presbyterian ministers serving with Scottish regiments is itself an old one, dating back to the religious wars of the seventeenth century, but it is not an unbroken one, for it lapsed for much of the eighteenth century. Regiments sometimes improvised, finding assorted clergy to minister to their religious needs on a piecemeal basis, or like the 92nd (Gordon) Highlanders, employed 'schoolmaster sergeants', literate men who would take Bible classes and hold services as and when required.[10]

In 1839 the General Assembly of the Church of Scotland agreed to petition parliament on the matter of licentiates of the Church of Scotland being recognised by the War Office as regular chaplains to Scottish regiments.[11] Difficult times faced the church, however, and the move languished until the authorities in 1859 accepted the principle of granting commissioned rank to chaplains, a significant step in the development of a 'Christian militarism' identified by historians of the nineteenth century.[12]

This, in some Scottish regiments, could take the form of a regimental church with its own Kirk Session, though these were not formally ordained by the General Assembly. There was a long history of this in the Argyll and Sutherland Highlanders and when, in 1968, its First Battalion Commanding Officer, Lieut.-Colonel Colin Mitchell, left the army in controversial circumstances, his departure was lamented by the regimental magazine as the loss of a good elder.[13] After the Second World War, Lieut.Colonel Bernard Ferguson, later Lord Ballantrae, who had become Commanding Officer of the First Battalion of the Black Watch, threw his weight behind the formation of a battalion Kirk Session, partly because he was troubled by the implications of compulsory church parades being ended by the army.

In the submission which he prepared for the General Assembly in

1950 he argued that 'the system of government within a Scottish parish would lend itself ideally to the life of the unit,'[14] and two years later the Assembly passed a more general Act 'anent the Institution of Services Kirk Sessions in Scottish Units of HM Forces'. By this time the battalion was bound for the war in Korea and full ordination of its new Kirk Session finally took place in Nairobi in 1954. At the present time the Gordon Highlanders and the King's Own Scottish Borderers also have their own Kirk Sessions. These comprise officers, warrant officers and senior NCOs whose links to their battalion chaplains can make for much improved guidance to soldiers with ordinary personal or family problems.[15]

Had a denominational recruitment pattern ever been central to the Scottish regimental tradition, then the army's extended involvement over the years with Ireland would have tested it to breaking point. It has for long been recognised as an over-simplification to describe events at the Curragh camp in Kildare as a mutiny, but there was certainly a degree of sympathy with Ulster Loyalist resistance to Home Rule which alarmed serving officers who valued above all the army's allegiance to the civil power. One of these was a young Captain (later Field Marshal) Wavell who, at the height of the crisis, wrote to his father,

> Once it comes to civil war every man has a right to choose his own side but we haven't got there yet and I hope will still steer clear. The idea of the officers of the army going on strike, which I think is what it really amounts to over this business, is to my mind absolutely disastrous. What about the men? They can't resign whatever their opinions are.[16]

Wavell, who was serving with the Black Watch, made no assumptions about what his men's views on the Ulster question might be, but other officers in Scottish regiments were in little doubt. One Second Lieutenant in the King's Own Scottish Borderers wrote in March 1914 that

> These Labourites and Socialists seem to imagine that the entire feeling [i.e. of aversion to the coercion of Protestant Ulster] was amongst officers only, but I know for a fact that it was not. Amongst the sergeants and other better educated NCOs the feeling was the same as that of the officers and I feel sure that if they had promoted the NCOs to officers they would also have declined to go North.[17]

On the same day a Royal Scots major wrote to the Conservative leader Bonar Law of how, in his battalion, 'the whole of the Sergeants and Lance Sergeants, with the exception of three, are heart and soul with Ulster ... I feel equally certain that the same feeling pervades the other ranks from Corporals to Privates.'[18] In fact the reaction within the army as a whole of those who identified this strongly with the cause of Ulster was out of proportion to any real military plans drawn up by the Asquith government to enforce Home Rule, as events were soon to prove.

All the Scottish regiments have served in Northern Ireland's renewed troubles since 1969 under pressures no different from those faced by the rest of the army in that intractable conflict, and some of their testimony has begun to be recorded.[19] There are those amongst them, in the army and out of it, still much troubled by the experience and Scottish regiments have at times been singled out by the republican movement's propaganda offensive. This happened, for example, in 1970 when the Royal Scots had the task of searching houses for arms in Balkan Street in Belfast's Lower Falls area. Reaction to the searches led to rioting and the imposition of a curfew in the whole area, backed up by the use of heavy reinforcements and CS gas. In reply to accusations about the Royal Scots' search and interrogation methods, as well as their alleged wrecking of religious objects in people's houses, the battalion defended itself by issuing a statement showing that around 40 per cent of its other ranks were in fact Catholics themselves.[20]

Political campaigns in Britain to bring the army out of Northern Ireland have never targeted the position of either Scots or Catholics in particular. Army training, regimental loyalty and an IRA enemy neither able nor willing to make denominational distinctions in its attacks upon crown forces, have all served to minimise the problems a Catholic background might create for soldiers in the province. One Catholic ex-corporal in the Argyll and Sutherland Highlanders recalls growing anger and incomprehension at fellow-Catholics being able to justify the violence of the IRA, and adds that on foot patrols in west Belfast, his last thought about the man covering him was whether he was a Catholic or a Protestant.[21]

Denominational relations within Scottish regiments might have suffered if Freemasonry was as strong an influence as some present and former soldiers claim. By its very nature it is something not easy to identify or substantiate within a milieu where rank and ritual are already important; in some regiments, however, its existence has been readily acknowledged. A serving officer in the Royal Scots published in 1934 a detailed history of masonic activity in the regiment's regular, volunteer and territorial battalions, tracing it back to the Grand Lodge of Ireland's granting of a warrant for a lodge to be formed by the First of Foot when it was serving there in 1732.[22] This lodge endured for over a century and 352 soldiers of all ranks at one time or another belonged to it.

Both it and another lodge formed in the regiment's Second Battalion became victims of the authorities' fear of Orangemen infiltrating the army, given the fine dividing line between the rituals of masonry and of the Orange Order after its formation in Armagh in 1796. A Parliamentary Select Committee was set up in 1836 to root out Orangeism from the army,[23] and masonic lodges in other regiments fell victim to the scare, but in the Royal Scots this appears to have been no more than a temporary reverse, with the craft flourishing until well into this century. One former Royal Scot who served a three-year engagement with the the First Battalion in the 1950s recalls rumours that the strength of Freemasonry was the cause of unease to some officers at that time. He himself, however, has no recollection of being asked to join a battalion or depot lodge.[24]

One regimental history that does single out a masonic tradition is that of the Highland Light Infantry. This had always been strong in the 71st Foot which in 1881 was incorporated within the new regiment of 'Glasgow Highlanders'. A '71st' lodge retained a vigorous life of its own in the amalgamated regiment's First Battalion, which between 1918 and 1922 had a Commanding Officer, Lieut.-Colonel H. C. Singleton, who liked to entertain the mess with the tale of how, when he had been captured on irregular service behind enemy lines in South Africa, a Boer firing squad had at once spared his life when he made a masonic sign to them.[25]

Masonic, and indeed Orange Lodge, influence has been blamed recently for the well publicised problems of the First Battalion of the KOSB in Colchester and in West Berlin in 1986-7. These involved sadistic and obscene initiation ceremonies for new recruits which, once made public, led to a series of courts martial, the battalion CO being relieved of his command, two company commanders being suspended, and the RSM being posted back to Army Headquarters, Scotland, near Edinburgh. One newspaper article sought to link these practices both to a shift in the regiment's pattern of recruitment and to Protestant sectarianism.

This was the *Observer* which, in a full-page article entitled 'The Battalion that went rotten', suggested that

> recent intakes have included a high proportion of Glaswegians who, true to the regiment's origins, come from a tradition of Orange Lodges and Protestant ascendancy that is almost as strident as Belfast's. It is a world where initiation ceremonies are not unknown and it is possible that some of what has gone on with the Borderers' battalion is some sort of twisted, adolescent fantasy of this.[26]

While the KOSB was raised in 1689 as the Earl of Leven's Regiment to harry and defeat Jacobite rebels, the fantasy was as much in the mind of a journalist who ignored how equally degrading initiation rites and vicious bullying were being reported at the same time in other regiments with no comparable traditions to those of the KOSB.

Scottish military and regimental traditions are a product of much that is common to the army as a whole and predate the best-known additions to them like the requirement to wear tartan. Only in 1881 were venerable Lowland regiments, who in 1715 and 1746 had faced and broken not a few clan charges, required by the War Office to don tartan trews and highland-style doublets. This brought them into line with Highland regiments, much their junior in age, who had been permitted, when raised in the late eighteenth century, to wear 'government tartan' to which over time some of them made their own additions and alterations. This 'military victory of Highlandism',[27] as it has been called, is a clear enough instance of the 'invention of tradition', but over time it has become another symbol of Scottish regimental identity.

As important as any tartan is a regiment's colours and the theft of the KOSB's, after a mess party at Redford Barracks in Edinburgh in 1961, was a national news story in Scotland. One of those responsible subsequently owned up and returned the colour, and later committed suicide after resigning from the Glasgow Stock Exchange. A corporal with eighteen years' service was reported to have broken down and wept at the news, and the culprit's apology, read out on his behalf, was converted into a solemn event which the entire battalion paraded to hear.[28] They were addressed by the second-in-command of the battalion who said,

> We have served in many places where it was necessary to guard our colours night and day. We did not think this would be necessary in our own country. But, on Saturday night, three men took advantage of our hospitality and removed the colours from their rightful place. I am now convinced that they did not appreciate the gravity of their act. They looked on it as an enterprising prank. They had not served in a famous infantry regiment and they did not appreciate this was an act of sacrilege.[29]

Along with the more obvious symbolism of a regiment's tartan and colours there has also been a tenacious family tradition reflecting itself in the recruitment especially of officers and NCOs. Wavell, while with no aspirations of his own for a military career, felt it natural once out of Sandhurst to take a commission in the Black

Watch as 'a son of the regiment'[30] and in the aftermath of the amalgamation in 1961 of the Seaforth and Cameron Highlanders, their successor regiment, the Queen's Own Highlanders, produced a booklet which stressed family continuity, with a group photograph to prove it.[31]

A new commanding officer of the Argyll and Sutherland Highlanders who took over in January 1967 was following in the footsteps of a father who had been commissioned in and decorated with the regiment in the First World War. He already felt the Argylls to be his second family. 'In the Highlands', he wrote later,

> the county or rather tribal regiment still survives and we were essentially a family regiment. Of the thirty-three officers I took with me to Aden, more than half were sons or nephews of former officers of the regiment. It was the same with the non-commissioned officers and soldiers, and we had a father and son serving together in Aden – one a sergeant and the other newly joined from the depot.[32]

In the King's Own Scottish Borderers, who are celebrating their Tercentenary at the time of writing, a family tradition remains strong, despite the enlargement of the regiment's recruiting area to take in the former territory of the Cameronians in Lanarkshire. Several of the First Battalion's officers and NCOs are sons and grandsons of the regiment, and one man is directly descended from piper Laidlaw who won the Victoria Cross in 1915. Until recently there were two brothers serving as officers in the battalion, and five sets of brothers serving in the ranks. There are relationships formed through marriage as well: one Company Quarter-Master Sergeant is married to the daughter of a former Colour Sergeant and the former Commanding Officer's driver is married to the sister of a corporal in the battalion.[33]

Each regiment creates a style of its own, a senior officer argues, and he claims that this enables him almost at a glance to tell a 'KOSB wife' from one 'married into' a different regiment.[34] Family feeling within the regiment is something he values immensely, and for him, after twenty-five years in the army, returning to serve out his time with the KOSB, has been both homecoming and fulfilment.

Sir Fitzroy MacLean, MP and former Brigadier, was eloquent on this aspect of the regimental system's durability when he spoke in 1968 in a debate in parliament prompted by a Ministry of Defence White Paper on regimental disbandments and amalgamations

> To this day the Scottish regiments have remained an essential part of Scottish national life and in many senses, both at home and perhaps even more abroad, a living symbol of Scotland.

To my own father for instance, who as a regular soldier spent most of his life abroad, his regiment, the Cameron Highlanders, was for many years his closest link with Scotland. When in due course I myself came temporarily to leave civilian life, it was to the same regiment, with which I had spent the early years of my childhood, that I naturally returned, and when I did it was like coming home. That is an experience which I share with innumerable other Scots.[35]

Part of the controversy created by Robert Lawrence's book on his Falklands experiences was the clear inference that the family tradition of his regiment, the Scots Guards, had done little to prevent him being treated, in his view at least, as some kind of non-person or pariah because of the disabling wounds which cut short his army career.[36] The Scots Guards' relationship to the army as a whole is, of course, different in some important respects from that of the Scottish line regiments, but service with them creates for many of all ranks, ties that are just as strong.

Closely woven into the fabric of Scottish military tradition is the extraordinary courage often shown by the regiments in action. The courage that earns Victoria Crosses, like that of Fusilier Donini in 1945, aged nineteen and only six months in the army, who, in action in Germany, carried a wounded comrade to safety while wounded himself, then re-engaged the enemy with his bren-gun to draw diversionary fire which killed him but let his platoon take their objective,[37] is often, in the last resort, a purely individual matter but can be shaped and strengthened by regimental traditions that will often bring out reserves of bravery and stamina as readily as will larger loyalties to Crown and nation state.

Nowhere is the anatomy of morale and the courage that emanates from it better analysed than in Sir John Baynes' study of a Cameronian regular battalion going to war in 1914.[38] Yet these very qualities can often co-exist with a more generalised ferocity that is the reverse side of the coin where the reputation of some Scottish regiments is concerned. This was certainly the case with the Cameronians, for example, whose off-duty exploits at times created problems for army public relations around the world.

As one observer of their arrival in India during the Second World War wrote:

They recruited most of their men from the streets of Glasgow and had the reputation of being one of the toughest regiments in the British army in peacetime. They waged street fights with secreted bayonets and broken bottles, and on at least one occasion in Calcutta, with rifles and ball ammunition. They carried razor blades in the peaks of their caps, with which to wipe the grin off opposing faces by a careless backhand swipe of the cap, and potatoes in their pockets in which razor blades were stuck. No one but their own officers could handle them, and their touchy discipline vanished altogether for a week around the great Scottish fiesta of Hogmanay, New Years Eve.[39]

Twenty years later in West Germany, a new generation of Cameronians were stereotyped as *Giftzwerge* or 'poison dwarfs' by a citizen of the town of Minden interviewed on television after disturbances in which some of the First Battalion had been involved. This unleashed an avalanche of adverse publicity for the regiment and gave newspaper cartoonists a field day, though in fact the battalion's relations with the town survived the episode quite well. The Commanding Officer took firm action, and as his divisional commander put it, 'there is no doubt there were quite a large number of unsavoury characters in the battalion which made his task all the more difficult. He competed with all this with efficiency and equanimity despite the fact that he was hounded by the press daily.'[40]

Although in recent years and since the ending of national service, Scottish regiments have a good recruiting record, this should not be incorporated within any national myths about Scotland's uniquely martial qualities. Indeed, there were many points at which, in the nineteenth century, Scottish regiments could not recruit up to the minimum they needed. There were, of course, more of them than now, but in 1878 for example, of nineteen regiments only three drew 60 per cent of their officers and men from Scotland.[41]

If anything, Scotland came to be under-represented in relation to its population, in the Victorian and Edwardian army. Irish recruitment went down too, but in 1914 had settled at a level close to Ireland's proportion of the British Isles' total population. As Dr K. Jeffrey, the historian of Britain's pre-1914 regular army, has put it: 'The British army both before and immediately after World War I was predominantly and disproportionately an English army.'[42]

Actual aversion to army service because of low pay, long separations from home and family, and what was felt to be its brutalising nature was certainly something that complicated army recruiting in central and lowland Scotland. In the highlands, clearance and depopulation stretched regiments to the limit in finding an adequate minimum of men within their catchment areas, and for a time the Cameron Highlanders became known in army circles as the 'Whitechapel Highlanders' because of the number they were alleged to be accepting from the East End of London.[43]

A pacifist element within Scottish liberalism, strongly influenced by dissenting Protestantism and the Free Church secession of 1843, has also been cited as a reason for the army's problems,[44] but at the same time, military service in the form of the Volunteer units launched in 1859 was hugely popular to an extent that baffled the movement's historian.[45] This accustomed many working-class Scots to an acceptable form of military service outside the corrupting influence of the regular army and, indeed, linked such service in the minds of many with heroic liberators like Garibaldi of continental nations 'rightly struggling to be free' and celebrated accordingly in flights of Gladstonian rhetoric. Here perhaps was a liberal militarism easily adapted to the creation of the Territorial Army in 1908 and then to the manpower needs of a war in 1914 which added hugely to the Scottish regimental mystique.

Scotland's military and regimental tradition is now inextricably woven into popular culture thanks to song writers, entertainers and the annual Edinburgh Tattoo with its combination of dazzling pageantry and popular religiosity. It is a tradition which in fact owes little to sectarianism or denominationalism as such but everything to Scotland's relationship to an imperial state in which the army as a whole, not just its Scottish component, ceased to be a pariah body and moved much closer to the community as a whole. It was greatly aided in this process by the popularity of part-time soldiering, paramilitary youth movements like the Boys' Brigade, a cheap circulation press and popular writers ready to reinforce its altered self-image. With political nationalism developing late in Scotland, these forces along with two world wars made the Scottish regiments an embodiment of a British Scotland which writers or politicians challenged at their peril.

One who dared to do just this is himself a scion of a family that contributed its part to Scottish military history by raising, in the Covenanting period, a cavalry regiment which later became the Scots Greys. Its origins as an instrument with which its founder, Sir Thomas Dalyell of the Binns, could hunt down Covenanters, was not forgotten by some who reacted in incandescent fury to a descendant of Sir Thomas, Tam Dalyell MP when, in 1968, he went so far as not merely to dispute the case for a Scottish regiment's retention when others were being disbanded, but to criticise its record in a messy rearguard action in the long post-war march home from empire.

Other regiments like the Cameronians and the Highland Light Infantry and Royal Scots Fusiliers accepted their fate reluctantly, and in the HLI's case, only after a major campaign against the actual terms of amalgamation,[46] but only the threat to the Argyll and

Sutherland Highlanders in a Labour Government White Paper in 1968, unleashed an outcry which became the focus of a confused and angry set of emotions in Scotland and beyond.

Prior to the Ministry of Defence's announcement in July 1968 that the Argylls were to be disbanded, the regiment had been at the centre of controversy over its operational role in Aden during the final stages of Britain's withdrawal from the old Crown colony, which in 1958 had been incorporated within a federation of South Arabia in which feudal sheikdoms predominated. Opposition by nationalists and trade unions in the port of Aden to the idea of federation found support both from Cairo and the new republic of the Yemen, which had been set up the previous year, and the resulting violence made the military and naval bases in Aden a diminishing asset for Britain. Political indecision, however, exposed British troops there to increasing guerrilla attacks, while other units, including the SAS, were extensively deployed to neutralise nationalist guerrilla insurgency in the wild sheikdoms of Aden's hinterland.

The Argylls were sent to Aden as a highly experienced battalion under a Commanding Officer with a taste for plain speaking who did not shy away from the media. This was Lieutenant-Colonel Colin Mitchell, 'Mad Mitch' as the British press soon christened him once his uncompromising methods against unrest in the colony became known to it. Decisive in its influence upon his attitude to the situation was the loss of some members of his battalion's advance party who were killed, along with a larger number of English troops, in a guerrilla ambush on 20 June 1967 after authority in the Crater area had virtually collapsed in the aftermath of a mutiny by the local police.

This episode enraged Mitchell, who felt firm action by the local commander could have prevented it, but confirmed his resolve to minimise casualties to his men while reasserting British control pending actual withdrawal. The culmination of his period in command was the battalion's retaking of the Crater on 3 July 1967, an operation which took the British command as much by surprise as it did the local population. The pipes and drums of the battalion played to proclaim the Argylls' presence. 'In an internal security operation against a lot of third-rate, fly-blown terrorists and mutineers [in Crater on 3 July 1967] it seemed utterly appropriate',[47] Mitchell wrote afterwards, and thereafter 'Argyll law' reigned in the Crater.

Exactly what 'Argyll law' could involve for the Crater's population has been disputed since, but 'Battalion Notes' from Aden in the regimental magazine for 1967 give a hint of attitudes to them which became the focus of some criticism. One entry in these notes profiles

a 'typical' Crater inhabitant as 'Name, Abdul, Seyid, Yussifa, Alia —
alias Gollie, though more commonly referred to as "You, you black
—"'. The profile goes on to cover 'VDM' or very distinguishing
marks, 'a flattering translation for very dirty marks, which are never
lacking'; favoured tactics, 'running away'; personality, 'lazy and
unintelligent – who would throw a grenade when you can get fifty
pounds for it?'; place of business, 'the market, convenient roof top,
or street corner. If he is not available, try the mosque. Armed with
the above information any would-be Gollie-hunters should now
have no trouble finding their man.'[48]

Mitchell himself, both in his autobiography and elsewhere, never
betrayed any doubts over tough measures having paid off and saved
lives. Writing more generally four years later on colonial emergencies in
which British troops had been involved since 1945, he declared:
'The military lesson then, as for the future, is that the way to destroy
terrorism is to terrorise the terrorists.'[49] The difficulty of this formulation is, of course, for the armed forces of a democracy, in drawing
a distinction, or trying to, between the terrorists and the community
of which they are likely to be a product and which will in some
measure either be terrorised by them or will identify with their cause.

Mitchell cultivated favourable press coverage though there are
still conflicting opinions about some of the methods used during
searches, arrests and interrogations. The Argylls left as part of the
British withdrawal, returning to barracks in Plymouth at the end of
November 1967, and in late January 1968 a large number of awards
for bravery in Aden were announced, but the Argyll's Commanding
Officer received only a Mention in Despatches, not the DSO which
an officer of his rank might have expected. The *Scottish Daily Express*
led the way in denouncing this as an insult to the battalion as well as
to Scotland, with the *Daily Record* taking up the story strongly as
well.[50]

The next day it described Mitchell as the 'iron man of the Crater'
who preferred dead terrorists to dead Argylls,[51] and it and the *Express*
were soon vying with each other for coverage of a story which rapidly
turned Mitchell into the post-war army's best known and most
photographed officer. The *Express* reporter, Jack Webster, wrote of
a whispering campaign within the Ministry of Defence to discredit
Mitchell and the Argylls[52] and the paper initiated its own opinion
poll among readers as to whether the Colonel had been badly
treated. This produced nearly 20,000 replies, 18,982 of which took
his side.[53]

The 'quality press' warned against attempts to turn Mitchell's
treatment into a 'Dreyfus case'[54] but it was the popular Scottish

papers which made the running on the issue, helped by the Lieut.-Colonel's being given the 'Scot of the Year' award[55] and by the intervention of Mrs Winifred Ewing, heroine of the great nationalist by-election victory at Hamilton the previous November. She promised to pursue the matter,[56] though many in her party had been critical of imperial rearguard actions in Cyprus, Aden and elsewhere.

What really brought feelings to the boil, however, were two developments: the Ministry of Defence Supplementary Statement on Defence Policy which was published early in July 1968,[57] and the comments its recommendations on the future of the Argylls prompted in parliament from Tam Dalyell. On its final page, this document announced that, as part of a further slimming down and rationalisation of the army's unit structure, the Highland Brigade would be reduced by one battalion, namely the Argylls. This led to an opposition censure motion with a three-line whip on 15 July, and it was in this debate that the storm broke.

The censure motion predictably was defeated after a series of eloquent speeches by Scottish Conservatives in praise of regimental tradition and of the Argylls in particular. Before them, however, Tam Dalyell challenged the idea that the regiment's case against its disbandment should be linked to its recent role in Aden. The operation there had been, in larger political terms, a futile one, he argued, and he went on to deplore the remarks Lieut.-Colonel Mitchell had made to the press at the time about the healthy discipline handed out by early British settlers in Aden who had hung the recalcitrant mayor of the Crater district off the mast of a ship: 'I simply remark that I do not want to be represented abroad in the Arab world by this kind of man',[58] Dalyell declared and went on to claim that many young people shared his view.

Posing a series of leading questions about the way in which the Crater had been reoccupied and how hand grenades for use in a built-up area had been issued to companies and platoons of the battalion, allegedly without proper authorisation, he put the question: 'Is it not true that the Argylls in Aden, far from being the superbly disciplined force which they were claimed to be by the British press, in fact suffered from a lack of discipline? Is not that the actual truth of what happened?'[59] Compounding this offence, he went on to question the merits of the regimental system as a factor in army recruiting, responding to one former Argylls officer, George Younger MP for Ayr, by saying, 'I do not take that evidence about a huge percentage wanting to join a particular "tribe" which he gave us quite as seriously as he does.'[60]

One or two other members took a similar line, notably Emanuel

Shinwell, who disputed the notion that the regiment was in any real sense Highland at all, given its recruitment area. Most real highlanders, he argued, joined the police in Glasgow, which was now where the Argylls recruited much of their manpower. It was Dalyell's intervention in the debate that drew a storm upon his head, however, not just for his remarks about Aden and the Argylls, but because he called in aid his own military lineage. In doing this he referred to his ancestor who 'founded a troop of cavalry with a clear and definite operational requirement in his view, namely to restrain the activities of some seventeenth-century Scottish religious bigots'.[61]

This last reference to the Covenanters infuriated some people as much as his criticism of the Argylls and brought him an avalanche of hostile mail, much of it viciously abusive and highly personal. Twenty years later, Tam Dalyell still has some 250 of these letters about which he remains philosophical. His intervention in the Defence White Paper debate was, he claims, an unplanned one, but he still feels that Lieut.-Colonel Mitchell already in 1968 had political ambitions in the furtherance of which Aden and the threat to the Argylls were a godsend. Indeed, he wonders now whether his much publicised criticisms did not in fact assist the Colonel's early entry to parliament. This is contrary to the view at the time of Richard Crossman, whose Parliamentary Private Secretary he was at the time and who thought the whole episode might 'quite possibly be a useful spoiling operation against the Tories'.[62]

The letters themselves repay reading, though many do not go much beyond virulent personal abuse and crude racism. 'A wog respects a kick round the stern more than a pound note', wrote one ex service correspondent from Carlisle. 'It took men with the spirit of Mitchell three hundred years to build an empire, you and your colleagues have frittered it away in five years.'[63] Another declared that 'homos, ponces and nig-nogs are all you scum care about. Bravery and guts you don't want to know.'[64] Advice to emigrate to the Congo[65] came in another letter along with recurrent accusations of being a 'wog' or 'nigger' lover. These latter insults tended to be coupled to more generalised and usually crude invective over the Labour government's alleged inaction on the issue of Commonwealth immigration into Britain.

Raw racism of this kind was often linked to a macho-Scottish pride in the country's reputation for producing 'real' soldiers. Mocking Tam Dalyell's own national service, one ex-regular in the Royal Scots Fusiliers wrote to him: 'You are not fit to lick the boots of a private in the Argylls who done [sic] the job the English could not do in Aden.'[66] Another correspondent sent him a coloured photograph of Lieut.-Colonel Mitchell in full kilt with the message: 'Here is a man. Take a good look at it because you won't see one when you look in your mirror.'[67] Many more enlarged on his unfitness to clean, shine or lick the Lieut.-Colonel's boots and fifteen of the letters still in his possession single out his own failure to get a commission during his own national service. One ex-KOSB man went further, writing, 'Mitchell could shite better things than you.'[68]

As many letters in this vein came from Scotland as from south of the border, and some of these were written by Scots. A few attempted a reasoned defence of the regimental system and of the case for retaining the Argylls, and just under thirty writers identified the issue as a nationalist one in the sense that they saw it as proof of the need for some form of Scottish self-government. They were often as angry over the regiment's threatened disbandment by a London government as they were over Dalyell's 'slander' of brave compatriots. One St Andrews woman was, in fact, at pains to deny SNP allegiance but finished her letter by saying, 'Give us our rights. Leave our kilted army alone. Scotland for ever.'[69]

Other correspondents were incensed by Dalyell's references to his ancestor's campaigns against the Covenanters and their rage was fuelled by an *Express* article which made the connection for them between his criticism of the Argylls and family history: 'He shows a vindictiveness that he may have inherited from his near-Muscovite ancestor, General Tam Dalyell of the Binns, who earned a fair part of his bloody reputation helping the Russian Czar oppress the Tartars and suppress the Turks', the paper declared, adding that 'the charming skills he learned in this notorious company he later found a use for in persecuting the Covenanters with an evil relish that revolted even his friends'.[70] Some sent him copies of this article and a few referred in offensively personal terms to his marriage to the Catholic daughter of a Scottish judge, Lord Wheatley.[71]

Besides the 250 hostile letters, Tam Dalyell also has sixty-five written in support of his stance. They form an interesting antidote to the campaign being sustained by the *Express*, which had produced the formation of an action committee to organise a national petition to 'save the Argylls'[72] and a pledge a few days later to back the campaign from the Central Council of Scottish Conservative and Unionist Associations.[73]

Some came from writers with experience of Aden, both as administrators and in the services, who did not share the popular press view of the Argyll's role there. One, a marketing director of a major industrial concern, described himself as a Tory with a brother who was commanding officer of an armoured regiment and alleged that in fact Lieut.-Colonel Mitchell had been a weakling, obsessed with publicity and ready to court popularity for the wrong reasons with an unsavoury element in his battalion while it was in Aden.[74] A Liverpool journalist of Greek-Cypriot descent supported the Dalyell allegations and recalled some of his own family's experiences of the regiment in action ten years previously during the emergency in Cyprus.[75] He was supported in another letter by a former member of the regiment who recalled reprisals he himself had witnessed by its First Battalion back in 1939 against a recalcitrant locality in Eritrea.[76]

Some simply found the whole spectacle of Aden repugnant and politically an anachronism: 'I for one hated to see British soldiers shooting and bullying Arabs. We were told that Aden was essential for Britain's security but since we left no Arab has invaded Britain, the oil still flows and young soldiers died for nothing.'[77] This was the view of a London woman, also of a leading Church of Scotland minister who declared in his letter: 'The agitation on this decision [i.e. to disband the Argylls] is, in my opinion, completely synthetic... I was particularly glad that someone came out in the open about Mitchell and I only wish the Church of Scotland had done so. There were reports from Aden by our people which, to put it mildly, were not uncritical of Mitchell and his leadership.'[78]

Using the Argylls as part of a nationalist argument particularly angered some with proven allegiance to the cause of Scottish self-government. As Professor Douglas Young, the St Andrew's University classicist and poet, put it: 'I have never been an enthusiast for enlisting Scottish patriotism, or local clan sentiments, to recruit for English imperialism. What I would like to see is the sort of attitude the modern Swiss or Norwegians have to their defence requirements.'[79]

Despite the SNP's refusal the previous year to support a resolution opposing the disbandment of Scottish regiments, some prominent party members had in fact given full support to the campaign to keep the Argylls in being. One of them was the party's first ever MP, Robert McIntyre, victor at the Motherwell by-election of April 1945, and in 1968 Provost of Stirling, where the presence of the Argylls' depot gave an obvious focus for the national petition to save the regiment. This confirmed for some letter-writers their doubts about the image of Scotland that existed in the minds of some nationalists. 'Mitchell's remarks on Aden', one wrote, 're-vealed all the stupidity, prejudice and arrogance of the mediocre military mind: it was sickening to see the SNP feting him as 'Scotsman of the Year', and indicative of nationalism's real roots in a particularly shoddy ersatz cultural jingoism compounded by historically illiterate nostalgia and bigotry.'[80]

Many hostile correspondents echoed the *Express* in predicting electoral disaster for the member for West Lothian at the next General Election. Some encouragement for them came in the form of a written answer made in parliament by the Minister of Defence, Denis Healey, on 25 July to some of the questions which had been raised about the Argylls and their Commanding Officer in Aden. He advised the House that there was no evidence of operational orders having been disobeyed, except possibly over the unauthorised possession of grenades by some platoons in the Crater. Nor, he stressed, had Lieut.-Colonel Mitchell at any point been reprimanded, for this was a punishment which could only be issued to an officer of his rank by a court martial. It had, however, Healey's statement went on, been necessary to emphasise to Lieut.-Colonel Mitchell that the maintenance of law and order with minimum force leading to an orderly withdrawal from Aden with minimum casualties was the policy that had to be followed'.[81]

No special report on Lieut.-Colonel Mitchell's conduct had been required from his Commander-in-Chief in Aden, the Minister stressed, and in a sentence seized upon by all those who had joined in the outcry against Tam Dalyell, he added, on the allegation of indiscipline by the Argylls, 'I cannot accept this charge. I am assured that although they were tough and spirited they were also extremely well led and disciplined.'[82] Preoccupied with his own censure by the House's Committee on Privilege over a different matter, Tam Dalyell did not take part in the following day's debate on Healey's statement but he made it clear to the press that he was unrepentant over raising the issue.[83]

The actual campaign to save the regiment, hugely assisted by Lieut.-Colonel Mitchell's own much publicised retirement from the army in August, quickly took over from the more specific matter of what had or had not happened in Aden twelve months previously. Tam Dalyell's reaction to the whole episode brought him scant support from fellow Labour MPs, except for Emrys Hughes, the member for South Ayrshire, something identified by one supporter who went into print on the controversy while the excitement was at its height. This was Allan Campbell McLean, a highland Labour activist who had stood for parliament in the two previous general elections for the Inverness-shire and Ross and Cromarty constituency and who was also the author of a powerful novel based on his own military experiences.[84]

He described the Parliamentary Labour Party as the dog that

didn't bark, given the isolation in which Tam Dalyell found himself over both Aden and the retention of the Argylls. 'We all know', McLean wrote, 'the Argylls employed strong-arm tactics in Aden, but the moderation, the restraint, the good humoured tolerance of "the Jock" overseas have been too long ingrained in the national consciousness to be susceptible to doubt. And who can question the emotional boost to a people deprived of Empire of Mitchell re-occupying the Crater district with pipes playing?'[85] He went on to ask how the indigenous population of Campbeltown in 1967, had they been colonised by Arab invaders the previous century, would have reacted to anyone claiming virtue for the hanging of their Provost from a mast-head, and described Lieut.-Colonel Mitchell as 'possessed of a terrifying innocence, seemingly unaware of the social revolution that has convulsed Asia, the Middle East and Africa in the last two decades'.[86] Correctly, as it turned out, he also dismissed predictions of Tam Dalyell's political demise, finishing his comments with the thought that 'the venomous disapproval of the *Daily Express* is an infallible guarantee of ultimate success'.[87]

'Saving the Argylls' did indeed become a popular cause in the last months of 1968, whether or not the organisers had the million signatures they claimed when the petition against disbandment was finally delivered to Parliament on 13 December 'One million Scots just can't be wrong' was the *Express* headline that day,[88] and along with its stable-mate the *Glasgow Evening Citizen*, it had certainly kept the campaign in front of the public. Politically it became a largely Conservative attack upon a faltering Labour government, though one weakened by the record of previous Conservative Defence Ministers on the issue of regimental disbandments and reorganisation. This was brandished against them by the Scottish Nationalists who did not, as a party, support the campaign, though one of their leading spokesmen, Arthur Donaldson, was as infuriated by Tam Dalyell's criticisms of the Argylls as any Tory. Disbandment of famous Scottish regiments, he argued, was yet another Tory policy carried on by Labour, like the closure of Scottish railways and mines.[89]

Some senior officers still serving with Scottish regiments who were in the army in this period express strong reservations and, in one or two cases, outright distaste at a campaign which they feel it was unprofessional and even 'ungentlemanly' (the word one uses) for a former Commanding Officer to associate himself with so publicly. They feel the Argylls were no more a special case than regiments senior to them which had already lost their separate identity and that they were used in a way which might have compromised the necessary political neutrality of the army.[90] In the event, the Ministry of Defence decided to reduce the regiment to single-company strength, and this unit, named Balaclava Company, was formally designated at Stirling Castle in late January of 1971, the rest of those still with the First Battalion being transferred to other regiments.

Lieut.-Colonel Mitchell, as many had predicted he would, entered politics in the Conservative interest, not as a nationalist as some of Tam Dalyell's hostile correspondents had expressed the hope he would, and was adopted for a then safe seat, West Aberdeenshire, which returned him to Parliament in the 1970 General Election. His career in parliament was something of an anticlimax and he declined readoption in 1974. He did make a name for himself by calling for draconian measures by the security forces in Northern Ireland's renewed troubles, and it was indeed these which were instrumental in 'saving' the Argylls and restoring them to full battalion strength in 1972. The decision in principle to do this was announced by the new Defence Minister at the Conservative conference the previous year and the news reached Balaclava Company of the regiment in Gibraltar where it was based.

The *Express*, whose journalists and leader-writers had done so much to support the retention of the Argylls, acclaimed this decision as 'a sensational victory for public opinion and the battering-ram of a million-signature petition'. It went on, however, to lament the circumstances behind the decision: 'What a tragedy it is that the restoration should be occasioned by the troubles on the British soil of Ulster.'[91]

The curious and conflicting cross-currents that characterised the campaign to save the Argylls revealed much about Scotland's relationship to a regimental system that had drawn strength from a certain image of Scotland. They were thoughtfully explored in one newspaper comment on the survival of the regiment:

> The threat to disband the Argylls stirred up emotion barely imaginable in softer, southern parts of Britain because it offended several Scottish idols at the same time: national pride, the ancient aptitude of the Scots for soldiering that has always made Scottish regiments the proudest and prickliest in the British army, and an impression that old values of authority and loyalty were being undermined by new winds from London.
>
> Indignation on behalf of the Argylls became curiously entwined with Scottish nationalism which has always had an uncomfortably ambivalent attitude about the famous regi-

ments of Scotland, and on the other side with Scottish Unionist pride in tradition.[92]

Despite a developing conflict there which, in March 1971,
claimed the first British lives, including three young off-duty Royal
Highland Fusiliers lured from a Belfast pub to their deaths at IRA
hands, recruits flowed in and by early 1972 the regiment was back to
battalion strength. Its first active duty was in fact in Northern
Ireland in that bloodiest year in the province's history. The need for
infantry on the ground there may have saved the regiment but it took
its toll in lives lost and men wounded. It also exposed it to publicity
more serious than any events in Aden had created.

Six years after the restored battalion's first tour of duty in
Northern Ireland, the Argylls were stationed at Catterick in Yorkshire during the succession of gruesome murders later proved to be
the work of Peter Sutcliffe. A telephone call to the police by a former
Argyll who had been with the battalion six years before claimed a
connection between the regiment and one of these murders, and this
launched a police inquiry. Many serving and former Argylls were
questioned but no light was cast on any victim of the man later to be
known as the 'Yorkshire Ripper'. Where the trail did lead, however,
was back to an isolated farm near Newtonbutler close to Ferman-
agh's border with County Cavan in the Irish Republic.

There, in late 1972, a farmer and farm labourer had been found
by the RUC, dead with multiple stab wounds. Loyalist militants,
enraged by a recent IRA killing of a part-time Ulster Defence Regiment soldier, were blamed and the RUC accepted the army's story.
The anonymous telephone call to the Yorkshire police, and the
intensive questioning of soldiers it led to, reawakened RUC interest
in the case and in 1981 two sergeants, a former lance-corporal and
a captain, who had all been part of a patrol near Newtonbutler at the
time of the murders, were brought to trial in January 1981.

The two sergeants and the former lance-corporal were found
guilty of murder and the captain, Andrew Snowball, was dismissed
from the army for not giving voice to his suspicions, over a period of
six years, so shielding the three men. Snowball was from a well-
connected army family, held a staff appointment at the time of the
arrests and was considered to have a promising military career in
front of him. Belfast Crown Court accepted that he had acted as he
had done to protect his regiment, while of the informant whose
approach to the police had set in motion the whole process, a
detective in the RUC had this to say: 'We feel he is in a rather
delicate position. He belonged to a regiment with a great family
tradition, probably the strongest in the British army, and loyalty

amongst the men is something of which they are extremely proud. I am sure some of them know who he is, and as far as they are concerned he broke a strict barrack-room rule and squealed.'[93]

The trial was a reminder, twelve years on into Northern Ireland's troubles, of the pressures soldiers could come under and the ferocious way in which some could react to them. To that extent, it helped prevent Scots who had served there, and still did, from becoming forgotten men, but it also aroused uneasy and angry argument, reminiscent of the Aden controversy eleven years before. Some felt the men had been victimised, others were appalled at how regimental loyalty could protect murderers. The easiest and most logical response came from those Scots who saw no place either for British troops in Northern Ireland, or for Scots in an army other than their own. As one contributor to the debate put it: 'An army's proper honour lies in its readiness to defend the homeland and is best preserved when it remains within its own borders; in the present case that postulates a different army from the one an imperial history has saddled us with – and a separate entity called Scotland for it to defend.'[94]

The absence of such an entity since 1707 and its incorporation within an Anglo-British state which took on a global military role was decisive in shaping a Scottish regimental tradition, or Scottish militarism as some Socialists would prefer to call it. It was more decisive than a popular Protestant tradition which is the connecting theme of these essays, though religious beliefs and observances have been, and still are, important to the collective life of some Scottish regiments. Given modern Scotland's changing social and religious geography, the army's recruitment needs prevented these traditions from ever becoming exclusive or sectarian any more than they did in the long period over which all of Ireland raised regiments for Crown service. In so far as affirmative feelings towards Scottish military tradition became a potent part of the nation's popular culture, this was a process reinforced by an age of empire and world wars. If that age is really behind us, then Scotland's relationship to its regiments and what they stand for may become an uncertain element in our image of ourselves as people.

ACKNOWLEDGEMENTS

In preparing this essay, I have been greatly helped by staff at the National Library of Scotland and the Scottish United Services Museum Library at Edinburgh Castle. I also owe a debt to all those whose help I have acknowledged, especially Mr Tam Dalyell, MP, for so willingly making his correspondence available to me.

NOTES

1 Baynes, J. *The Cameronians (Scottish Rifles)*, vol. 4, *The Close of Empire, 1948-1968* (London: Cassell, 1971), pp. 220-8. See also *The Covenanter*, June 1968.

2 *Scottish Daily Express*, 19 July 1967.

3 Sir J. Baynes, former Second-in-Command, First Battalion the Cameronians, in conversation with the author, 12 October 1988.

4 Former Cameronian Rifleman, conversation with the author, 10 October 1988.

5 Stewart, D. *Sketches of the Character, Manners and Present State of the Highlanders of Scotland*, vol. 2 (Edinburgh: Constable, 1825), p. 321.

6 Gardyne, C. G. *The Life of a Regiment: A History of the Gordon Highlanders*, vol. 1 (London: Medici Society, 1929), pp. 268-69.

7 I am indebted to Lieut-Colonel Finlay MacLean, Commanding Officer of the Scottish Division Depot, Glencorse, for these figures.

8 *Ibid.*

9 Major H. M. Dove, formerly of the First Battalion, the Royal Scots Fusiliers, in conversation with the author.

10 C. G. Gardyne, op. cit.

11 A. C. Dow, *Ministers to the Soldiers of Scotland* (Edinburgh, London: Oliver and Boyd, 1962), pp. 265-270.

12 O. Anderson 'Christian Militarism in Mid-Victorian Britain, *English Historical Review*, 1971.

13 *Thin Red Line*, January 1969.

14 N. W. Drummond, (1979) *The Kirk Session of the First Battalion the Black Watch: the first Twenty Five Years, 1954-1979* (Perth: Woods, 1979), pp. 5-10.

15 Lieut-Colonel Finlay MacLean.

16 J. Connell, *Wavell – Scholar and Soldier* (London: Collins, 1964), p. 85.

17 I. F. W. Beckett, *The Army and the Curragh Incident* (London: Bodley Head (for the Army Records Soc., 1981), pp. 124-5.

18 *Ibid.*, 288.

19 M. Arthur, *Northern Ireland – Soldiers Talking – 1969 to Today* (London: Sidgwick and Jackson, 1987).

20 Lieut-Colonel Finlay MacLean.

21 Former corporal, First Battalion, Argyll and Sutherland Highlanders, conversation with the author, 10 October 1988.

22 T. R. Henderson *Freemasonry in the Royal Scots* (Aldershot: Gale and Polden, 1934).

23 H. Senior, *Orangeism in Ireland and Britain 1795-1836* (London: Routledge and Kegan Paul, 1966), pp. 267-73.

24 H. Cowper, former corporal, First Battalion, Royal Scots, conversation with the author, 15 June 1989.

25 L. B. Oatts, *Proud Heritage: The Story of the Highland Light Infantry, vol. 4, 1919-1959* (Glasgow: Grant, 1963), pp. 52-3.

26 *The Observer*, 27 September 1987.

27 *Observer Scotland*, 8 January 1989.

28 *Scottish Daily Express*, 28 June 1961.

29 *Ibid.*

30 J. Connell, op. cit.

31 Sir J. Cassells, *The Queen's Own Highlanders* (Morecambe: Morecambe Bay Printers, 1964), pp. 31-5.

32 C. Mitchell, *Having Been a Soldier* (London: Hamish Hamilton, 1969), p. 158.

33 A senior officer, First Battalion, King's Own Scottish Borderers, conversation with the author, 16 May 1989.

34 *Ibid.* See also R. Woollcombe, *All the Blue Bonnets* (London: Arms and Armour Press, 1980), p. 7.

35 Parliamentary Debates, vol. 768, 15 July 1968, para. 1065.

36 R. Lawrence, *When the Fighting Was Over* ... (London: Bloomsbury, 1988), pp. 189-90.

37 J. C. Kemp, *History of the Royal Scots Fusiliers 1919-1959* (Glasgow: Robert MacLehose & Co., 1963), pp. 292-4.

38 J. Baynes, *Morale: a Study of Men and Courage* (London: Cassell, 1967).

39 J. Masters, *The Road Past Mandalay*, quoted in J. Baynes, op. cit., p. 5.

40 Letter quoted in J. Baynes, op. cit., p. 163.

41 H. J. Hanham, 'Religion and Nationality in the Mid-Victorian Army'. In Foot, M. R. D. (ed.), *War and Society* (London: Paul Elek, 1972).

42 I. F. M. Beckett, and K. Simpson, (eds.), *A Nation in Arms* (Manchester: Manchester University Press, 1985), p. 218.

43 A. R. Skelley, *The Victorian Army at Home* (London: Croom Helm, 1977), p. 288.

44 M. Fry, *Patronage and Principle: a Political History of Modern Scotland* (Aberdeen: Aberdeen University Press, 1987), pp. 68-9.

45 H. Cunningham, *The Volunteer Force* (London: Croom Helm, 1975), p. 175.

46 L. B. Oatts, op. cit., pp. 425-30.

47 C. Mitchell, op. cit., p. 179.

48 *Thin Red Line*, September 1967. For accounts of operations in Aden involving the Argylls, see G. Blaxland, *The Regiments Depart* (London: William Kimber, 1971), pp. 445-65. See also S. Harper (1978). *Last Sunset: What Happened in Aden* (London: Collins). This author, a journalist, describes the regiment's response to a grenade attack on their Commanding Officer. Five Adenis were shot in reprisals and he was taken to see their bodies in a local mortuary. '"We got a couple of brace', said a wickedly grinning lieutenant."

49 *Thin Red Line*, August 1971.

50 *Scottish Daily Express*, 14 January 1968; *Scottish Daily Record*, 24 January 1968.

51 *Scottish Daily Record*, 25 January 1968.

52 *Scottish Daily Express*, 6 February 1968.

53 *Glasgow Herald*, 15 February 1968.

54 *Scottish Daily Express*, 11 May 1968.

55 *Ibid.*, 1 February 1968.

56 Supplementary Statement on Defence Policy, 1968, Cmnd. 3701.

57 Parliamentary Debates vol. 768, 15 July 1968, para. 1068.

58 *Ibid.* paras. 1087-8.

59 *Ibid.*

60 *Ibid.*, para 1091.

61 Conversation with the author 1 November 1988.

62 R. H. S. Crossman, *Diaries of a Cabinet Minister, vol. 3* (London: Hamilton Cape, 1977), p. 138.

63 Undated.

64 Undated.

65 20 July 1968.

66 Undated.

67 Undated.

68 Undated.

69 16 July 1968.
70 *Scottish Daily Express*, 16 July 1968.
71 Two letters, 16 July 1968.
72 *Glasgow Herald*, 20 July 1968.
73 *The Scotsman*, 27 July 1968.
74 Undated.
75 16 July 1968.
76 18 July 1968.
77 16 July 1968.
78 12 July 1968 (from the Revd Dr D. M. Steele).
79 16 July 1968.
80 16 July 1968.
81 Parliamentary Debates vol. 769, 25 July 1968, paras. 138-40.
82 *Ibid.*
83 *Glasgow Herald*, 26 and 29 July 1968.
84 A. Campbell MacLean *The Glasshouse* (London: Calder and Boyars, 1969).
85 *Tribune*, 2 August 1968.
86 *Ibid.*
87 *Ibid.*
88 *Scottish Daily Express*, 13 December 1968.
89 *Scots Independent*, 27 July 1968.
90 Private conversations with the author.
91 *Scottish Daily Express*, 14 October 1971.
92 *The Times*, 16 October 1971.
93 *The Scotsman*, 16 January 1981.
94 *Ibid.*, 20 January 1981.

8

'There's not a team like the Glasgow Rangers': football and religious identity in Scotland

GRAHAM   WALKER

Football is central to popular culture in Scotland. No other leisure pursuit can generate the passion, the colour, and the fanaticism which football has been responsible for in Scotland since the late nineteenth century. It is a recurring theme in folklore and the stuff of millions of dreams. In common with continental and Latin American countries, Scotland romances the game; the average Scottish fan is widely believed to be among the most knowledgeable and appreciative of the species.[1] The game is played competitively at a bewildering number of levels in Scotland, and the nation has one of the largest numbers of professional (full-time and part-time) league clubs, in proportion to its population, in the football-playing world.

Rangers Football Club are central to Scottish football. In terms of domestic honours they are the country's most successful club. They are, however, far more than this: they are an institution in Scottish life which attracts devotion and antipathy in roughly equal parts and with about the same degree of intensity. They are, for example, the best-supported team with average home attendance in the last three seasons (1986-9) of just under 40 000. On the other hand, and quite apart from the hatred of supporters of rival teams, most notably Celtic, they have provoked the charges of being 'a permanent embarrassment and an occasional disgrace' to Scotland,[2] and *'the institution that perpetuates all that is reactionary in Scottish life'.*[3]

The latter charges were levelled at Rangers primarily on account of the club's Protestant exclusivism, a tradition recently terminated (or perhaps interrupted) by the present management's decision to sign, in July 1989, the Roman Catholic player Maurice Johnston.[4] This event stunned the Scottish public, so improbable had it seemed hitherto that Rangers would choose to buck tradition by signing a player who, on top of his religious upbringing, had played for Celtic and had, in May 1989, declared his intention of returning to the same club. The acquisition of Johnston by Rangers was a revolution-

ary act and its ramifications for Scottish society will take time to be
assessed.

This chapter comments on the new phenomenon which Rangers
represent under the guidance of Graeme Souness, who became
team manager in 1986; However, the chapter primarily discusses the
club's changing role in Scottish football and society through its
history, focusing on specific episodes, historical questions and conceptual themes. The unifying theme will be that of the club's
Protestant image and the sense in which Rangers have stood for a
powerful current of popular Protestantism. The nature of this
'popular Protestant' phenomenon will thus be illuminated.

Rangers, of course, are the Protestant half of Scottish football's
internationally known religious rivalry. Celtic stand for the Catholic
cause, although the club have fielded many Protestants. The 'Old
Firm', as they are commonly referred to, have dominated Scottish
football for a century. They have also made Glasgow synonymous
with religious tensions, an image which the commercial and cultural
re-casting of the city in the last decade has not obliterated. The
development of both clubs has, to a large degree, been symbiotic,
and discussion of Rangers necessarily entails some discussion of
their greatest adversary.

The Old Firm phenomenon has been the subject of scholarly
investigation recently by Bill Murray.[5] Murray's work has clarified
many issues, particularly in relation to the roots of the rivalry; his
analysis of Celtic's origins (in 1887) in the context of the immigrant
Irish Catholic community of Glasgow and the West of Scotland
demonstrates the symbolical potency which football held for these
people. Celtic, from their inception,were more than just a successful
football team – they were a cause, the standard-bearer of a poor
community. About a decade after Celtic's formation, Rangers (in
existence since 1872) assumed a mantle of similar social and cultural
significance: nicknamed 'the Light Blues', they had by this time
come to be seen as the home-grown team to challenge most successfully and keenly 'the Irishmen'. Home grown' meant Protestant,
just as 'Irish' was synonymous with Catholic.[6]

The Catholic community was culturally and politically vigorous,
with Irish concerns to the fore, but socially and economically
disadvantaged.[7] It would be some time before they attained a degree
of significant social mobility, and the extent to which anti-Catholic
discrimination was primarily responsible for this will continue to be
debated by scholars and laymen alike.[8] Certainly, prejudicial notions of the Irish Catholics as priest-ridden, feckless, idle and

criminally-inclined wielded a tenacious grip on the indigenous population's outlook. Anti-Catholic feeling had been prevalent in Scotland for a long time before the advent of the religious tensions which accompanied industrialisation and erupted spasmodically in Glasgow and in the mining areas of Ayrshire and Lanarkshire in the second half of the nineteenth century. In the case of Rangers and Celtic, the spectacular growth of football as a mass spectator attraction was the spark which ignited the combustible material of religious-based divisions in Lowland society.

The Old Firm epitomised the fact that football could be good business in this early phase of its commercialisation. In this respect, Celtic, contrary to legend, were never a poor club, however poor their followers were. Some five years after their inception, for instance, their income (and expenditure) was the highest in Scottish football, and roughly double that of Rangers.[10] As the aura of religious sectarian rivalry grew around the Old Firm in the early twentieth century, so did both clubs' profits increase.[11]

The respective profiles of the clubs' followings can be tentatively sketched out from Club membership and shareholding records and other fragmentary evidence. Wray Vamplew, in his excellent study of professional sport in Britain in the period 1870-1914, provides the former: from this it transpires that in 1899 some 35 per cent of Rangers club members and 31 per cent of shareholders were drawn from the skilled manual occupational group; the next highest figures (25·2 per cent and 18 per cent) were drawn from the clerical group, and the third highest (14 per cent and 12·5 per cent) from the proprietors and employers group. The figures for Celtic in 1897 show that the skilled manual group also provided most members and shareholders, but that a considerable percentage of shareholders (24·7 per cent) were proprietors and employers and that a further 23·3 per cent of shareholders were proprietors and employers specifically connected to the drink trade. On the other hand, in comparison with the other Scottish clubs, the semi- and unskilled occupational groups were better represented in the ranks of club members.[12]

Celtic's connections with the drink trade are well discussed by Murray[13]; this was one of the most tried and trusted avenues of economic opportunity for the Irish Catholic community. The same community, however, was rather short on skilled labour, so it is something of a surprise that this group should be so well represented; the strong showing of the semi and unskilled labour groups in the members' figures is far more in line with expectations. Turning to Rangers, the strong showing of the skilled manual group seems to confirm the impression gained from anecdotal evidence and contemporary observation that Rangers drew much of their support from this sector. In their book *Glasgow in 1901*, the three authors compositely known as 'James Hamilton Muir' portray the typical skilled craftsman as a member of a Rangers supporters' Brake Club who discharges the frustrations of the working week on a Saturday at the match.[14]

Rangers were also associated with Govan, the area where their stadium, Ibrox Park, was situated. This was an area of relatively high skilled working-class density. In some ways it symbolised the economic power of Clydeside in this peak period of empire, with its shipyards and heavy engineering firms. Across the River Clyde lay Partick and Whiteinch, areas of similar skilled working-class character, which had witnessed Protestant – Catholic riots at periodic intervals in the nineteenth century. It seems that Rangers also drew much support from these quarters: in 1914 the football correspondent of the popular newspaper, *The People's Journal*, noted that many former Partick Thistle supporters 'are now Rangers adherents, and the rising generation Whiteinch way find it much handier to cross the river to Ibrox than to travel to Queens Cross [to see Partick Thistle]'.[15] It may also have been the case that the strong Protestantism of many skilled craftsmen, recalled by 'Red Clydesider' Harry McShane among others,[16] was finding expression through support for Rangers.

This hypothesis is strengthened by consideration of the likely social and cultural impact made by the opening of the Harland and Wolff shipyard in Govan in 1912. This Belfast company, by setting up in Govan, immediately began a two-way traffic in shipyard workers between Belfast and the Clyde, and an as yet unquantified number of Ulster (Protestant) workers settled in Glasgow as a result.[17] This development has been cited by several people including the Celtic manager of the time Willie Maley, as the factor which injected the decisive note of religious bitterness into the Old Firm rivalry and which determined an all-Protestant signing policy at the Rangers club. Murray, while noting Rangers' close relationship with the shipbuilding industry, is not convinced by this and sees the development as merely speeding up what had already begun.[18]

However, the Harland and Wolff factor may well be seen as decisive if considered in conjunction with the issue of Irish Home Rule. The impact of this issue on Scotland was to sharpen ethnic division; the despair of the Labour movement at the time is eloquent testimony to this.[19] Glasgow Irish politics were galvanised and, on the other side, the Orange Lodges recruited for the Ulster Volunteer

Force and pledged their support for Edward Carson's campaign of resistance. The Orange Order had been introduced to Scotland in the 1830's and had grown rapidly both in the mining areas of Ayrshire and Lanarkshire, and in the skilled-working-class areas of Glasgow such as Govan and Partick.[20]

It seems likely, as Moorhouse has suggested,[21] that aspects of the Ulster sectarian culture became more deeply rooted in Lowland Scottish life at this juncture. Against this background Celtic's open identification with the cause of Irish Home Rule – several club spokesmen had been prominent in Home Rule politics[22] – may well have resulted in Rangers becoming a rallying point for Ulster Unionist sentiments. To a clear if undemonstrative Protestant image there might have been grafted, at a period of political tension, a boisterous Unionism energised by the Ulster crisis and underpinned by a faith in the material progress of empire – 'a social imperialist' outlook.

Certainly there is evidence that soon after this, if not before, Rangers became a popular team in Ulster, vying with the Belfast team Linfield for Protestant affections. As the Ulster poet John Hewitt, writing of his childhood in the early 1920s, put it:

> *We had our cricket team, our football team;*
> *Our jerseys blue, our heroes, I should say,*
> *were Glasgow Rangers, Linfield. Like a dream,*
> *McCandless passed once, home on holiday.*[23]

If the 1912-14 period is viewed as crucial in the 'firming up' of Rangers' Protestant image and in grafting on to it what might be called 'Unionist militancy', there have to be qualifying remarks nonetheless. It was the case, for example, that Rangers supporters (along with Celtic's) had acquired by the 1890s a reputation for fanaticism. This seems to have been the result of an Old Firm supporters' subculture which focused on the Brake Clubs, horse-drawn carriages which transported the fans to matches. These brakes were invariably decorated in the team colours and banners were flaunted from them by the supporters. One Rangers player of the 1890s reminisced about the Brake Clubs in the Supporters' Annual of 1952:

> I cannot end without a word of appreciation for all the kindness and encouragement I received in my playing days from Rangers supporters, and particularly from the members of the Old Brake Clubs. I can still see in my mind's eye that wonderful procession of four horse brakes filling the length of Buchanan Street, on the evening in 1897 when we celebrated

our third cup victory that season. Every brake was packed with jubilant Rangers supporters, and I still look with pleasure on a silver salver and tea service given to me one happy evening in Govan Town Hall through the combined generosity of those same Brake Clubs.

A certain rowdiness was another feature of the Old Firm supporters from an early period. Comment was passed on Rangers' rowdy element as early as 1887, the year of Celtic's establishment [24] The history of both clubs thereafter is peppered with their fans' occasional excesses, most commonly the invading of the playing pitch. In 1912 fighting Rangers fans invaded the pitch and forced the abandonment of a match played against another Glasgow club, Clyde.[25] By the 1920s the brake clubs had become a by-word for public terror; the arrest of an entire Celtic brake club was made after an Old Firm game in 1923 and weapons were found. It seems also that the bulk of the brake club members by this time, if not before, were young, in the 18-25 age group.[26]

The First World War triggered a fervent 'King and Country' patriotism in Scotland as elsewhere in Britain. Allegiance to empire was strong, not least on account of the economic benefits it had brought to the Clyde. There was an imperial popular culture reflected in the romantic image of Scottish regiments in the British army, in music hall, and in the popularity of youth organisations such as the Boy Scouts and the Boys' Brigade.[27] The latter in particular was Protestant in character, its activities usually bound up with a parish Church. Protestant children (especially boys) growing up in urban Scotland tended to undergo an education both in school and at church which celebrated empire and the moral example of imperial heroes such as David Livingstone;[28] in addition, they were likely to join an organisation like 'the BB, which further reinforced this 'loyalist' ethic. It was a cultural conditioning shared by the middle and working classes but one which the sons and daughters of the skilled and generally more 'respectable' working class were more vigorously encouraged to adopt as a symbol of their sense of integrity and self-conscious social worthiness.

This loyalist culture might be said to have embraced Rangers. It is probably no coincidence that a Royal Investiture took place in 1917 at Ibrox Stadium. The club's chairman at the time was Sir John Ure Primrose, a local Unionist politician and wealthy businessman who was certainly proud of Glasgow's reputation as 'Second City of the Empire'. Primrose, moreover, had sat on the platform at Carson's anti-Home Rule rally in Glasgow in 1913.[29] In the 1920s, if not before, Rangers fans appropriated the Union Jack as something of a club emblem.

As ever, however, their behaviour has to be viewed in the context of the Old Firm rivalry; Celtic fans flaunted flags and emblems proclaiming their Irish nationalism and were prone to characterising their rivalry with Rangers in terms of Ireland's troubles. Thus the banner on a Celtic brake after an Old Firm game in 1921 which read: Rebels 2 Black and Tans 0.[30] Moreover, as Murray points out,[31] instances of IRA activity in Glasgow at this time aroused justifiable alarm among Protestants, particularly the working class of Glasgow; hostility to Catholicism and Irish nationalism, and what might have been seen as a defensive reaction to IRA militancy, found expression in a popular cultural sense through football.

It also found expression in the inter-war period through gang warfare in Glasgow. The most notorious razor gang of this Chicagoesque episode was the 'Billy Boys' from Bridgeton in the city's east end. As the name suggests, the gang were Ultra-Protestant, and they hitched themselves to the Orange Order. Ferocious street battles with Catholic gangs in the east end, most notably the 'Norman Conks' of the Gallowgate area, usually erupted during or after Orange parades . The 'Billy Boys' were led by one Billy Fullerton who inevitably took the soubriquet 'King Billy'. It has been established that Fullerton and his gang were keen supporters of Rangers,[32] and it was very likely they who constituted the group who sang Orange 'party' songs on the east terracing at Ibrox in the 1930s. Today, at Ibrox, their memory is celebrated in a battle hymn with the following chorus: 'Hello, Hello, we are the Billy Boys/Hello, Hello, you'll know us by our noise/We' re up to our knees in Fenian blood surrender or you'll die/For we are the Brigton Billy Boys'.[33]

Bridgeton, indeed, has remained an area of strong Rangers and Orange Order loyalties, despite its proximity to Celtic Park. In the 1930s it was an area of high unemployment; in this period there were many thousands of Protestant unemployed, in absolute terms more than there were Catholic. A steep decline in the shipbuilding and engineering industries left many skilled workers on the dole, sometimes for long periods. This apart, the strength of Rangers loyalties in Bridgeton indicated that their support also included many unskilled and semiskilled workers as well as unemployable 'flymen' who lived on their wits. Bridgeton lay across the River Clyde from the largely Catholic Gorbals. Both areas were full of poverty, violence, colourful characters, human generosity and religious and football mania. Such characteristics still prevailed in the 1960s (both areas were then redeveloped) when the folk singer Adam MacNaughton immortalised their Rangers and Celtic loyalties:

> *Oh don't wear a green scarf in Brigton,*
> *Or a blue one in Cumberland Street,*
> *Unless you're a heavyweight champion,*
> *or helluva quick on your feet.*[34]

Billy Fullerton died in 1962 and hundreds attended his funeral. The occasion prompted a poem entitled 'King Billy' by Glasgow's Edwin Morgan. Its closing lines are as follows:

> *Go from the grave. The shrill flutes*
> *are silent, the march dispersed.*
> *Deplore what is to be deplored,*
> *and then find out the rest.*[35]

It might he said that too many have been content simply to deplore where the Old Firm, and particularly Rangers, are concerned. The ideological dimension to this question will be discussed below, but at this point it is sufficient to note that few commentators have bothered to 'find out the rest' – to explore the extent to which Rangers and Orange marches and a sense of group belonging and loyalty to something traditional with roots in previous centuries filled a great social and popular cultural need in economically harsh and often brutalised existences.[36] It might be suggested that bigotry should be condemned where it is simply bigotry, but that where complex phenomena are operating in a bigoted context there should be an attempt made first to understand the dynamics involved.

Overall, the inter-war period was marked by a decidedly sectarian character in Glasgow – political manifestations of this were the emergence of a populist Protestant party, the Scottish Protestant League, and attempts to start a Catholic party;[37] socially, there was a plethora of Catholic organisations which, in many ways, mirrored the phenomena of Orangeism and Freemasonry among Protestants.[38] There was no doubt about Rangers' identification with the former: in 1930 (as reported in *The Belfast Weekly News*, 3rd April) a club director James Bowie addressed an Orange Order social gathering on Glasgow and praised the Order's "traditions" and "principles".

Freemasonry has also been associated with Rangers in the public view. In the last analysis the extent of the association cannot be clearly measured, but there are many indications of it. Murray has noted the masonic-sounding language employed by the official historians of the club,[39] and in some accounts by past Rangers players of their careers at Ibrox, words like 'brotherhood' abound.[40] Among supporters, given the high rate of masonic membership among skilled workers in Scotland – it is much more working-class in composition than in England – it is inevitable that there has been, and remains, such a link. The better dressed Rangers fans often sport a masonic lapel badge or tie. In 1953, in the course of a correspondence in the *Glasgow Herald* about the way .Rangers were being managed, some fans wrote using pseudonyms such as 'Cupid' and 'Atlanta'.[41] For many of those who believe that freemasonry exerts an important influence at authority and decision-making level in society, and on job opportunities and distribution, the masonic dimension to Rangers is proof of the club's complicity in a 'hidden agenda' in Scottish life which is fundamentally Protestant and anti-Catholic.[42] Today it is vehemently asserted by some Rangers fans that a very different one operates – namely, the favouring of Catholics in public service employment and the media harassment of Rangers, the Orange Order and other aspects of a perceived Protestant way of life. Such an attitude is very much part of a more recent sub-cultural outlook built around Rangers, something discussed below.

However, there was a general sense of self-confidence about Rangers' Protestant identity from the 1920s through to the 1960s, perhaps personified in the dominant personality of William Struth who managed the club from 1920 to 1954. Struth was a disciplinarian who, more than anyone, created a daunting mystique around Rangers which carried with it an arrogance and a typically dour Scottish approach. Such an approach was in a way a hostage to fortune for, when the lean times came on the field and criticism was levelled at the club off it, it found sympathy scarce; the club had alienated many people in Scottish football and society.

It was, perhaps, understandable that an arrogance should emerge, given Rangers' very considerable feats in the domestic football scene. In addition to this, of course, they commanded a huge support organised after 1949 into the largest federation of supporters' clubs in Britain. The fanatical devotion of these supporters was almost palpable; in 1962, for example, between 10000 and 15000 turned up at Renfrew Airport to welcome the team home from a successful close-season trip to Russia.[43] Rangers, indeed, became Scottish sport's premier institution, acquiring international recognition and featuring in such matches of immense public interest as the clash with Moscow Dynamo of Russia in 1945. Not least, the club's fame was broadcast throughout the British Commonwealth by those fans (mostly skilled workers laid off in periods of economic decline) who had emigrated. Emigration was a significant feature of both the inter-war and post-war eras. To exiles in Canada or Australia, following Rangers' fortunes was a way of keeping in touch with home and a way in which, socially, through supporters' clubs, they held on to their Scottish cultural identity. In the Commonwealth countries there was something of a social holy trinity of St Andrews, Burns and Rangers clubs; the exiles were also regularly visited by Scottish entertainers who were usually Rangers fans.

Rangers, especially in the post-war era, were thus part of a celebration of Scottishness which was underpinned by a strong unionism or loyalism. It can be argued that the Unionism was viewed as essentially an expression of Protestantism, following the traditional Orangeist rhetoric of loyalty to the crown and constitution and the defence of civil and religious liberties. Rangers fans often sang the national anthem and used pictures of royalty to adorn banners. In 1952 on the Saturday after the death of King George there was a special tribute at Ibrox. This Unionist sentiment was certainly not the product of a warm relationship with England; anti-English feeling, however superficial, was and is rife throughout Protestant Scotland.[44] Rangers fans for a long time considered themselves the backbone of the support for the Scottish national team, and for many the primary reason for joining a supporters' club was to get a ticket for the bi-annual pilgrimage to Wembley for the match in London against the 'Auld enemy'.[45] Lion Rampants were frequently waved by Rangers fans along with Union Jacks.[46] Celtic supporters, by contrast, were largely indifferent to the national team till the 1970s; they viewed the Scottish football authorities as biased towards Rangers.

The style in which Rangers were celebrated by popular entertainers and journalists says much about their cultural context. In the early 1960s, for example, the popular singer Andy Stewart recorded a song, 'Rangers for Me', which was a straight adaptation of 'A Gordon for Me', a song in praise of a Scottish regiment. In his book *We Will Follow Rangers*, the journalist Hugh Taylor also used the military metaphor; Rangers, he wrote, 'could be called the Scots Guards of football in this country'.[47] The most famous Rangers song, 'Follow Follow', was adapted from a Salvation Army hymn and has a decided martial air to it. Moreover, in the early 1970s, Rangers fans contrived to render 'The Lord's My Shepherd' as a battle hymn by adapting the tune to the words of 'Derry's Walls'. Up until at least the mid-1960s, Rangers were thus saluted in a popular cultural manner redolent of the 'kailyard'[48] with imagery of a romantic military kind, and their followers often sang their praises in the religious idiom to which many had become accustomed through their Sunday School and Church-going experience, however short-lived.

Hooliganism at Old Firm games continued – indeed increased – during the 1940s and 1950s when there were some spectacular outbreaks of bottle-throwing and terrace fighting. The press acknowledged that religious rivalry was the root cause but, excepting the oblique comments of the *Glasgow Herald's* Cyril Horne,[49] Rangers were not taken to task over the issue of the signing of Catholic players. Indeed, the most adverse publicity concerned Celtic' s insistence on flying the Eire tricolour (then in splendid isolation) from the roof of their enclosure at Celtic Park. All this seemed to reflect a continuing suspicion of the 'Irish' Catholic community in Scotland; correspondingly, there was a willing acceptance on the part of many of an overtly Protestant assertion of identity to counter what was viewed as the exclusivist and still rather alien characteristics of the Catholics. Issues like education (Catholics had been granted state support for their schools back in 1918) continued to arouse sectarian emotions.

This situation changed quite dramatically in the cultural and moral flux of the 1960s. In the climate of this era religious antagonisms began to be considered antiquarian and the signing policy of Rangers Football Club discriminatory and unjust. The disjunctive effect of the sixties has probably been exaggerated, but nonetheless there has seldom been a time in which young people have felt so emboldened, for better or worse, to reject the values and standards of their elders. In short, in relation to Rangers, it stopped being fashionable around the mid 1960s to support a club with its associations. Of course, many young people continued or started to support the team; however, in the new hyper-critical times Rangers' Protestant image was more vulnerable to attack and those imbued with the liberal or even anarchic spirit of the youth culture of the period were, generally, not attracted to the club. It might also be said that the Rangers supporters on the terracing developed a more crudely anti-Catholic repertoire in the 1960s with obscene chants about the Pope prominent.

More importantly – for at root Rangers are about football – the club was spectacularly upstaged on the field by its old rival. In 1965 Jock Stein, a former player, took over as manager of Celtic. He was the club's first Protestant manager, an indication that Celtic were prepared to go further in relegating the significance of religion in Scottish football. In just over two years Stein led Celtic to the pinnacle of club football: a European Cup triumph in Lisbon against the Italian champions Inter Milan. For all the mutterings about the Celtic supporters' displaying of Irish flags, this was a victory hugely celebrated in Scotland as a Scottish achievement. Stein had taken

Celtic out of something of a Catholic ghetto, and made the team
attractive to Protestant as well as Catholic Scots. In domestic
competition too, Rangers fell into their rival's shadow, a state of
affairs which lasted nearly a decade. Suddenly, on and off the field
Rangers were on the defensive and showing clear signs, in both
respects, of panic.

The 'no Catholics' issue was finally highlighted by the press in a
way which could not be ignored from around 1969 onwards. These
critical attacks usually followed displays of hooliganism by Rangers
fans such as in Newcastle in 1969, Barcelona in 1972, Manchester
in 1974 and, most crucially, Birmingham in 1976. The Ibrox Disaster[50]
of 1971, in which sixty-six Rangers fans were crushed to death after
an Old Firm game, had the effect of intensifying the wider (British)
public and media scrutiny of the character of the club.

The riot in Barcelona followed (and tarnished) the considerable
achievement of the team in winning the European Cup Winners'
Cup. The fans fought a pitched battle with General Franco's police,
for which some of their customary detractors back home forgave
them much. However, the generally middle-class readership of the
Glasgow Herald was outraged; a stream of letters excoriated the fans'
alleged bigotry and their anti-social behaviour, and identified them
as the kind of people who went on strike, drew state benefits and
cheated employers by taking time off to go to football matches.
Amidst this anti-working-class furore, the Labour Party journalist
Brian Wilson urged that Rangers be banned on account of their
sectarian signing policy.[51]

Rangers had their defenders in this correspondence, however,
and their comments make interesting reading. One correspondent
was obviously a military enthusiast: 'One knows how old soldiers
speak of pride in their various Scottish regiments and in particular
the now non-existent Highland Light Infantry and I would suggest
the very same qualities are evident in the fighting men of that famous
regiment as were evidenced in Barcelona by another generation of
Glaswegians.'[52] Not for this reader, then, anything so prosaic as
football hooliganism; and there is another indication here of the
aforementioned tendency to use military metaphors and images in
connection with Rangers as doughty fighters on behalf of Scotland.

Brian Wilson was taken to task by another reader who alleged that
Celtic's ethos was Catholic and sectarian, and went on to argue:
'The fact is football clubs win support by appealing to existing
loyalties, be they religious, national or parochial.' This correspondent then asked if Wilson was suggesting that 'the only people who
should not be allowed to express their loyalties in this way are

Scottish Protestants?'[53]

These comments arguably summed up the views of a lot of Rangers fans. By now they felt themselves embattled and more than a little bewildered at the extent of the criticism their club was taking. Whatever their own personal feelings towards Catholics – and, for many, religious friction simply went habitually with the Old Firm rivalry on a Saturday and could be put aside for the rest of the week – they felt that Rangers should be able to stand for Protestantism in a Protestant country and that Celtic, for all their Protestant players, still carried the banner for the Catholic cause without incurring the same criticism. For those more fervid in their Protestant loyalties, it seemed that it was the Protestants in Scotland – through such campaigns of criticism against Rangers – who were being discriminated against. In an interview with the author in May 1989, Rangers season-ticket-holder and Orange Order trustee, Danny Houston, advanced essentially this view: Protestants in Glasgow, he claimed, were a forgotten people with no-one to speak up for their rights; he considered that the signing of a Catholic (this was before Maurice Johnston) would be a betrayal of Protestantism and a surrender to a concerted media campaign which did not spend the same time and energy in highlighting instances of Roman Catholic sectarianism. For Danny Houston there was nothing wrong in a football club signing players with a view to preserving a specific identity; he pointed to the examples of Atletico Bilbao who only signed Basques, and to the Jewish club Maccabi.[54] These opinions would not have been shared by those Rangers supporters (perhaps more numerous than is often thought) who considered the religious issue an embarrassment; however, for these people too, it seemed that the issue of segregated schooling was of more moment in causing sectarian discord in Scotland, and the spectacle of Rangers in the media dock often triggered defensive reactions.

The feeling of being embattled was felt by Rangers fans all the more keenly in the 1970s and 1980s for the criticism from people they may fondly have regarded as being on their side. Hence the sense of 'et tu Brute' when some influential figures in the Church of Scotland began to call the club to account. In 1974 representatives of the Glasgow Presbytery challenged the club to state openly whether or not they operated a discriminatory policy.[55] In 1978 *The Bush*, the Church of Scotland journal, published articles condemning Rangers as sectarian and claimed to possess a dossier compiled on the subject.[56] Such pressure from the Church was considered evidence by those of a fundamentalist disposition of the baleful effects of ecumenism in watering down true Protestantism and making Protestants apologetic about their identity. For these people Protestantism – under siege in Ulster by the IRA and the Catholic Church – was being undermined too in Scotland, often from within.[57] In this battle for survival, defending Rangers' right to remain exclusively Protestant was central to the upkeep of morale. Friends within the church, however, there still were – *The Bush* suffered a serious drop in circulation; and Rangers could also rely on a clerical defender in the redoubtable Reverend James Currie, a minister with a populist touch who took the view that his colleagues were losing touch with the sentiments and values of working-class members of the kirk.[58]

Perhaps, too, the church's attacks on Rangers indicated that many middle-class Scots, by the 1970s, were no longer prepared to be associated with the club. For many years it had been the case that Rangers' fortunes were discussed avidly by business and professional people in coffee rooms, as well as by working men in pubs. By the 1970s this had changed; there remained well-off Rangers fans, but they tended to be men with working-class origins who had made good in business and who still clung to the values and loyalties of their past. In the middle class generally there had developed a disdain for the crude religious bigotry associated with Rangers; rugby was a more favoured recreational outlet and the religious discrimination practised by golf clubs was discreet and thus more acceptable. By contrast, the Catholic middle-class in Glasgow has never lost touch with Celtic; old social and economic grievances are not forgotten, and support for Celtic – for all the excesses of their working-class fans – is still seen as a way of giving vent to them.

On the basis of such developments, it is perhaps unsurprising that there has recently emerged a tendency to 'ideologise' the Old Firm rivalry, with Celtic cast in the role of progressives on account of their roots, and Rangers in the role of the reactionaries or oppressors. In Scotland there is a left-of-centre ideological consensus and the Labour Party enjoys political dominance. The Labour Party, in Glasgow at least, is predominantly Catholic, and – more than most places in Britain – enjoys considerable middle-class support and participation, both Protestant and Catholic. In addition to this there is a strong strain of left-wing nationalism which has arguably wielded great influence intellectually in the 1970s and 1980s. Among these political activists and opinion-formers, there is no doubting the Celtic loyalties and/or hostility to Rangers. Brian Wilson, a Labour MP since 1987, wrote the official Celtic centenary history in 1988; Scottish Labour MPs clamoured to table congratulatory motions in the House of Commons on Celtic's centenary and their feat of winning the double in their centenary year; a celebratory article about Celtic appeared in the same year in the left-wing cultural nationalist journal *Cencrastus*. The latter article, by Simon Pia, lauded Celtic as a popular cultural antidote to Calvinism and Unionism, and levelled the usual charges at Rangers regarding sectarianism. It seemed to this author that the piece represented an attempt to transplant characteristics of Irish nationalism (apparently viewed as more 'virile') into the Scottish consciousness; fuelling a fashionable and politically sound 'cult' around Celtic (which also seems to be an objective of the Celtic supporters' fanzine *Not the View*) might be one way of serving such an end.[59]

This is not the place to discuss the question of whether Celtic's record can bear the weight of a 'right on' political endorsement.[60] However, it must be stressed that the sectarian hatred which is part of the Old Firm rivalry is mutual, and the anti-protestant and pro-IRA songs sung at Celtic Park cause great offence. There are Rangers fans who admit that anti-Catholic songs and chants are in bad taste, but who exonerate themselves on account of what is heard from their rivals. Moreover, charges of racism levelled by politically-minded people at Rangers supporters over the years rather backfired in 1988 when Rangers signed a black player who was racially abused by Celtic fans on his debut.

The objection made here to the above characterisation of the Old Firm in pseudo-political terms is that it is the kind of exercise which only leads us to misread our history and to fail to understand fully the dynamics of sectarian loyalties in our society. Firstly, there is the implication that Rangers, by virtue of their Protestant loyalism, have been a right-wing institution supported by bigoted reactionaries. As in Northern Ireland, the equation between loyalism and right-wing politics is not that simple. Certainly, Rangers have had Chairmen who were Conservative politicians and there seems little doubt about the political inclinations of their board members through the years. However, it is far less clear that Rangers have been used for any right wing, as opposed to Unionist or Loyalist, purpose (although the Prime Minister's visit to Ibrox in March 1990 has been interpreted in this way). Certainly, Rangers have been supported by some prominent Labour men over the years; in the 1950s for example, a Labour Lord Provost of Glasgow, Tom Kerr, was an avid attender at Ibrox. Kerr, indeed, was an avowed pacifist who had led the unemployed of the Govan area in the early years of the century.[61] More recently, the Rangers Chief Executive from 1986-9 David Holmes, has made no secret of his socialist background and leanings, and Graeme Souness attended an anti-Poll-Tax concert in March 1989.

Assessing the political loyalties of Rangers' vast support is, of
course, an impossible task. However, there are pointers: for example,
there is the evidence of areas renowned for their 'bluenose' (allegiance to Rangers) character such as Bridgeton and the mining area of
Larkhall which consistently vote Labour overwhelmingly; there is also
the historical evidence of the Rangers supporters' documentation
which shows that supporters' clubs in the 1950s met in Labour Halls as
well as in 'Unionist rooms' or Orange or Masonic halls.[62] Today, in
spite of some Young Conservatives' well-publicised Rangers leanings, the editor of the Rangers' fanzine *Follow Follow* is of the view
that most Rangers supporters could be labelled 'right-wing Labour'.[63]

Certainly, given the current state of the Tory Party in Scotland, the
vast bulk of the Protestant working class *must* be voting Labour (and
some Scottish Nationalist). In the past there was a strong working-class
Tory vote which resulted in the seat of Govan, for example, being
captured by the Conservatives in 1951. However, there is as much, if
not more, historical evidence to link the Protestant working class
(particularly the skilled section of it) with Liberalism in the nineteenth
century and Labourism after the First World War.[64] It is merely common sense to conclude that many of these working men would have
been Rangers fans; whatever the consensus may have been among fans
around issues like Protestantism and Unionism (and it is not entirely
clear), it is likely that there were many political differences. Football in
Scotland, however, has never been an arena for distinctively political
issues to be fought over.

There is, therefore, a danger in imposing retrospectively a sim-
plistic view of the Old Firm which caricatures both clubs in quasi-
political terms and ignores the socio-cultural context in which the
rivalry developed and in which, until the mid-1960s, Rangers were
not generally viewed through the medium of disgust about sectarianism. There is a further danger in linking Old Firm loyalties to
certain kinds of political behaviour and opinions since, arguably,
these do not neatly coincide. Indeed, it might be contended that in
Scotland, Rangers and Celtic loyalties and sectarian behaviour are
to a large extent compartmentalised. Sectarian thinking is nowhere
near as pervasive as in Northern Ireland, however much the troubles
of that place seem to dominate the thoughts and behaviour of many
Old Firm fans. There is in Scotland, possibly to a greater degree than
in any other part of the UK, a tendency to separate different sets of
loyalties or to live with sets of loyalties which may conflict or, at the
very least, sit uneasily with one another. We need to be aware of such
complexities of modern Scottish life and to appreciate both the
importance and the *limits* of sectarianism and Old Firm allegiances.

These limits were pointed up in newspaper reports concerning two Rangers fans arrested for singing obscene sectarian songs in 1976. Both were instructed by the court to write explanations of their conduct. The newspaper reported that: 'Both youths agreed it was wrong to introduce religion when supporting their team, but said they had been carried away with the atmosphere in which everyone around them was singing "the Sash" and making abusive remarks about the Pope.' One of the youths wrote: 'I don't like abusing religion, 'cause I have nothing against it. Most of my friends are Catholics and we get on great. My mother's side of the family are all Catholics. It is just at a football match … it must be the atmosphere, and the Rangers football team doesn't help any with their 'No Catholics' policy.' The other youth explained: 'I don't mean anything or hold anything against any other religion when I sing these songs. I just like singing along with the rest of the fans. To my mind when you hear the fans singing at a football match it makes the players feel good as well as the fans.'[65]

Too much stress should not be laid on statements obviously designed to encourage the Sheriff of the Court to be lenient. Nonetheless, these statements warn us that too much can be read into the singing of sectarian songs and that for many Rangers (and Celtic) fans such songs and chants were primarily viewed as creating an electric atmosphere at the match and part of the fun. The Old Firm phenomenon is thankfully about love of football, humour and banter, and a commendable spirit of loyalty and dedication, as well as religious feuding and violence.[66] It has also been one of the most distinctive aspects of a Glasgow working-class upbringing and has been portrayed at once critically and sympathetically in the works of fiction by Alan Spence and the plays of Hector McMillan and Peter MacDougall. Beyond the ugliness of the sectarianism and everything there was, and is, to 'deplore', lies something else. It is implicit in the following passage of Spence's:

> The night before I had sat up late with my father, the two of us talking about football. He told me his legends, of the great Rangers teams of the past. He told me of Alan Morton, scoring a goal direct from a corner kick, of Jerry Dawson, leaping backwards to make an impossible save, of Willie Thornton, face down in the mud after diving full length to head a last-minute winner against Celtic. It didn't matter that I heard it all before. These were the myths we shared. The fire was blazing in the hearth, and we stared into it, my father was the teller of tales, he was the weaver of fables, and his heroes strode before me and were real.[67]

Among the songs of praise to Rangers penned by one 'Billy King' in his *Loyalist Song Book*,[68] there is one entitled 'Rangers Canny Sign a Catholic'. Its first verse concludes: 'We can sign a Hindustani/a Russian or a Fin/ But we canny sign sign a Tim.'[69] Mr King's reaction to the signing of Mo Johnston was not put on record, but it probably would have echoed that of those who felt so betrayed as to renounce publicly their loyalty to the club at the time. The signing was the culmination of Rangers' evolution, under Souness, into a cosmopolitan, nationally, racially and religiously mixed squad of players;[70] Souness, as promised, had given the club a more worldly and less hidebound look. However, for the protesters it was also the final act of betrayal of the club's Protestant traditions, a process they had detected at work earlier in such actions as the refusal to allow the Orange Order to hold its divine service at Ibrox.

The spectacular nature of scenes of scarf-burning and of apocalyptic graffiti led many to fear for Johnston's safety and to doubt whether Rangers could, in practice, transcend their past. Inevitably, the question arose as to whether or not the club could prosper after contravening the unwritten law of Protestant exclusivism. It was suggested that fanatical elements would desert in droves, leaving embarrassing spaces in the majestic stands of the stadium. The remarkably hostile reaction of the Secretary of the Supporters' Association, David Miller, only strengthened such conjecture.[71]

The sceptics, however, were confounded. Johnston was well-received by a packed Ibrox on his first appearance there, and has been lauded many times since, none more so than when he struck a sensational winning goal against Celtic. His own phlegmatic approach to the matter undoubtedly helped, for it is quite clear that he is someone who does not take sectarianism seriously and who probably laughed with the rest of the nation at the plethora of jokes generated by his decision to cross the great divide.

However, if outright bigotry has been dealt a body blow, it would be going too far to conclude that this historic move has diluted Rangers' Protestant image. Rather, it seems, at the time of writing, to underline the extent to which popular Protestantism is a cultural current independent of its most obvious recreational focus in Scotland. As the editorial of the *Follow Follow* put it in the wake of the Johnston transfer: 'Signing Maurice Johnston changes nothing ... Having Mo in the team will make about as much difference as Roman Catholic cleaners and office workers at Ibrox have made. Rangers, as a club have never done anything publicly to encourage Protestantism or Unionism. The club has remained a Protestant one because the supporters wanted it. No-one else.'[72] Across the Irish

Sea, one of Rangers' Ulster fans wrote as follows to the *Belfast News-Letter*: 'Rangers are bigger than Mo Johnston, and we can maintain our Protestant Loyalist identity. Our presence at Ibrox … keeps the tradition going, and cements the bond with Protestant Scotland.'[73]

To effect a total change in the club's character, Rangers would have to lose these fans. Signing Catholic players has evidently not led to the loss of more than an insignificant minority. However, whether in conscious pursuit of such an aim or not, Rangers have, since Souness took over, embarked on a course of action off the field which *has* forced many of their traditional fans to question their loyalty. This course of action has been concerned with the cultivation of a super-club status beyond the field of play; commercialism has become predominant and the aim of becoming a flourishing business enterprise vigorously pursued without reference to supporters. This trend received further reinforcement in November 1988 when the self-made millionaire David Murray bought out Lawrence Marlborough, marking the end of Rangers' long connection with the Lawrence family and building concern. Murray's business empire is already impressive and is set to expand still further. Murray was never a supporter of the team, so Rangers' traditions seem unlikely to hold up plans he may have to maximise the club's earning potential.

Rangers, under Souness, first with David Holmes in overall charge (as Marlborough's man) and now with Murray, have distanced themselves discernibly from the ordinary supporter. The club, in these years, has assumed an even more Olympian sense of detachment than before. In Souness's early years there were unedifying rows with the press which led to temporary bans of certain journalists from Ibrox. A defensive attitude prevailed at top level and spread to the supporters who adopted the chant 'No One Likes Us, We Don't Care'. For a while management and supporters seemed united in their belief that the world, in its envy of them, was out to put the knife in at every turn.

However, it soon became clear to many fans that their loyalty to the club and their sacrifices for it were not uppermost in the minds of those at the top. The fanzine *Follow, Follow* soon became a vehicle for much of the discontent felt by supporters on matters such as admission prices, ticket allocations, the role of Rangers' police liaison officer Alistair Hood, communication between club and fans, and the question of what kind of stadium the fans themselves wanted. Despite obvious popular support for the retention of a standing area in the stadium, recent reconstruction plans unveiled by the management have confirmed what most Rangers fans had long suspected: that Ibrox would soon be all-seated and even more expensive to gain admittance to.[74] While all Rangers fans shared the dream of the club becoming one of Europe's elite, there was the fervent hope that this could be done without jeopardising the club's popular base of support among those of limited economic means. It seems highly questionable now if this will turn out to be the case.

Rangers might, before long, have to decide between the types of supporter they wish to attract. If they opt for the moneyed kind with business or professional clout they will have to accept that such people do not, in general, 'follow follow' everywhere. If they want the game, in the age of the global village of satellite television, to remain with the people and to be played in front of large attendances in a passionate atmosphere (and Ibrox has often been noticeably less than passionate in the last couple of years), they will have to ponder the implications of their business and commercial strategies, whatever the successes of these may be.

If the ordinary fan is not driven away by commercialism, Rangers will in all probability remain the Protestant club in Scotland just as Celtic have remained the Catholic club for all their past and present Protestant employees. The significance of religious labels – however nominal – shows no sign of waning in large parts of Scotland. The roots of people's need for such an identification lie deeper than football, although, such is the game still a national obsession and such is the Old Firm's cultural domination of it,[75] that the fusion of religion and football is a remarkable social force, both divisive and cohesive, in itself. Rangers and Celtic will probably never just be football teams, but in Scotland football will never just be a game, unless, that is, it is totally hijacked by business tycoons or politicians.

ACKNOWLEDGEMENTS

With thanks to, in alphabetical order: Stuart Bathgate, Robert Burns, Mark Dingwall, Jack Geekie, Danny Houston, Robert McElroy, Alan McKnight, Bill Murray and Iain Patterson. None are in any way responsible for the views advanced here. The supporters' documentation referenced is privately held by the author. The research for this article was aided by a grant from the Central Research Fund, University of London.

NOTES

1 See the view of English football writer Simon Inglis in *Scotland on Sunday*, 10 September 1989.
2 Ian Archer in the *Glasgow Herald*, 11 October 1976.
3 Stuart Bathgate in *The Absolute Game* (Scottish football fanzine), Number 10.

4 Rangers have, contrary to popular belief, signed several Roman Catholics in the past, especially in their early years. See the *Rangers Historian*, Vol.2, No.5.

5 Bill Murray, *The Old Firm* (Edinburgh, 1984) and *Glasgow's Giants* (Edinburgh, 1988).

6 There was, however, considerable Protestant Irish emigration to Scotland. See the point about Harland and Wolff Shipbuilders in Govan, below.

7 See T. Gallagher, *Glasgow: The Uneasy Peace* (Manchester, 1987) and Murray, *The Old Firm*, chapter 4.

8 See Sean Damer's review of Gallagher, op. cit. in *Cencrastus* No. 32 (New Year, 1989).

9 An excellent account of the sectarian strife in the mining districts is provided by A. Campbell, *The Lanarkshire Miners* (Edinburgh, 1979).

10 *Scottish Sport*, 26 May 1893.

11 See Murray, *The Old Firm* chapter 2.

12 W. Vamplew, *Pay Up and Play the Game* (Cambridge, 1988), pp. 287-91.

13 Murray, *The Old Firm*, pp. 103-4.

14 James Hamilton Muir, *Glasgow in 1901* (Glasgow, 1901), p. 194.

15 *People's Journal*, 4 July 1914.

16 H. McShane, *No Mean Fighter* (London, 1978), p. 56.

17 See *Govan Press*, 25 July 1913 for comment on this.

18 Murray, *The Old Firm*, pp. 84-5. See also letter to *Glasgow Herald*, 15 July 1989. No Catholic was signed by Rangers between 1919 and 1951. Two were signed in the years 1912-19 but neither remained long. See *Rangers Historian*, op.cit.

19 See, for example, report of municipal elections in *Forward*, 9 November 1912.

20 The best source of information on the Orange Order in Scotland is an unpublished dissertation: W. Marshall, 'The Development of the Orange Order in Scotland' (Glasgow Room, Mitchell Library, Glasgow).

21 H. F. Moorhouse, 'Professional Football and Working Club Culture: English Theories and Scottish Evidence', *Sociological Review*, Vol. 32, No. 2 (1984).

22 See Murray, *The Old Firm*, pp. 66-75.

23 From 'On Dunmore's Waste' in John Hewitt, *Kites in Spring* (Belfast, 1980). McCandliss was an Ulsterman who played for Rangers in the 1920s.

24 See the quote from *Scottish Athletic Journal* in Moorhouse, op. cit. See also *Rangers Historian*, vol.2, No. 6 for comment on the Kinning Park 'foulmouths' who followed the club in the late 1880s.

25 *Glasgow Herald*, 12 February 1912.

26 *Glasgow Herald*, 29, 30, 31 October 1923.

27 The Boys' Brigade centenary celebrations (for the whole of the UK and including visitors from abroad) was held at Ibrox in 1983.

28 See John MacKenzie's article in this volume.

29 Primrose had been a Liberal Unionist. See Strathclyde Regional Archives, AGN 356 for a profile. For a report of Carson's rally see *Glasgow Herald*, 2 October 1913.

30 Murray, *The Old Firm*, pp. 172-3.

31 *Ibid.*, p.129

32 *Ibid.*, chapter 6

33 'Fenian', from the Irish Republican movement of the nineteenth

century which believed in the necessity of force to secure its goals, is a
term used commonly, and usually derogatorily, in Glasgow to refer to
Catholics. The Bridgeton and Calton areas of Glasgow's East End saw
an influx of Protestant Irish immigrants – many of them weavers – in
the early nineteenth century. This is probably the root of the area's
strong Protestant and Orange tradition. Similarly, the well-known
Rangers area of Larkhall in Lanarkshire was a mining area which
attracted the Protestant Irish in the mid-nineteenth century. See
Campbell, op. cit.

34 'The Derry and Cumberland Boys' from Adam MacNaughton's LP
record, *The Glasgow I used to know* (Greentrax).

35 'King Billy', in E. Morgan, *Selected Poems* (Manchester, 1985).

36 However, note the very telling points made in *The Scotsman* editorial
on religious bigotry, 7 May 1973.

37 See chapter 6 in this volume. For the Catholic party see *Irish News*, 5
May 1933.

38 See Gallagher, op.cit., especially chapter 3; Murray, *The Old Firm*,
p.128.

39 Murray, op. cit., p.77.

40 See especially the articles by Jimmy Millar and Ralph Brand in *The
Rangers Players Story* (1962).

41 *Glasgow Herald*, 22 December 1953.

42 See Gerry Finn's chapter in this volume.

43 The late James Sanderson, then a journalist, described this as 'the
greatest home-coming of any sportsmen to Scotland', *Rangers Supporters' Association Annual 1962-3*.

44 See the story in the *Sunday Telegraph*, 1 May 1988, about the police-
man who was a mason and a Rangers fan and who had 'a pathological
hatred of all things English'.

45 The Rangers Supporters' Annuals of the 1950s contain remarks about
membership falling off after the Wembley internationals.

46 A Rangers supporters' song of the 1950s, 'The Ballad of Willie
Woodburn', mentions both the Lion Rampant and the Union Jack as
supporters' emblems. See also photograph of supporters in the Supporters' Association Annual of 1961-2.

47 H. Taylor. *We Will Follow Rangers* (London, 1961), p.12.

48 This was the term given to the late Victorian school of popular fiction
(which included J. M. Barrie) which celebrated sentimentally what
were seen as traditional Scottish virtues and values.

49 See, for example, *Glasgow Herald*, 14 February 1952.

50 Perhaps the most significant sympathetic published responses to the
Disaster have come from two Glasgow celebrities steeped in the Celtic
tradition: see John Cairney, *The Man Who Played Robert Burns* (Edinburgh, 1987), pp. 113-14; and the late Matt McGinn's 'The Ibrox
Disaster' in *McGinn of the Calton* (Glasgow, 1987). Both of these indicate the instinctive fellow-feeling which exists between the best Old
Firm (and, indeed, football) fans, and also, in a positive sense, the
integrity of the Old Firm quarrel. See also John Burrows' evocative
account in his *Frontline Report* (Edinburgh, n.d.).

51 *Glasgow Herald*, 7 June 1972.

52 *Ibid.*, 10 June 1972.

53 *Ibid.*, 7 June 1972.

54 Interview with Danny Houston, 21 May 1989.

55 *Glasgow Herald*, 10 October 1974.

56 *Ibid.*, 25 August 1978.

57 Interview with Danny Houston.

58 See W. Coffey, *God's Conman* (Moffat, 1988) pp. 154-64.

59 For Pia's article see *Cencrastus*, No. 30 (Summer 1988); for reply see *Cencrastus*, No. 31 (Autumn 1988}.

60 But see the critical article written by Celtic fan Peter Brougham in *The List*, No.65. Also Murray, *The Old Firm*, especially pp. 104-16.

61 For information on Kerr, see Strathclyde Regional Archives, ACN 355; see also comment in Rangers Supporters' Association Annual 1953, and report of his speech at the Association's annual rally in the 1954 issue.

62 See, for example, the Supporters' directory in the Association annual of 1952.

63 Interview with Mark Dingwall.

64 See chapter 6 in this volume.

65 *Glasgow Herald*, 17 September 1976.

66 The Old Firm have been a staple part of the repertoire of Scottish comedians such as Lex McLean and Andy Cameron (both 'bluenoses') and Glen Daly (a Celtic fanatic).

67 From the story 'Blue' in the collection *Its Colours They Are Fine* (Edinburgh, 1983}.

68 The *Loyalist Song Book* (privately printed, n.d.).

69 'Tim' is a colloquial Glasgow expression for Roman Catholic, mistakenly viewed as an offensive term by those who have recently discovered the Old Firm phenomenon.

70 Most of Souness's signings have been English, but there have also been two Israelis and a Dane, and, in Mark Walters, the first black player to turn out for the team.

71 *Glasgow Herald*, ll July 1989.

72 *Follow, Follow*, a Rangers fanzine, No.8.

73 *Belfast News-Letter*, 21 August 1989.

74 See *Evening Times* (Glasgow), 20 February 1990. In February 1990 the Taylor Report into the Hillsborough disaster recommended the phased introduction in British football of all-seater stadia. Rangers have subsequently used this to justify their decision in response to fans' complaints.

75 Witness the replication of the Old Firm rivalry at other levels of the game in Scotland, and also the extent to which the character of the Old Firm rivalry is reproduced in its Edinburgh counterpart – Hearts v. Hibs.

9

In the grip? A psychological and historical exploration of the social significance of freemasonry in Scotland

GERRY P. T. FINN

INTRODUCTION

This chapter presents a preliminary, and necessarily limited, summary of ongoing research into the psychological and historical significance of Scottish freemasonry.[1] Various research approaches have been used in an attempt to explore and reflect the multi-layered complexity of masonry. Informal interviews and open-ended questionnaires have been used to identify the images freemasonry conjure up for non-masons. Media reports and masonic publications have been analysed. And a small number of masons have been interviewed. Those interviewed represent the range of masonic involvement and the continuum of masonic experience. They included a former lodge official, now antagonistic to the order, and the sympathetic son of a mason who, however, took the first masonic degree only out of respect for his father and the family's masonic tradition. Some active master masons were also interviewed, and very senior office-bearers in Scottish freemasonry gave in-depth interviews, which were tape-recorded.

The senior masons were all members of the Grand Lodge of Scotland and also occupied other important masonic offices. One was presently a Provincial Grand Master; another was an elected member of the Grand Committee of the Grand Lodge of Scotland, and a Past Provincial Grand Master. The remaining two had exceptionally impressive records of masonic service, one being a Past Depute Grand Master Mason of Scotland who has occupied other high offices at both national and provincial level, and the second, Mr J. M. Marcus Humphrey, having held many prominent positions, culminating in his being Grand Master Mason of Scotland, 1983-8.

Influential figures in Scottish masonry occupy important offices in other masonic orders. Marcus Humphrey (who had also been Senior Grand Warden in the United Grand Lodge of England) illustrates this pattern: he was Provincial Grand Master of the Royal Order of Scotland and, as a member of the Supreme Council of the Ancient and Accepted Scottish Rite, he is one of only nine 33° (degree) masons in Scotland. The status of these other masonic organisations is frequently misunderstood. Honours achieved in one order are largely irrelevant to a mason's position in another body. Craft or St John's masonry, with its masonic lodges, is the fundamental masonic order in Scotland. A mason can hold the 33° of the Scottish Rite, but he still has to adhere to the discipline of Craft masonry when attending his masonic lodge; when there, he has to obey the lodge office-bearers who may be simply master masons.

None of the four leading Scottish masons requested anonymity. But only those subjects identifiable because of publicity elsewhere will be named. Some interviewees, particularly among the non-masons, expressly requested that their names not be given. A request for anonymity may suggest to some that interviewees can not substantiate their accounts, but the subjects were worried about being known to have spoken about freemasonry, which demonstrates the real emotions aroused by this particular topic. Their fears may be unrealistic, but research ethics demand that the researcher does not additionally worry subjects who have participated voluntarily in the study. Guaranteeing anonymity for subjects is common practice in social scientific research, and that practice will be followed here, as much as is possible, whether anonymity was requested by interviewees or not.

The fears expressed confirm that research in this area poses some extra problems, even if they are normally overstated. Some non-masons have worried that, by writing this chapter, I am placing my life in danger, or, at the very least, seriously damaging my future career prospects; similar reasoning led to the requests that some participants remain anonymous. Beliefs about the powerful hidden hand of freemasonry are common. In his sequel to *The Brotherhood*, Short discussed at some length Stephen Knight's death at the young age of thirty-three, only eighteen months after the publication of his book which many masons saw as an unfair attack on masonry. Short eventually dismissed the suggestion that Knight's death was the result of masonic vengeance; but his lengthy treatment of the matter endowed claims of this type with a doubtful credibility, and partly legitimised the murky imagery of freemasonry as an organisation party to criminal intrigue [2] Many masons worry when outsiders (termed the 'profane') write about freemasonry, and they suspect the motivations that lie behind these attempts to understand masonry. Masons see the books by Knight and Short as attempts to smear masonry by making the organisation as a whole responsible for the actions of a few.

Paradoxically, the fears of masons parallel those of the 'profane', and some masons still believe that no assistance should be given to those wishing to study freemasonry. A senior mason expressed strong suspicions about the motivations behind this study. He was concerned it would inflict more serious damage upon the reputation of freemasonry and, perhaps, affect the lives of individual free-masons. The strong feelings displayed by masons and non-masons alike reveal much about the perceptions of the social significance of masonry for Scotland. Very powerful emotions, both positive and negative, are aroused by the order in Scotland. Serious study of an organisation which produces such intense feelings is long overdue, and an objective examination of the types of images conjured up by Scottish masonry is an important starting point.

COMMON IMAGES OF FREEMASONRY

Comments from community education students in the West of Scotland unveil the content of the common images of freemasonry, and this content reveals the reasons for the strong feelings engen-dered. Previous experiences, social backgrounds, age range, and career choice ensure that these subjects are more representative of the general population than many student groups. Anonymous students wrote replies to questions on why men became masons and on what they believed to be the most important aspects of freema-sonry. Questions were left open-ended to ensure that the descrip-tions used came directly from the subjects, who also reported on their contacts with, and knowledge of, freemasonry, and their age, gender and religious affiliation. Table 9.1 summarises the various descriptions volunteered by respondents. Subjects provided a vari-ety of descriptions of freemasonry. One common set was revealed by terms like 'an old boys' network', 'exclusive', 'elite', 'hierarchical', 'power', 'prestige', 'status'. Comments like these were taken to reveal an underlying dominant view of freemasonry as a traditional, powerful elite, which operated on exclusive and hierarchical princi-ples. Images of a closed, influential network seemed to imply secretive operations, perhaps explaining why only 36 per cent explicitly associated masonry with secrecy – despite this being the issue about which most concern is expressed.[3] Masonic influence was perceived to be particularly helpful in obtaining jobs and promotions. Some recognised that the decision to become a mason was influenced by a family tradition of masonic membership. A few acknowledged that masonry could be misused by anti-Catholic

Table 9.1 Images of freemasonry

	Female		Male	
	Catholic	Protestant	Catholic	Protestant
	(all figures below are percentages)			
Masonry as traditional hierarchical power-elite	88·9	100 All individuals: 94·3	100	90
Masonry seen as means of career advancement	77·8	83·3 All individuals: 79·3	100	65
Masonry identified with secrecy	22·2	41·7 All individuals: 35·9	41·7	35
Masonic membership as family tradition	11·1	33·3 All individuals: 28.3	41·7	25
Masonry associated with Protestant image	22·2	16·7 All individuals: 26·4	41·7	25
Claiming close masonic associations	44·4	33·3 All individuals: 49·1	41·7	65

Note: The sample of 53 subjects consisted of 9 Catholic women (age range from 20 to 42 years: average 26·4), 12 Protestant women (age range from 20 to 45: average 26·8), 12 Catholic men (age range 20 to 42 years: average 27·7) and 20 Protestant men (age range 21 to 40: average 27·0). The religious affiliation was determined by their own self-description of either their present beliefs or of the religious orientation of their upbringing. A male subject refused to divulge if he was a mason: all other subjects claimed not to be.

members, but over a quarter of subjects saw some association between masonry and Protestantism; and, again, this may have been implied in descriptions of masonry as an elite and exclusive, hierarchical network.

The number of subjects in each category is too small to allow any firm conclusions to be drawn, but the differences obtained may be indicative of some small variations in attitude as a result of gender and religious influences.[4] The Catholic men had a slightly more negative view of masonry and the Protestant men had a slightly less negative view than other subjects. Both of these viewpoints are probably influenced by the apparent significance of freemasonry for Scottish male culture, especially in typically male work-places where some link the order to protestantism. Some women did judge masonry to be a sexist organisation, but their comments could also include the disdainful, equating masonic membership with activities normally enjoyed by 'wee boys'. However, the most striking finding is that negative images of freemasonry predominate among all subjects, regardless of their religion or gender. Most were highly suspicious of freemasonry and its perceived power and influence, which they assumed were used by members for personal advancement.

Close personal contact with masons, claimed by almost half the sample, did not necessarily lead to more positive views either; most of these subjects held strong, negative images as well. One of the more positive responses came from a woman in her mid-forties, whose father and brothers were all masons. She saw masonic membership as resulting from family connection, but even she depended on a negative cliché when she summarised its most important aspects as being: 'Collective help. It is also a tradition to help each other, like the "Old Boy Network".' A woman in her late twenties whose brother was a mason used the same cliché and described it as a 'closed organisation with privileges such as employment'. One woman judged masonry to be for 'personal gain', as well as being bigotedly anti-Catholic, both conclusions drawn from her experiences with her former boyfriend who had been a mason. Another woman, a Catholic also with a mason as a former boyfriend, stated that, though some masons were bigoted, anti-Catholicism had no real place in masonry; but a (Protestant) man related how his uncle had left the masons because of the bigotry he found there.

The views of other Protestant males, those claiming most contact with masons, were also substantially negative. Most of those with family members or friends in masonry expressed the common view. A twenty-nine year-old claimed that 'most male members of my family' were masons, and declared that men became masons 'to gain promotion in certain occupations'. A twenty-three-year-old explained that a close friend had joined 'to enhance his business links', a motivation he judged to be the most important in freemasonry. A student in his mid-twenties, whose father and close friends were members, considered the reasons for joining masonry to include 'business contacts, employment'; and a thirty-three-year-old, with father and uncles in the order, wrote that: 'It's elitism. Reinforcing belief in the Protestant (in this country) superiority.'

In his thirties, and brought up as a Catholic, a former shipyard worker claimed to have had the opportunity to observe freemasonry closely in the workplace. Although he had a mason as a close friend, he believed freemasonry was for 'the protection of WASP culture, God and the Queen', and that it discriminated against 'women, Catholics, Asians and other minority groups': he described 'freemasonry in action' as the 'acquirement of career goals and promotion'. But another Catholic in his mid-twenties, also with a close masonic friend, wrote that men became masons for 'a mixture of reasons, brotherhood, a sense of belonging, getting a job, charity work. A lot of men join for the wrong reasons i.e. bigotry against Catholicism, promotion, to further their own aims.'

Overall, the views demonstrate a very negative set of images of masonry and these views are fairly general, regardless of gender, religion or even masonic friends or family associations. Instead, it appears as if some of these relationships actively reinforce a negative image of masonry. The subjects confirm that masonry is an object of suspicion, and is generally seen as a society that conspires to confer power, privilege and advantage on its own, to the detriment of those outside of the order, particularly Catholics and, inevitably, women; though some believe that these accusations might be more properly made against individual masons rather than masonry.

The views of this small sample provide some objective evidence of the suspicions many have about the role of freemasonry in Scottish society. It is no overstatement to say that the dominant descriptions reveal an underlying reliance on conspiracy theories to explain the operations and appeal of freemasonry. Many other Scots seem to take a similar stance. Commentators on Scottish social and economic life have come to similar conclusions, suggesting that freemasonry operates to confer advantages on masonic brothers and to act prejudicially against non-masons, especially when they are Catholic. A relationship between freemasonry, religion, politics and self-advancement is assumed by many, and Scottish masonic membership has been linked to support for Tory politics. Similar perceptions can be found throughout Britain, with anti-masonic feeling being even stronger on the political left than the right.[5]

MASONIC 'GLASNOST'

European mainland masons did use freemasonry for political and religious ends: British masonic bodies have condemned this behaviour, which they believe illegitimate and characteristic of what they judge to be 'irregular' masonic organisations with which they have no associations. 'Regular' (British-style) masonic organisations claim to outlaw any masonic bodies engaging in political activities, or adopting sectarian religious positions. There is a determined effort by masonic organisations to make the public more aware of the general principles of masonry, with the intention of ending confusions of this type. Leading masons urge that members be less unnecessarily secretive about their activities. This masonic version of 'glasnost' can not be dissociated from the realisation that freemasonry has to look to, and amend, its public image. The three Grand

Lodges of Scotland, Ireland and England now acknowledge that the interest and suspicions that their activities arouse among non-masons demand some response. Public perceptions of freemasonry are believed to have developed from partial information about the order. Seldom do the 'profane' have little more than snippets of real information, which are then transformed into various tales of variable (and dubious) accuracy. The Grand Lodges have adopted their new position in an attempt to remedy these problems.

Thus, within Scottish freemasonry there is a welcome trend towards a greater openness. Marcus Humphrey, when Scottish Grand Master, encouraged others to be more open about masonry, and he led by example. Having previously granted interviews to newspapers, he became the first Scottish Grand Master to be interviewed on radio.[6] Despite his own efforts, he is under no illusions about the problems masonry faces. He believes that it will be 'a long haul to overcome the preconceptions' of the public and that, as the three Grand Lodges only took the decision to be more open four or five years ago, there remains much to do. Commenting upon the views of the wider public, he said: "It's public perception. We have suffered from a bad public perception for a very long time. And we are all now trying to change this perception. It's going to take a very long time.'

The student views described above show the enormity of the task facing masonry; and there also remain masons at all levels who are very suspicious of openness and of discussions with non-masons. One senior mason argued that freemasonry should retreat to its long-held and trusted position of ignoring comments made about it by outsiders, and should not respond to criticism. But Humphrey, like other senior masons supporting 'glasnost', points to Scottish masonry's past record of openness. Until the 1930s considerable newspaper coverage was devoted to masonry; today some local newspapers publish small reports of masonic events. Humphrey was convinced that in the smaller Scottish communities everyone knew who the masons were, and recognised the good social and charitable work they carried out there; unjustifiable worries about masonic malpractice and the wielding of unfair influence were characteristic of larger, more anonymous communities.

Ironically, however, freemasonry has probably brought some of its negative image upon itself by its previous attempts at openness and positive self-publicity. The Craft tends to give considerable publicity to its adherents from the more prestigious sectors of society. Originally this was a response to the accusations, derived from the activities of 'irregular' masonry, that freemasonry was a subversive conspiratorial organisation. To counter this image, masonry in Britain identified itself with the ruling elite. A central element of this masonic strategy was to reveal the identities of those masons who were prominent members of the elite, with the intention of demonstrating that masons had a vested interest in the maintenance of the *status quo*.[7] Ever since masons have drawn special attention to wealthy and powerful members of the order, even to the extent that it distorts the history of the movement. Stevenson has pointed out the contradiction in an organisation that asserts that it disregards social status, but which persists in minimising the role of the ordinary craftsmen, who were not operative stone-masons, in its evolution: historical accounts by masons rely 'on the snobbish assumption that it is only when the gentry take over the movement that it becomes freemasonry'.[8] Yet prior to the accusations of subversion and conspiracy, masonry had already courted power and influence. As early as 1630 Scottish masonic lodges sought the patronage of the local gentry. It was the introduction of individuals other than stone-masons into operative masonic lodges that produced the transformation to speculative masonry or freemasonry. Although freemasons have overstated the role of the gentry, they are correct to identify their presence in lodges as significant. The order became popular and was taken up in England, where the gentry played a greater role, introducing various innovations into freemasonry. Masonic exchanges between the two countries also led to some Scottish adaptations;[9] but the English example of a masonry with strong aristocratic associations, and royal patronage from the early eighteenth century, made the order much more acceptable and attractive to Scotland's own elite classes.

The Craft seemed increasingly to cut across some class boundaries, while still recognising class distinctions. Scottish masonry appeared a united body, which ran from skilled artisans through the middle classes to the aristocracy, with the added attraction of royal patronage, as exemplified by the Prince of Wales (later George IV), who was Scottish Grand Master Mason from 1805-20. Masonry stressed its powerful and famous members from the aristocracy and royalty (and still does so in contemporary publications).[10] Throughout the eighteenth and nineteenth centuries masonry attracted more and more gentleman masons, and appeared more and more interesting, attractive and influential to the middle and artisan classes who also increasingly applied to join. By 1900 Scottish freemasonry could give the appearance of exclusivity while containing most of the important members of society; and masonry could call on prestigious figures to publicise their patronage of masonic events, and to assist directly at them in a variety of ways.

The Glasgow Provincial Grand Lodge held a 'Grand Masonic Bazaar' in the St Andrews Hall which ran for four days in October 1903. Special train fares were introduced for those wishing to attend: the masonic affiliations of the railway directors can not have hindered this helpful decision. Among the masonic patrons was the Lord Provost, Sir John Ure Primrose, leading Rangers shareholder and holder of a handful of company directorships. Former Lord Provosts were not neglected: the shipowner, Sir James Bell and Sir Samuel Chisholm, a wholesale grocer and active member of a number of religious, charitable and temperance societies adorned the list of patrons. The official patronage of the Grand Lodge, with its aristocrats and two members of parliament, was only to be expected. Other masonic MPs with local connections openly gave support. They were: Bonar Law, later to be Prime Minister; Col. J. M. Denny of the Denny shipbuilding company; the industrialist, Alex Cross; Sir John Stirling-Maxwell and M. Hugh Shaw-Stewart, local lairds and landowners with a range of commercial and social interests; and the much smaller landowner, J. Parker Smith of the Jordanhill estate. Sir Wm George Pearce, sometime English south-coast MP, and son of Sir William Pearce, the deceased owner of the Fairfield shipyard and Provincial Grand Master of Glasgow, was another patron. Education and religion were not neglected in the array of talent brought together for the occasion. The Very Revd Story, the Principal of Glasgow University, and former Moderator of the Church of Scotland, and Sir John Neilson Cuthbertson, evangelist and chairman of the Glasgow School Board featured, along with the minister of Glasgow Cathedral. Various other local industrialists and Volunteer officers gave their support. Different patrons were called upon to open each day's proceedings; and, as a token of support, the King sent a floral bouquet from Sandringham.[11]

A similar event in Bathgate was organised by the town's Lodge Torphichen Kilwinning in 1901 to raise £2,000 for a new masonic hall. They obtained comparable support, showing that the centrality of masonry to local community life was not restricted to Glasgow; loyal, prestigious masons were to be found all over Scotland, and in Bathgate their wives were named as official patronesses of the event. From up to sixty miles from the town, the return fares were reduced to a quarter of the normal price by the North British Railway Company. The Grand Lodge of Scotland gave its support. Elected representatives were again to the fore: 'The Provost and Magistrates of Bathgate' were patrons; some of them, including the Provost, served on special lodge committees. Local MP, Alex Ure, gave his support, as did his wife. Many local landowners and businessmen were directly involved, with others supporting the bazaar through advertising. 'With what must have been most of Bathgate's businesses taking space,' states a recent masonic historical account, 'the souvenir handbook was packed with advertisements.'[12]

Events of this sort gave Scottish masonry considerable publicity. For example, both received considerable press coverage, with the prestigious members being highlighted. Newspaper reports identifying very prominent local and national figures with masonry were common. Reading newspapers from around the turn of the century yields the impression that masons were very significant in all sections of the community.

In Govan, then one of the largest burghs in Scotland, the construction business seemed to be almost exclusively in the grip of masons:[13] architects, measurers (surveyors) of various types, and the promoted and skilled employees of the building firms were masons. So were businessmen of all sorts and at all levels. In some areas of commerce, masonry seemed especially strong. From the licensed and hotel trade to banks and insurance companies, masons seemed to predominate, as they did in engineering companies. Shipyard owners and managers and foreman were all brothers together. Doctors, dentists, lawyers, teachers and ministers were masons. Well-known entertainers and theatrical personalities were even grouped in their very own Lodge Dramatic, No. 571, based in Glasgow. Footballers, bowlers and other sportsmen were masons. Politicians of a unionist true blue hue were masons; but so were liberals and a surprising number of ILPers; and so were the councillors, and the policemen, and the undertakers; and so often were the newspaper proprietors, which may explain why masonry seemed to be so important: for these impressions come from the *Govan Press*, owned by a mason who gave considerable coverage to masonic events, including reports of lodge meetings.

Press reports revealed no masonic secrets; but the masonic presence in Scottish society was no secret. The order was presented as having considerable influence, power, status and prestige. Professor Story could proclaim to masons that they were working 'secretly to be a power in the land'. What this actually meant is unclear, but such claims were not uncommon; and other reports also stressed the mutual assistance masons owed to one another.[14] The irony, given the contemporary masonic glasnost, is that much of the present image of masonry results from past public campaigns aimed at creating a positive masonic image. The aura of power and influence wafting around masonry was very strong – and seductive. Many applied who wished to become part of an elite and to experience the feeling of being in a secretive organisation to which so many important figures also belonged. The imagery was irresistible to some, but the imagery was also clear to the large number who, for whatever reason, remained outside the order.

FREEMASONRY THROUGH THE TWENTIETH CENTURY

Masonry believed that it commanded respect because of the size and especially the quality of masonic membership: James Hozier, MP, the Grand Master Mason claimed 100,000 Scottish Constitution masons in 1903, but he emphasised the importance of selectivity, stating that they could increase the number ten-fold if they took in all who applied. The epithet of 'the mafia of the mediocre' was highly inaccurate.[15] Masonry contained most of the elite of Scottish society. The Craft publicised its prestigious membership, and the wider masonic membership which had always had a substantial skilled working-class element grew, despite some concern about the loss of exclusivity. Members were increasingly drawn from all sections of the *male, skilled, Protestant* Scottish population, and the numbers probably peaked sometime in the inter-war period.[16]

Throughout this century masonic lodges have spread, with more being established in Scotland and abroad. In mid-1989, there were 1,135 Scottish constitution lodges, with 661 in Scotland itself, geographically widespread enough to cater for most of the inhabitants of Scotland; and, elsewhere in the world, the Scottish expatriate community can often also attend a Scottish lodge. (See Appendix A.). But some time since the heady days of the inter-war period, there has been a decline in members, which probably became more marked in the mid-1960s. Scottish freemasonry, with a considerably greater working-class proportion of members, is much less of a middle class phenomenon than English masonry. Many observers have judged the Scottish brotherhood to be less formal and snobbish and more democratic than their English brethren; this image has been one of the special attractions drawing masons to Scottish constitution lodges abroad.[17] Now, though, there is some concern that there is an under-representation of masons drawn from the professional and upper middle classes in Scotland.[18] There are no hard figures to demonstrate this problem. Masons can still be found in many professions, and there is still support from aristocratic families with a long family tradition of membership; but the strong impression is that there are fewer masons, especially younger masons, coming from these sections of society.

Even obtaining an accurate figure of overall masonic membership is not possible: the Scottish Grand Lodge itself can not provide precise figures, as there are a number of complicating factors. In his radio interview, Marcus Humphrey estimated there to be somewhere around 100,000 masons in Scotland. However, Scottish masons can by choosing to pay a once-only fee, which is fifteen times the annual subscription fee, obtain life membership. With age or illness or other life changes, many stop attending lodges, but they are still masons; the proud masonic claim is, 'Once a mason, always a mason'. Certainly, there are many more men obligated by their masonic vows than those simply attending lodges. The Grand Secretary confirmed that an estimate taking account of this possibility could lead to a membership figure nearer 150,000. But these estimates probably set the extremes of present masonic membership in Scotland.

Membership figures within this range do not show an organisation in terminal decline. Membership is higher than in 1903. Many other Scottish bodies would be delighted to claim as high a proportion of the population as members, and Humphrey has claimed that in recent years there has been an increase in interest.[19] Yet, given the high points of masonic membership, there are signs that, like other traditional societies, masonry now faces increased competition for membership and attendance as a result of the more varied leisure activities available; a challenge that may be being lost among the more prosperous sections of Scottish society. A university lecturer stated that he was withdrawing from any masonic involvement because he had much better things to do with his free time. He was also scornful of the suggestion that masonry was a means of obtaining influence and assistance; Scottish freemasonry was much less influential than in England, where he had been first initiated. Because of the large working-class membership in Scottish masonry, he believed that belonging to former-pupil associations of the fee-paying schools or to organisations like Rotary would offer much more in the way of useful contacts for advancement. Yet, like others, he was aware that some did join masonry in pursuit of personal advantage.

As the sample of students demonstrated, this is a common belief among non-masons: their responses revealed an underlying model of masonry as a conspiratorial organisation. Past publicity about Scottish masonry emphasised the powerful and elite masons who were members, and the supposed power and influence of Scottish freemasonry. Although the intention was to create a positive image for freemasonry, the presentation of masonry as a secretive organisation, which included and supported the British elite, and worked to achieve unspecified masonic ends, could only fuel suspicions about how it used its apparent power and influence. It can be no surprise that the perception of masonry as an establishment conspiracy seemed to be confirmed in some eyes, an image which claims even more support today; but the same conspiratorial image, so repellent to some, would prove to be an attraction for other potential recruits.

Present-day images are based on those of the past. The ruler of masonry, the Scottish Grand Master, was largely chosen from among the aristocratic or landowning classes, and many in the last century were active Unionist politicians in the Commons or the Lords. (See Appendix B for a list of Grand Masters over the last century.) Their prominence added to the mystique surrounding freemasonry, and further suggested that it was a right-wing, establishment club, despite its considerable working-class following and the presence at lower levels of active members of the Scottish Labour movement. Grand Master Masons still come from this section of Scottish society. Marcus Humphrey, a landowner, is a Conservative councillor on Grampian Regional Council. In Wolridge Gordon's case, his brother was the Conservative MP; Sir James McKay, a member of the anti-Labour coalition, the Progressive Party, was Lord Provost of Edinburgh in 1969-72. But the best known political figure in Grand Lodge, Viscount Whitelaw, former deputy Prime Minister, holds no important office within Scottish masonry. Scottish masonry still receives great support from across class and political divides: the senior men in Scottish masonry have been consistently unrepresentative of the organisation as a whole. Recent Scottish Grand Masters come from similar social backgrounds to their predecessors but, capable as they are, they are less well-known in contemporary Scottish society than their predecessors. And there can be no doubt that turn-of-the-century *Provincial* Grand Masters were much more representative of the Scottish establishment than is now the case.[20]

The tendency to publicise prominent adherents is not only a characteristic of masonic bodies: many organisations have believed that the personal achievements of members reflects on them; but few other societies can have such an image of mystery and intrigue surrounding them. Pride in the social status of masons increases suspicion among the 'profane'. Public concern about freemasonry cannot be divorced from the apparently secretive nature of the organisation. Freemasons deny that they are a secret organisation. Some used to define the institution as a 'society with secrets'. Now the apparent preference is for masons to style themselves only as people who 'value their privacy'.[21] Perhaps some criticism will now be deflected by the adoption of a strategy of greater openness. However, enveloped in the often self-created images which mix power, privilege and secrecy, the masonic orders can expect to remain objects of suspicion and criticism. To overcome these images will be very difficult, regardless of the reality of actual masonic principles and practice. And masonry faces another serious problem here; some aspects of masonry cannot be revealed, and much of the meaning of masonry is a question of interpretation.

Masonry cannot be totally open, or issue definitive interpretive statements, and still remain masonry. Masonry, claiming to be a 'progressive science', depends on 'initiatic secrets' which can only be revealed to the applicant in the process of his being made a mason; the interpretive flexibility of the Craft is at the core of its very existence. Applicants to become freemasons prepare for their ritual examination in the lodge by learning to respond to a routine series of questions with the correct answers. One of these answers gives the order's own definition of freemasonry which is that: 'Freemasonry is a peculiar system of morality veiled in allegory and illustrated by symbol.'[22] The masonic rites and rituals, which rely heavily on allegory and mystic symbolism, offer a very general and vague framework for the masonic moral code which masons are obligated to follow. The meaning of masonry is therefore a very personal matter, and this poses a variety of problems for anyone, supporter or detractor alike, wishing to utter the definitive statement about the meaning of masonry in principle or in practice.

MASONRY AND THE USE OF CONSPIRACY THEORIES

Uncertainty about the precise nature of freemasonry does help those detractors who rely on conspiracy theories, persistently seeing masonic influence determining Scottish society. By itself, the decrease in support for freemasonry from the elite of Scottish society ought to challenge the crude conspiracy theory of freemasonry. But any ready reliance on a conspiracy theory is worrying; conspiracy theories are often a very unattractive form of explanation of social events.

The consistent use of conspiracy theories as an explanation often indicates prejudiced thinking. Psychological research has begun to explore the use of conspiracy theories as explanations for the perceived injustices of everyday life.[23] A conspiracy theory can be seen as a very powerful attribution of responsibility for the cause of events, which identifies the machinations of a particular group of people as the underlying explanation for what occurs. By revealing the conspiracy to others, individuals using the conspiracy theory as an explanation also appear to display their own special and privileged understanding of the world. Unlike others, they are not going to be deceived by how events might appear, or indeed how they have been designed to appear. Conspiracy theorists believe that they can see through what they judge to be the manipulations and deliberate diversions of the conspirators, and detect the actual underlying influences of the group that is really determining events.

The machinations of some specified group of others is postulated to lie behind many problems and injustices in contemporary society; this minority is judged to discriminate actively against the majority, resulting in disproportionate benefits being attained by the minority. Numerous events can be explained by their actions, so the conspiracy theorist appears to have an important analytical concept which makes sense of the social world. Even when the evidence seems to direct attention to some other social organisation or social causation, the conspiracy theorist interprets this as a deliberate sowing of confusion in order to cover the tracks of the real conspirators. The inability to provide evidence to substantiate the claims of a conspiracy need cause no embarrassment; this simply serves to show how clever and powerful the conspirators are. And the presence of some circumstantial evidence is almost ideal – it truly reveals nothing, but allows attributions of a conspiracy to appear credible.

Exploration of the ideology of conspiracy theories emphasises the need for caution in exploring freemasonry, and raises the issue of whether concerns expressed about freemasonry reveal widespread prejudice *against* freemasonry, rather than an objective pronouncement that the order is itself a conspiratorial society and a source of prejudice. Certainly many who condemn freemasonry in no uncertain terms seem to know little about the organisation. The subjects whose definite views were reported above included 66 per cent who declared that they did not know much about freemasonry. And all of the remainder, bar one, accepted that they had limited knowledge. Only three (6 per cent), one Catholic woman and two Protestant men, answered that they did not know why men became masons nor what were the most important aspects of masonry. All the rest volunteered motivations for men to become masons, though a few did admit ignorance of masonry itself. Subjects can only be responding on the basis of the generally accepted and socially dominant beliefs about freemasonry found in this society.

Few realise that fears about masonry have featured in some of the most prejudiced and irrational movements in history.[24] Even more intriguingly, given the assumptions of an anti-Catholic bias in freemasonry, many anti-masonic movements in the USA constructed conspiracy theories in which masons and Catholics were presented as being different heads of the same conspiratorial hydra, with the freemasons being believed to be heavily influenced by, amongst others, the Jesuits! Although it is difficult to imagine such a concoction of beliefs having much success in Scotland today, the question remains as to whether contemporary beliefs about freemasonry are any the less absurd.

The historically common portrayal of freemasonry as a conspiracy, and the relationship between prejudice and the use of conspiracy theories, deliver strong warnings against any uncritical reliance upon common preconceptions about masonry. Yet it would be wrong to dismiss accounts of events simply because they invoke conspiracies, which are, by definition, difficult to prove. A *consistent* reliance on conspiracy theories reveals a prejudiced attitude, unrelated to real life events, but this does not mean that all allegations of a conspiracy are unrelated to reality.[25] Conspiracies do occur. Systematic research into Scottish freemasonry, with the aim of testing the descriptions of masonry obtained from non-masons and masons alike, is required before any valid judgement can be passed on the impact of freemasonry on Scottish life and before any accusations of conspiratorial behaviour are justified.

MASONRY AND DISCRIMINATION

Masons are themselves aware that, just as non-masons have seen the order as a means of self-advancement, so have some who have become members. If the common belief is that masonry serves this purpose, then it is inevitable that there will be those attracted to become members because they believe this to be true. Presumably, there are members who become masons because they see masonry in conspiratorial terms. However, the order is convinced that the lessons communicated by masonic teaching and ritual ensure that masons know that such behaviour is unmasonic. It is accepted that there will remain some masons who will, despite these strictures, misuse the organisation, and senior masons express strong views on the need to remedy this problem.

Perhaps paradoxically, senior masons do also accept that masons will tend to show some preference towards other masons. Preferential behaviour is excused by them as the unavoidable result of having something in common with another person, and is argued to be a feature of most social organisations, but they judge masonry to be less prone to actions of this sort than other groups. Most of the concern expressed by non-masons is about masonic favouritism, and masons become very irritated by what they see as unfair accusations. However, one master mason, who savaged the wrong types who joined freemasonry for the wrong reasons, identified and then defended a practice that he thought open to misinterpretation by outsiders. Like other masons, he believed preferential hiring in the labour market based on common group membership to be inevitable; he also claimed to know of two businesses, each owned by masons and in one of which he was himself employed, that broadly pursued a policy of employing only brother masons. One firm, in engineering-related trade, he believed to employ only masons when selecting male staff. The other was in the service sector, and employed a number of women, but the men were masons.

The practice was apparently defended by the accountant of one of the businesses, who was also a mason. The interviewee stated that he believed, along with the accountant, that a mason employing only masons ought to be able to ensure greater harmony and loyalty in the work-place, and that their masonic bonds should determine that employer and employee could have a greater trust in the other. Similar statements were made by 'Vindex', the pseudonymous, masonic English clergyman, who further believed that masonic membership was, in itself, an additional qualifying attribute for a job applicant because, having been accepted by masonry, the man could be assumed to be of an upstanding and moral character.[26] However, it was on this very point that the interviewee presented his own reservations about the employment policy. He was concerned that there were too many who had joined masonry for the wrong reasons; too many who had joined to exploit their membership of masonry, with the result that masonic membership no longer provided an absolute guarantee of a man's character to either prospective employer or employee. If masonic membership was not a true measure of a man's upright character, then he was not sure that employing only masons was a justifiable practice.

No evidence to support his claims of masonic discrimination was provided by the interviewee. The most important point is that he clearly believed this to be the practice where he worked, and he believed it to be defensible, as long as masonry selected applicants for membership carefully. The problem is that, if this practice does occur, men will choose to become masons because of the practice rather than because they wish to be good masons! Numerous stories of this type have been volunteered. None can be properly substantiated. But one is very striking, demonstrating the unusual range of careers supposed to have been sometime in the masonic grip. The very reliable informant occupies a highly responsible post in a Scottish college of education, and had a close friend who retired some time ago as one of Her Majesty's Inspectors of Education. The friend had become a mason because of his very firmly-held conviction that this was necessary in order to be appointed as an HMI in the immediate post-war period; and he claimed that his experiences once in the inspectorate confirmed this belief. Again, his beliefs were genuine, and consistently expressed. Masonry has been prominent in British educational circles, and the retired HMI's account could even fit into the 'Kirriemuir career', the recent description of the shared set of experiences common to those small town, male, Protestants who formed the loyal, cohesive group, including HMIs, that administered Scottish education until the mid-1960s. Again, without firmer evidence, suggestions of masonic influence in educational circles remain hypotheses that require further exploration.[27]

Prominent masons tend to be outraged at suggestions that masonry is used in this sort of way. They assure non-masons that an individual who flaunted his masonry at a job interview would get short shrift from them, or from other masons faced with such a situation. There is little reason to doubt that their views are honestly held; senior masonic office costs individuals considerable time and often money. One senior mason pointed out that masonry had not helped him in business; his business would be much better off if he had spent less time on masonic duties. But there is a problem for freemasonry when tales of the importance of masonic influence come from masons themselves. If masons can believe that masonic discrimination can not only happen, but be justifiable; and if men can become masons to obtain important positions in which their experiences lead them still to believe that masonic membership is an essential prerequisite for the post; then the 'profane' can be excused from having doubts about the possible effects of masonic influence, though they cannot be excused the suspension of all of their critical faculties. It is absurd to believe that masonic membership inevitably implies a conspiracy. But if some masons can also believe that masonry can be used for conspiratorial purposes, then presumably others can, as these examples suggest, transform that belief into action. Masonry used to discriminate positively effectively discriminates negatively against non-masons; this also raises the possibility that some might use masonry as a mechanism to discriminate deliberately against specific groups of people.

SCOTTISH MASONRY AND ANTI-CATHOLICISM

Catholics are the group most commonly assumed to be discriminated against by freemasons. Despite the official eschewal of sectarianism by Scottish freemasonry, there can be little doubt that many

masons are deeply anti-Catholic. The BBC Radio Scotland interview with Marcus Humphrey produced the biggest listener response
the programme had ever received.[28] Some argued that masonry was
not anti-Catholic, and that Catholics could join. Programme pre-
senter Colin Bell recounted information from Donny McLeod, a
Perth mason 'that in his lodge in Fiji there were Scots, Fijians,
English, Irish, Fijian-born Indians… and TWO Roman Catholics!'
Other listeners included a Renfrew Catholic, Mr McDermott, who
had applied to join a masonic lodge and had been refused membership, and Derek McCulloch, a former mason, who categorically
stated that Catholics are excluded from freemasonry in many
Scottish areas. McCulloch, a former masonic lodge office-bearer,
had earlier expressed in interviews[29] his own dismay at the extent of
anti-Catholic prejudice displayed by masons. Even masonic social
events could be marred by some who insisted on singing sectarian
songs, a practice which too many other masons had simply seemed
to accept. Bell's co-presenter, Lesley Riddoch, gave her judgement
on the issue:

> I must admit, it also seems odd, if no prejudice at all exists, that
> we should have got quite so many calls like these… George
> Porter of Irvine wants us to have a discussion on the Catholic
> societies such as the Knights of St Columba, and complains
> that it is always the masons who are discussed… John
> Peterson, of Hamilton, who is a mason, wants a full and frank
> discussion of the Knights of St Columba – with, he adds, two
> *Protestant* interviewers, which is a fairly obvious, and wildly
> inaccurate, innuendo.[30]

The students' images of masonry demonstrated that suspicions
about masonry were common, with religious affiliations irrelevant as
an explanation of their beliefs. Yet many masons readily dismiss any
suggestion that masons discriminate in favour of brother masons,
implying such suggestions to be Catholic in origin; and, just as
readily, masons themselves suggest that Catholics conspire in favour
of their own co-religionists. Accusations that a minority group
conspires against the wider society are often a characteristic of
prejudiced majority group members who are themselves guilty of
conspiring against the rights of the minority.[31] If some masons do
hold to the prejudiced view that Catholics form a conspiratorial
social group which threatens the position of the majority in Scotland, then the use of masonry to counter this perceived threat could
well follow. And prejudice against Catholics in masonic lodges can
be very strong, as the responses to BBC Scotland suggested. Masons
are not Orangemen: the two organisations have no formal connec-

tions; although the evolution of Orangeism in Ireland was sponsored by northern Protestant masons, physical fights between members of each order occurred in early-nineteenth-century Ireland.[32] Yet Scots Orangemen, and other anti-Catholic Protestants, can believe masonry to be a parallel organisation to the Orange societies, and masonic lodges can become conduits for anti-Catholic sentiment.

The Past Depute Grand Master confirmed that, suffering from this delusion, anti-Catholic men do join but he claimed Scottish freemasonry 'was not prejudiced as a body'. Scottish masonry attempted to ensure that members learned that religious prejudice was opposed to masonic principles, but he knew there were serious problems to overcome in communicating that message. He said: 'In some areas even senior office bearers don't know much about it; and they haven't thought very clearly about it. And they can have this anti-Catholic bias.' He knew that it is relatively easy to find masons making strongly anti-Catholic statements, some of which have even appeared in past masonic publications. He commented that: 'We've always had these sorts of people, who would make statements like that. But I don't think that that would be an attitude which would be held today, or supported today. In fact, it would be condemned today.'

The problem remains for Scottish freemasonry that, by the actions of its own members, it is tainted by anti-Catholic prejudice, and the fears that some masons may use the order to assist in discriminating against Catholics appears to be a hypothesis requiring further investigation. Rangers Football Club has been seen by some to be a possible example of this practice. Though he believed his hypothesis to be untestable, and evidence too difficult to obtain, Murray suggested that the traditional policy of not recruiting Catholic footballers could be the result of a masonic grip on the Ibrox club.[33]

It is possible to uncover various inter-relationships between Rangers and freemasonry; they are personified by John (later Sir John) Ure Primrose, who first became involved with Rangers in 1887, and was the club patron by 1888. Primrose was an ardent Unionist, breaking with the Liberal Party over Irish Home Rule in 1886, which he staunchly opposed throughout his life. Like many others associated with Rangers, he was also an active and energetic mason. By 1890, Primrose had involved the club in a fund-gathering event for the Grand Lodge of Scotland organised by his mother lodge, Lodge Plantation, No. 581. Here, he publicly pledged himself and Rangers Football Club to support the masonic cause. Primrose remained a crucial influence on the club for all his life.

Though he stepped down as club chairman in 1923, he was still a director when he died in 1924.[34] The close relationship between Rangers and freemasonry seems to have continued ever since then. Don Kitchenbrand, who played with Rangers in the mid-1950s, thought that it was expected that players would be initiated into freemasonry.[35] Both Marcus Humphrey and the Past Depute Grand Master were aware of this practice, with the latter also commenting that:

> They do tend when they bring people like Terry Butcher up, or Roberts, or what have you – you'll find that they'll appear in some lodge around, and they'll be made a Scottish mason up here. That is, I think, just part of the, sort of, the Ibrox set-up, which has existed for a very long time. I am very pleased to see it broken down at last – I wouldn't want the masons to be associated with Rangers policy, though a lot of them are masons.

Exactly how this use of masonry fitted into the anti-Catholic recruitment policies of Rangers requires much further analysis and discussion, but masonic affiliation appears to have been meant to bond players together, and to ensure loyalty to the club's and the supporters' particular value system. Senior masons may not wish masonry to be associated with behaviour of this sort, but other masons have clearly thought and acted otherwise. And if some masons could believe that this was an acceptable interpretation of masonic principles, and use their masonry as an appropriate mechanism for this purpose, then other masons may have come to similar conclusions. If, for some, this was masonry at leisure, then masonry could also be put to work. Freemasonry may have been used by *some* masons to block Catholics from being employed or promoted in other areas of Scottish life, as some commentators have proposed. But it would be a fundamental error to blame principally Scottish freemasonry for anti-Catholic prejudice.

SCOTLAND AND ANTI-CATHOLICISM

Both the Past Grand Master and the Past Depute Grand Master believed that historically freemasonry and anti-Catholicism had been linked because most Scots, and consequently most masons, shared the intense prejudices against Catholics and Irish, and that much of contemporary anti-Catholicism in masonry today is a relic of those sentiments. The Past Depute Grand Master, a retired doctor who had worked with the oil industry, gave an impressive example of what he believed to have been the active discrimination suffered by Catholics in Scotland, and he explained the beliefs which were used to justify this blatant prejudice. He revealed that: 'I was born and brought up in a Scottish Oils area. I was in practice there. Scottish Oils and BP, up to – not too many years ago, never promoted a Catholic up to the rank of foreman or above. Didn't matter how good his qualifications were! He never became a member of staff. He never became a foreman.' When asked how the policy operated, he replied:

> It was unspoken policy; absolutely unspoken policy – but it happened. It doesn't happen now, but it happened then. Any BP person of the older age group, of my age group, will tell you that. It was just unspoken policy. It just didn't happen. A man would be asked what his religion was before he was appointed to any job. And it was a definite bias. But it had nothing to do with masons. It was just to do with the fact that Scottish Oils and BP were controlled by old Presbyterian stock; and that was it! Just strong men as Protestants, who wouldn't allow these Irish immigrants and Catholics to go into any position where they could have advanced their friends. But in masonry that's never been a problem.

The overt justification for this blatant discrimination was the assumption that Catholics would conspire against Protestants, a belief that seems central to the structure of Scottish Protestant prejudice against Catholics. Individuals who consistently rely on conspiracy theories normally belong to the majority group within society; they believe the minority group to be conspiring, or supported by a conspiracy, to deprive majority group members of their privileged positions, and they believe themselves justified in operating in a conspiratorial manner against the minority group. Given the structure of these beliefs, and the beliefs about the nature of masonry contained within the common imagery, it cannot be a surprise that Scottish anti-Catholics were attracted to Scottish masonry. Though there is no reason to doubt the statement that masonry itself played no part in this particular example of anti-Catholic discrimination, the oil companies did give considerable assistance to masonic lodges in oilproducing countries, which were primarily for their employees when abroad.[36] Strong Protestants would no doubt wish to encourage an organisation seen to be fundamentally supportive of Scottish Protestantism and unsympathetic to Catholics. The association between the two may even have led some to believe, erroneously, that masonic influence was at work here just as it played ball with Rangers at Ibrox Park.

Although it was, in a strict sense, masons and not masonry that operated this way, Scottish freemasonry must still carry some re-

sponsibility for the anti-Catholicism historically associated with it as
an organisation. Some senior masons strongly disapprove of religious prejudice, but more could be done to tackle the issue. One
serious problem is that many masons themselves, as members of a
very traditional society, inhabit a world which relies on traditional
Scottish stereotypes. Masons discussing women or Catholics show
this most clearly. Masons give credit to their wives for their support,
which frees them as men to play their leading roles as masons: and
some also see masonry as a body which holds the line against
feminism, and allows men to limit (symbolically) what they see as
any further encroachments by women.

In a similar way Catholics in Scotland have been stereotyped, and
are seen as a 'problem' group within Scottish society, a stereotype
which inevitably influences the thinking in Scottish freemasonry.[37]
The historical antagonism between Catholicism and freemasonry
had some effect, adding to Scottish masons' antipathy to Catholics;
but freemasonry in Scotland appears to have identified itself with
Protestantism fairly soon after the Reformation.[38] Catholic condemnations of freemasonry were much later than this, and in other
countries prominent Catholics remained in freemasonry until well
into the nineteenth century. Daniel O'Connell, Ireland's 'Liberator'
was not only a mason, but undertook duties on behalf of the Irish
Grand Lodge;[39] and in other countries it seems that Catholics can be
found to belong continuously to masonic lodges. But in Scotland the
'problem orientation' to Catholics seems to have ensured that any
Catholic applicants were simply excluded from masonic membership or, for a long period of masonic history, if any Catholics were
allowed to enter, both they and the Craft kept it a close masonic
secret. In addition, though the only strong evidence comes from the
interplay of masonry and anti-Catholicism at Rangers Football
Club, masonry seems to have been enlisted as a mechanism to
exclude Catholics from sectors of Scottish life. But Scottish freemasonry is not the source of this anti-Catholicism, though in some
areas some masons appear to have turned their order into a bastion
of anti-Catholicism. The source lies deep in the mythology of
Scottish Protestant culture, from which masonry has taken such
sustenance.

Scottish freemasonry has to an extent sustained and enhanced the
prejudice against Catholics in Scotland. The masonic bond helped
band diverse Protestants together in mutual antagonism towards
Catholics, but masonry has also truthfully reflected the strength of
that prejudice buried deep within Scottish Protestant culture.[40] In a
similar manner, German freemasonry was riddled with anti-

Semitism and American masonry was profoundly racist, opposing black masonic recruitment.[41] These examples demonstrate very real limits to the practical implementation of the high principles claimed by freemasonry. The actual prejudice does not lie within masonry; it is embedded within the particular local culture, and the closer that masonry is bound to that culture, the more will masonry express the prejudices of that community. Like other identifiably Scottish organisations, masonry has had to shoulder an additional burden. A stateless nation, Scotland has had to express its national identity through a variety of other means. Presbyterianism, and the national church, preaching vigorous opposition to Catholicism, were exceptionally important in expressing a specifically *Scottish* identity. The increasingly globally organised, and globally recognised, *Scottish* variant of masonry seems to have been another means by which some could express a distinctively Scottish identity of sorts.

Traditionally, Scottish masonry has been closely allied to the Church of Scotland, which is why masonry, which recognises no particular religion, came to be seen as quintessentially Protestant. An apparently Protestant masonry could appear to be even more expressively Scottish, and a masonry which did not quickly take on this character would have been a object of great suspicion to the Kirk.[42] For many Scottish masons, Protestantism and freemasonry have been as close as brothers. When the 250th anniversary celebrations of the founding of the Grand Lodge took place in 1986, masonic ministers were prominent. The then Moderator, the Rt Revd Professor Robert Craig was in attendance, and the final masonic thanksgiving service of the Grand Lodge celebrations was held in Glasgow Cathedral with Dr W. Morris, minister of the cathedral, as one of the officiating ministers.[43]

Perthshire East Provincial Grand Lodge celebrated the same event with a thanksgiving service in St John's Kirk of Perth. The Revd F. Routledge Bell, formerly Grand Lodge Senior Chaplain, addressed the masons. He placed the Kirk and masonry at the heart of the nation, its culture and society; he eloquently expressed the belief in the strong influence of freemasonry, allied to the established Kirk, in the formation of contemporary Scotland: 'The history of our land is made up of the story of those institutions which have moulded Scotland, and Freemasonry is foremost amongst these.' He believed that masonry should be safe from attacks from within the Kirk: 'We ought always to remember that there is an inevitable relationship between Faith, the Church and the Craft.' Masonry, the Kirk, and Scotland were intertwined: 'In an age when there is much criticism of our Order these facts are at once our cause and our defence. Apart from the Church, from the works of which the Craft came, and with which it has been so long connected, there can be few institutions in Scotland of greater age and more noble purpose.'[44]

Thus, it was to the genuine offence of masons that an over-whelming majority of the 1989 General Assembly backed the report of the Panel of Doctrine that masons in the Kirk should reconsider their membership of masonic orders, on the grounds that masonic membership was theologically unsound for Christians.[45] The actual compatibility between membership of freemasonry and an individual church is a complex one, and the theological arguments are too complex to allow for present discussion.[46] In essence, masonic religious requirements are simple: all applicants must believe in 'a Supreme Being'. For Kirk members, this has inevitably been Christ, and they believe that freemasonry assists them in understanding their religion. They deny that masonry takes away from their belief. The Provincial Grand Master interviewed joined the Kirk as a result of masonry, and a master mason's wife confirmed that it was only after he became a mason that her husband seriously thought about religion and voluntarily attended normal church services.

However, the relationship between Scottish freemasonry and Protestantism is a very complex one. Much depends upon the interpretation of masonry made by an individual mason. The simple idea that Scottish masonry is inevitably Protestant is invalid. There are three masonic lodges established by the Jewish community in Scotland.[47] Moreover, evangelical Protestant churches have long been actively opposed to freemasonry. The 1989 Assembly was even visited by an anti-masonic demonstration led by Pastor Jack Glass and his Twentieth Century Reformation Movement.[48]

The studied indifference to attacks from fundamentalist Protestants, and the ready acceptance of members of these churches as masons, is further evidence that the antagonism to Catholics was not simply a response to the anti-masonic rulings of their church. Numerous other Christian churches have now adopted critical stances on freemasonry, on the basis that masonic membership is not compatible with belief in Christianity. A number still leave the final decision to their church members' individual consciences, and urge the need for pastoral care for those who remain masons. This is now the position of the Church of Scotland and the Methodists. Despite some considerable public confusion over their position, the Catholic Church has reaffirmed its opposition to freemasonry. The confusion seems to have arisen from attempts to stress pastoral concern for Catholics who are masons and from the open recognition that there are very good people in masonry doing very good charitable works. Ironically, given Scotland's history, contemporary Catholic theological criticisms of masonry are very little different from those of the Kirk, even though Catholicism takes a stronger position against membership, as does the Free Presbyterian Kirk, which has banned freemasonry outright since 1927.[49]

CONCLUSION

Scottish freemasonry is a complex phenomenon. A variety of interpretations of it can be made, and believed by some masons to be justified. There is much associated with masonry that can be criticised; masonry can be used in discriminatory ways. But more research needs to be reported before it is possible to identify the extent to which culpability can be attributed to freemasonry rather than to the actions of individual masons. The lack of an identifiable and agreed masonic message, the source of the personally satisfying complexity of masonry for individual masons, allows for a variety of interpretations of masonic practice. A fuller account of freemasonry must await analysis of the underlying ideology of the order, which will reveal the extent to which different interpretations can be legitimated; and more research must be reported on the organisation and actual operation of masonry. But some conclusions can be drawn.

Ironically, because of historical attempts to create a positive image to counter being seen as a subversive conspiratorial organisation, freemasonry now has the image of an establishment conspiracy which discriminates in favour of the dominant groups in society. The image of a powerful organisation based on mutual self-help has attracted some to join for reasons of self-advancement. In addition, the uncertainty about the precise moral nature of masonry has allowed some masons to construct versions of freemasonry which are self-serving, discriminatory and draw upon the deep-rooted prejudice against Catholics in Scotland. Masonry is not primarily responsible for these prejudices; they are part of traditional Protestant culture in Scottish society, though they are probably found more often in Scottish freemasonry, and certainly no less! But Scottish masonry does present an opportunity for men to band together and transform their anti-Catholic prejudices into collective discriminatory action.

Another point must be stressed: it is absurd to believe that masonic membership inevitably reveals an individual who is prejudiced or suffering from some other moral defect. The ready stereotyping of masons or the hasty recourse to general conspiracy theories of masonry are both unacceptable. Some do join masonry for self-advancement because of the very same beliefs that lead

others to criticise the order so readily. Freemasonry does have some
considerable heart-searching to do about how to stop some of the
practices of some of its own membership – but there are positive
motivations for joining and enjoying the masonic brotherhood. It is
an organisation which serves many human social needs, and it does
involve itself in projects which are beneficial to the community. The
Past Depute Grand Master should be allowed the last word; he
communicated just some of the good reasons for becoming a mason,
and his own pleasure in continuing as a mason, when he said: 'It's a
happy system: It's a happy business. It's voluntary. We don't get
paid for doing this. It's just great fun. Great fun! And you meet so
many nice folk from all over the world; that's what it's all about.'

ACKNOWLEDGEMENTS

I am grateful to the senior masons who agreed to be interviewed,
especially Mr Humphrey who helped me contact the other senior
masons. Thanks also to all those others, masons and non-masons
alike, who assisted but wish to remain anonymous. Special thanks to
Derek McCulloch who shared his views of masonry with me over a
number of discussions. BBC Radio Scotland helped by providing
the transcript of listeners' comments and information on the
response to the feature on the Knights of St Columba. Mr. Hazel,
Scottish Grand Secretary and Monsignor Docherty, Catholic
Church in Scotland, were both very kind to an inquisitive stranger at
the other end of a telephone line. The present account would have
been impossible without either the students who completed the
questionnaire or David Cornwell who distributed it, while I was a
temporary senior lecturer in psychology at the University of Ulster at
Coleraine - an institution which granted me the time to carry out the
interviews with the senior masons. Special thanks are due to Tom
Gallagher for his encouragement during the writing of this chapter.
I wish to dedicate this chapter to the memory of my nephew, Mark
Hamilton, who was seriously ill when it was being written and who
died soon after it was completed.

APPENDIX A

Table 9.2 Number of lodges in Scottish provincial Grand Lodges

Province	Number of Lodges
Aberdeen City	12
Aberdeenshire East	14
Aberdeenshire West	19
Argyll & the Isles	18
Ayrshire[c]	44
Banfshire	14
Caithness	4
Dumfriesshire	16
Dunbartonshire	21
East Lothian & Berwickshire	13
Edinburgh[ab]	40
Fife & Kinross	50
Forfarshire	32
Galloway	13
Glasgow[b]	85
Inverness-shire	15
Kilwinning[c]	1
Kincardineshire	6
Lanarkshire Middle Ward	42
Lanarkshire Upper Ward	16
Linlithgowshire	19
Midlothian	17
Moray & Nairn	11
Orkney & Zetland	8
Perthshire East	18
Perthshire West	14
Renfrewshire East	38
Renfrewshire West	9
Ross & Cromarty	11
Roxburgh, Peebles & Selkirkshire	11
Stirlingshire	24
Sutherland	6

Source: 1989 Yearbook

Notes

[a.] Because the location of the Grand Lodge is in Edinburgh, lodges in Edinburgh belong to a 'Metropolitan District' rather than a 'Province', and there is a chairman of the District Committee rather than a Provincial Grand Master.

[b] The number of Glasgow lodges is larger than this as a number of lodges actually within the present Glasgow boundary remain within the older masonic boundaries, even when established after the abolition of these boundaries. As a result some Glasgow lodges are to be found operating under neighbouring Provinces. A similar pattern exists in Edinburgh; and also perhaps Aberdeen.

[c] In 1983 it was agreed that Kilwinning lodge become a Province in its own right, set apart from the Province of Ayrshire.

Table 9.3 Location and number of lodges overseas under the Grand
Lodge of Scotland

Location	Number of lodges
District Grand Lodges	
Barbados	6
Eastern India	3
Eastern Province of the Cape of Good Hope	14[a]
Far East	10[b]
Ghana	29
Gilbraltar	3
Guyana	5
Jamaica & the Bahamas	20
Middle East	10[c]
Natal	25[a]
Newfoundland	16
New Zealand North	4
New Zealand South	7
Nigeria	65
Sierra Leone & the Gambia	14
Transvaal, Orange Free State & Northern Cape	104[a]
Trinidad & Tobago	11
Western Australia	8
Western Australia, Goldfields District	7
Western India	26
Western Province of the Cape of Good Hope	15[a]
Zambia	12
Zimbabwe	22
Under Grand Superintendents	
Bermuda	3
Chile & Peru	6
East Africa	6
Under Grand Lodge Supervision	
Belgium	2
Botswana	2
Fiji	1
Jordan	1
Lebanon	5
Malawi	4
Malta	1
Mauritius	1
Philippine Islands	1
Republic of Panama	2
Sri Lanka	1
Togo	1
West India Islands	1

Notes
[a] South African lodges, totalling 158, some operating in Namibia!
[b] Far East refers to Korea, Hong Kong & Japan
[c] Middle East actually refers to Thailand, Malaysia & Singapore!

APPENDIX B

A CENTURY OF GRAND MASTER MASONS

1885-92	Sir Archibald Campbell, later 1st Lord Blythswood
1892-4	George Arden, 11th Earl of Haddington
1894-7	Sir Charles Dalrymple of Newhailes, 1st Bart.
1897-1900	Alexander, 18th Lord Saltoun
1900-4	The Honourable James Hozier, later 2nd Lord Newlands
1904-7	The Honourable Charles Maule Ramsay
1907-9	Sir Thomas D. G. Carmichael, later 1st Lord Carmichael
1909-13	John George, Marquis of Tullibardine, later 8th Duke of Atholl
1913-16	Sir Robert King Stewart of Murdostoun
1916-20	Brigadier-General Sir Robert Gordon Gordon Gilmour, 1st Bart.
1920-1	Archibald, 16th Earl of Eglinton and 4th Earl of Winton
1921-4	Edward James Bruce, 10th Earl of Elgin and 14th Earl of Kincardine
1924-6	John James, 12th Earl of Stair
1926-9	Archibald Douglas, 4th Lord Blythswood
1929-31	A. A Hagart Spiers of Elderslie
1931-3	Robert Edward, 11th Lord Belhaven and Stenton
1933-5	Alexander Arthur, 19th Lord Saltoun
1935-6	Sir Iain Colquhoun of Luss, 7th Bart.
1936-7	HRH The Duke of York, later HM King George VI
1937-9	Brigadier-General Sir Norman A. Orr Ewing, 4th Bart.
1939-42	Robert Arthur, Viscount Traprain, later 3rd Earl of Balfour
1942-5	Captain John Christie Stewart of Murdostoun
1945-9	Randolph, 12th Earl of Galloway
1949-53	Sir Charles Malcolm Barclay-Harvey of Kinord (also GM of South Australia, 1941-4)
1953-7	Alexander, 7th Lord Macdonald of Sleat
1957-61	Archibald, 17th Earl of Elginton and 5th Earl of Winton
1961-5	Andrew, Lord Bruce, later 11th Earl of Elgin and 15th Earl of Kincardine
1965-9	Major Sir Ronald Orr Ewing, 5th Bart.
1969-74	David Liddell-Grainger of Ayton
1974-9	Captain Robert Wolrige Gordon of Esslemont
1979-83	Sir James Wilson McKay
1983-8	J. M. Marcus Humphrey of Dinnet
1988-	Brigadier Sir Gregor MacGregor of MacGregor, Bart.

NOTES

(The scope and number of the notes have been reduced on grounds of space.)

1. Masonry, Freemasonry etc, are given the lower key perspective advocated by T. Gallagher, *Glasgow, The Uneasy Peace. Religious Tension in Modern Scotland, 1819-1914* (Manchester: Manchester University Press, 1987).
2. S. Knight, *The Brotherhood: The Secret World of the Freemasons* (London: Granada, 1984); M. Short, *Inside the Brotherhood: Further Secrets of the Freemasons* (London: Grafton, 1989).
3. Open-ended questions ensure the use of subjects' own spontaneous descriptions. Masons complain that 'conspiracy' is the dominant image of masonry: see J. Hamill, *The Craft: A History of English Freemasonry* (London: Crucible, 1986). Secrecy: see titles of Knight & Short's books.
4. Differences in claimed contacts with masons between Protestant males and females suggest inadequately representative population samples; this alone could explain any response differences between the four category groups.
5. See H. McShane and J. Smith, *No Mean Fighter* (London: Pluto, 1978); Gallagher, op. cit.; Short, op. cit., chapters 25 & 34.
6. *Aberdeen Evening Express*, 8 April 1987; Radio Scotland, *Head On*, 23 October 1988.
7. Hamill, op cit., p. 154-5.
8. D. Stevenson, *The First Freemason: Scotland's Early Lodges and their Members* (Aberdeen: Aberdeen University Press, 1988), p. 9.
9. Stevenson, op. cit.; D. Stevenson, *The Origins of Freemasonry: Scotland's Century* (Cambridge: Cambridge University Press, 1988).
10. See G. Draffen (ed.), *Masons and Masonry: Selected Articles from the Grand Lodge of Scotland Yearbook, 1953-72* (London: Lewis Masonic, 1983).
11. Bazaar Programme, 1903; *Govan Press*, 30 October 1903.
12. 'Three Day Bazaar', *The Provincial*, 7, 34, 1987.
13. Masons exchange masonic grips, and not handshakes, with one another.
14. *The Scottish Freemason*, January 1895.
15. *Glasgow Herald*, 23 October 1903. As this includes all masons in Scottish *Constitution* lodges, there were well under 100,000 masons *in* Scotland. On mediocrity: P. J. Rich, 'Public-school Freemasonry in the Empire: "Mafia of the Mediocre"?', in: J. A. Mangan (ed.), *'Benefits Bestowed'? Education and British Imperialism* (Manchester: Manchester University Press, 1988).
16. See A. Donovan, 'The Great War Years', *Provincial*, 9, 33, 1989.
17. A. Cohen, 'The Politics of Ritual Secrecy', *Man*, 6, 427-48, 1971.
18. Humphrey, radio interview.
19. Humphrey, *Evening Express*, interview.
20. *The Grand Lodge Yearbook*, 1989.
21. J. Hamill, op. cit., p. 146.
22. G. Di Bernardo, *Freemasonry and Its Image of Man: A Philosophical Investigation* (Tunbridge Wells: Freestone, 1989); G. Draffen, *The Making of a Mason* (London: Lewis Masonic, 1978); Hamill, op. cit.; G. Draffen, 'On Ritual', in: G. Draffen (ed.), op. cit.; J. Mason-Allen, 'Masonic Initiation', in: G. Draffen (ed.), op. cit., p. 1.
23. C. F. Graumann & S. Moscovici (eds.), *Changing Conceptions of Con-*

spiracy (New York: Springer-Verlag, 1987), M. Billig, *Fascists: A Social Psychological View of the National Front* (London: Harcourt Brace Jovanovich, 1978); M. Billig, 'Methodology and Scholarship in Understanding Ideological Explanations', in: C. Antaki, (ed.), *Analysing Everyday Explanation: A Casebook of Methods* (London: Sage, 1988); M. Billig, 'Rhetoric of the Conspiracy Theorist: Arguments in National Front Propaganda', *Patterns of Prejudice*, 22, 23-34, 1988.

24. D. B. Davis, *The Fear of Conspiracy: Images of Un-American Subversion from the Revolution to the Present* (Ithaca: Cornell University Press, 1971).

25. E. Dwyer, 'The Rhetoric of Reform: A study of verbal persuasion and belief systems in the anti-masonic and temperance movements' (Ann Arbor: Yale University, History Ph.D. Thesis/Xerox University Microfilms, 1979).

26. 'Vindex', *Light Invisible: The Freemasons' Answer to Darkness Visible* (London: Regency Press, 1952).

27. A. F. McPherson, 'An Angle on the Geist, Persistence and Change in the Scottish Educational Tradition', in: W. M. Humes and H. M. Paterson (eds.), *Scottish Culture and Scottish Education 1800-1980* (Edinburgh: John Donald, 1983); A. F. McPherson & C. D. Raab, *Governing Education: A Sociology of Policy since 1945* (Edinburgh: Edinburgh University Press, 1988). Rich, op. cit, discusses masonry in British education.

28. Script of listener comments, *Head On.*

29. Derek McCulloch was interviewed on a number of occasions in 1986.

30. A subsequent interview with the Supreme Knight of the Knights of St Columba in Britain, *Head On,* 17 November 1988 aroused very little comment.

31. Billig, *Fascists* and *Patterns*; he also shows the conspiracy theorist attributes power to a group without power and discriminated against.

32. H. Senior, *Orangeism in Ireland and Britain, 1795-1836* (London: Routledge and Kegan Paul, 1966).

33. B. Murray, *The Old Firm: Sectarianism, Sport and Society in Scotland* (Edinburgh: John Donald, 1984). But see B. Aspinwall, 'Review of Bill Murray, The Old Firm, Sectarianism, Sport and Society in Scotland,' *British Journal of Sports History*, 2 (1985), 206-8; G. P. T. Finn, 'Racism, religion and social prejudice: Irish Catholic clubs, soccer and Scottish society', *International Journal of the History of Sport*, in press.

34. For a much more detailed analysis, including more positive aspects of freemasonry in sport, see: G. P. T. Finn, *Freemasonry and Scottish Sport: the Special Case of Rangers?* (in preparation). Primrose also embodied the active Unionism of many prominent Rangers officials.

35. *Daily Record*, 12 July 1989.

36. Lodge Pioneer, No. 1305 and Lodge Masjid-I-Suleman, No. 1324.

37. Finn, 'Racism/Irish catholic clubs' analyses this 'problem orientation'.

38. Stevenson, op. cit.; D. M. Lyon, *History of Freemasonry in Scotland: Drawn from the Ancient Records with special references to the Lodge of Edinburgh, Mother Kilwinning and other Ancient Lodges* (Edinburgh: W. M. Blackwood & Sons, n.d.).

39. See entry in F. L. Pick and G. N. Knight (revised by F. Smyth), *The Freemason's Pocket Reference Book* (London: Frederick Muller: 1983).

40. See: J. Handley, *The Irish in Scotland, 1798–1845* (Cork: Cork University Press, 1943). J. Handley, *The Irish in Modern Scotland* (Cork: Cork University Press, 1947); R. Miles, 'Racism and Nationalism in Britain', in: C. Husband (ed.), *'Race' in Britain: Continuity and Change* (London: Hutchinson, 1984); T. Gallagher, op. cit.

41. J. Katz, *Jews and Freemason in Europe, 1723–1939* (Cambridge, Mass., Harvard University Press, 1970); L. J. Williams, *Black Freemasonry and Middle-Class Realities* (Columbia: University of Missouri Press, 1980).

42. Stevenson, op. cit.

43. See R. S. Tait, 'The 250th Anniversary Celebrations of the Grand Lodge of Scotland', *Yearbook*, 1987.

44. F. R. Bell, 'Grand Lodge of Scotland, Thanksgiving Service Address, 250th Anniversary, *Yearbook*, 1988.

45. *Reports to the General Assembly* (Edinburgh: Church of Scotland, 1989).

46. The issue is complex. The classic works are: W. Hannah, *Darkness Visible: A Christian Appraisal of Freemasonry* (Devon: Augustine Publishing Co., 1988); W. Hannah, *Christian by Degrees: The non-Christian Nature of Masonic Ritual* (Devon: Augustine Publishing Co., 1984). Also see: J. Lawrence, *Freemasonry – A Religion?* (London: Kingsway Publications, 1987); W. J. McK. McCormick, *Christ, the Christian, & Freemasonry* (Belfast: Great Joy Publications, 1987). For masonic counter-arguments see Hamill, op. cit.; also see *Freemasonry and Christianity: Evidence on the compatibility of Freemasonry and Christianity* by the United Grand Lodge of England and other Masonic authorities, 1986; *Notes on the 'Contribution to Discussion' by a Working Group of the Standing Committee of the General Synod of the Church of England* (United Grand Lodge of England, 1987); M. S. Higham, 'Freemasonry – From Craft to Tolerance', talk given at St Margaret Pattens, London, 1 October 1985, reprinted in *Yearbook*, 1987.

47. Lodge Solomon, No. 1209, in Edinburgh; and Lodge Montefiore, No. 753 and Lodge Shalom, No. 1600 – both in Glasgow. All allow non-Jewish members.

48. *Glasgow Herald*, 22 May 1989.

49. Church responses: Lawrence, op. cit.; Short, op. cit.; and Monsignor Docherty, General Secretary of the Bishop's Conference, and formerly of the Sacred Congregation for the Doctrine of Faith, clarified catholic stance.

10

The press and Protestant popular culture: a case-study of the Scottish Daily Express

TOM GALLAGHER

The 1960s were a decade in which British institutions long accustomed to being treated with respect or even veneration began to come under attack for holding on to outdated values, for being repositories of indefensible privileges, or for being responsible in some way for Britain's relative economic decline.

Scotland was left virtually untouched by this anti-establishment upsurge, her universities being among the quietest in Europe during the 1960s. However, one institution did not escape unscathed. This was the Church of Scotland which periodically came under fierce attack for not upholding with sufficient vigour the Protestant values that had been embedded in Scotland's popular culture since the time of the Reformation. That the kirk came under such sustained attack and that it was indicted for seemingly deserting old values rather than for resisting winds of change may reveal a great deal about the Scottish national mood in the 1960s, as well as the diminishing regard with which the premier institution in shaping Scottish popular identity was coming to be regarded.

The kirk found itself locked in unaccustomed controversy as a result of efforts that were made to draw closer to the Anglican wing of protestantism. The modern union movement had its origins during the 1920s as an extension of the movement for Presbyterian Union. Negotiations led by Dr John White, the leading Presbyterian of his generation, failed in large part owing to the Depression. The process was revived after the Second World War; in 1947 a successful resolution at the General Assembly (hereinafter GA) urged that the question of intercommunion between the Church of Scotland and the Church of England merited full discussion.[1] At the inter-church talks that occurred over the next decade, a lot of previously contentious ground was covered so that, by the mid-1950s, it was commonly felt by the Anglican and Presbyterian delegates that an increased measure of tolerance and good feeling

between the churches was not sufficient; fuller unity was necessary
to spread more effectively the message of the Gospel and that
permitting immediate intercommunion was, in turn, a clear requirement if one church of Christ was to emerge from once dis-
cordant ecclesiastical traditions.[2]

Such a prospect did not involve any major alteration to Presbyterian doctrine which had long permitted any baptised, communi-
cant member of any branch of the church of Christ to receive
communion at its services. But the Anglican position was an altogether contrasting one: 'Anglicans conscientiously hold that the
celebrant of the Eucharist should have been ordained by a bishop
standing in historic succession and generally believe it to be their
duty to bear witness to this principle by receiving Holy communion
only from those who have thus been ordained.[3] The view that
intercommunion was impossible except on the basis of episcopacy
was so integral to the Anglican tradition that it was reiterated in the
above terms at the 1958 Lambeth conference of those churches
belonging to the Anglican communion, not long after the appearance of a joint report meant to clear a path for church unity.

Relations between Anglican and Presbyterian Churches was issued in
1957 by the Inter-Church Relations Committee of the Church of
Scotland. It identified as an attainable goal not a single 'Church of
Great Britain' but rather a 'Church of England and a Church of
Scotland in full communion with one another in the one Church of
Christ', both enlarged churches being the desirable outcome of a
union between the Church of Scotland and the Episcopalian
Church and a similar union in England between the Established and
the Presbyterian church.[4] The driving force for unity on the Pres-
byterian side was the inter-church relations committee and, in 1958,
it was prepared to recommend to the GA that the Church of
Scotland accept a form of Episcopacy, with each presbytery having
a 'Bishop in Presbytery' chosen by itself.

Firm opposition could have been expected from many in the kirk
ready to view this plan as a violation of fundamental Presbyterian
principles, but it is doubtful if the intervention of a popular daily
newspaper ready to depict itself as the guardian of a beleaguered
Presbyterian heritage could have easily been envisaged. In Britain
the mass circulation press had rarely fastened on to religious controversy, readers having shown little appetite for issues concerning
fine points of religious principle, least of all in the materialist 1950s,
with a British Prime Minister presiding over a consumer boom
shortly to announce to a citizenry tired of austerity that 'you've never
had it so good'. Scotland was far from exempt from these socio-

logical trends, but certain qualifications have to be entered which perhaps may explain why a popular newspaper could hope to sway its readers by appealing to certain deep-seated religious convictions in the late 1950s. Regular churchgoing, though in decline, was still proportionately higher than in the south, the parish kirk and its minister still played an important role in local communities, not just rural ones and, in a society where the economic boom and the pace of social change was notably slower than in the rest of Britain, Presbyterian values and underlying assumptions still exercised an undeniable appeal.

Founded in 1928, the *Scottish Daily Express (SDE)* geared its coverage of news and its editorial standpoint towards Scots who were conservative in their religious outlook as well as, very often in their politics and who preferred everyday human interest stories with an obvious Scottish flavour as against the brash sensationalism offered increasingly by its competitors. Thus it was not so out of character for it to run the Bishops in Presbytery story, the magnitude of which was first grasped by Ian McColl who, except for wartime service in the RAF, had spent his entire journalistic career with the *SDE* since he had joined as an eighteen-year-old cub reporter in 1933.

At the end of 1957 McColl alerted his editor, A. C. Trotter, who in turn informed Max Aitken, Lord Beaverbrook, owner of the Express group of newspapers, about the story.[5] Since emigrating from Canada to Britain before the First World War Beaverbrook, as befits a wealthy tycoon and successful political intriguer, had moved in top London circles and his direct contact with Scotland, the land of his forebears, was slight. Although he did not allow it to interfere unduly with the enjoyment of a colourful lifestyle, his Presbyterian background was an important reference-point in his life and 'he never forgot that he was the son of a Scottish Presbyterian minister'.[6]

According to McColl, Beaverbrook's response was 'fight, fight at whatever cost even if it means losing circulation'.[7] He 'instructed the *SDE* to put the facts and the rights and wrongs of the situation into the hands of the men and women in the pews'.[8] Minute instructions were given as to how the campaign should proceed. Thus on 22 April 1959, he wrote to Trotter: 'There are many in Scotland who are willing to sell the pass. You might wish to warn the Church that if there is any further effort in the direction of the movement for bishops, the Church may well suffer another disruption.'[9]

At Beaverbrook's insistence the resulting campaign drew heavily on John Knox for inspiration and the editor (an Episcopalian) soon received a recommendation from him to keep a copy of the Westminster Confession of Faith by his desk. Thus, on 25 May 1958:

> Please turn up the denunciation of bishops by John Knox.
> Then having printed it, conclude with the final sentence of the
> Scots confession of 1560, written by John Knox with the aid of
> other ministers: 'Arise, O Lord, and let thy enemies be con-
> founded. Let them flee from the presence that hate thy godly
> name: give thee servants strength to speak thy word in bold-
> ness; and let all Nations attain to thy true knowledge.[10]

In the 1930s Beaverbrook's Scottish heritage had allowed him to
promote the Scottish nationalist movement both financially and in
terms of press coverage,[11] but in the politically quiescent 1950s this
movement was dormant and the attempt to couch the bishops
debate in nationalist terms made by the novelist George Blake was a
relatively isolated occurrence, although it would prefigure language
commonly in use during a further stage of the controversy in the
1960s:

> Presbyterianism ... expresses the democratic leanings of the
> average Scott as Episcopalianism reflects the more feudal
> inclinations of the English. Many like myself, not notable for
> either piety or political fervour, would see acceptance of the
> Bishops report as a betrayal of a national heritage, of a disci-
> pline that has done so much to shape the best of what there is
> in Scotland and Scotsmen.[12]

The 1950s were not a period when Scottish national identity
seemed under any grievous threat and the campaign was largely
waged in religious terms by Ian McColl who produced pamphlets
called *Crisis in the Kirk* and *The Crux of the Matter* setting out in clear,
accessible language what was at stake under the changes proposed in
the Bishops Report. As an elder of the kirk and member of the
Presbytery of Glasgow, McColl was well able to perform this task.
On first reading the 1957 report, he claims that: 'my mind went back
to the Covenanters and then to the Covenant of 1638 and how
Scotland, for fifty bloody years, had fought the imposition by
Charles I and later Charles II of Episcopacy on the Presbyterian
people of Scotland.'[13]

Many thousands of pamphlets were published and given away at
the expense of the *SDE* – 'people wrote in for batches, congregations
snapped them up'.[14] The initiative passed to the opponents of
Bishops whose term for the offending report, coined by McColl,
became the accepted one. When the Bishops Report came up for
conclusive debate at the GA in May 1959, after nearly two years of
controversy, it had been thoroughly aired at public meetings and
through the medium of the press. Opposition was widespread, the

nucleus being located in the west where Dr George Dryburgh of Battlefield parish church, Glasgow 'made a tremendous impression' on the Glasgow Presbytery by using 'the Scots Confession of Faith' which reaffirmed the non-episcopal character of Presbyterian doctrine.[15] Paisley College, which then trained students for the ministry in the West, opposed bishops while New College, its Edinburgh-based counterpart, had provided the impetus for their adoption. A fierce critic of the Bishops scheme, Professor Ian Hen-derson of Glasgow University's divinity department, later explained this east – west dichotomy by dwelling on the class background and outlook of those who proposed it:

> The viewpoint which they represented was for the most part that of the Edinburgh professions and the fashionable Edinburgh churches ... It was that of upper middle-class Scotland. And the basic principle of the religion of upper middle-class Scotland is that English institutions are U and Scottish institutions are non-U. From that basic principle, a document like the Bishops Report follows with inexorable logic.[16]

Such hardbitten language would be a feature of *SDE* coverage of the 1960s controversy but, on the eve of the 1958 Assembly, the newspaper appealed to the 'rank-and-file of the Kirk' to speak out in boldness 'on this day of crisis'.[17] The commissioners of the GA, comprising equal numbers of ministers and elders, were asked to remember that not only were they 'spokesmen and legislators' of the Church of Scotland but they were its guardians too and that they should not hold back out of fear of offending 'the Presbyterian professors who signed the Bishops report or their Anglican collaborators'.[18] In the same article, commissioners were asked not to succumb to the conditioning whereby: 'you are being made to feel that you and your kirk are more to blame than the Anglicans for these divisions. Your strong answer must be that the communion table of the Church of Scotland is open to everyone whereas the Anglican communion is for confirmed Anglicans only.'[19]

The *SDE* had wished to see the Bishops Report thrown out by the 1958 GA but it still declared itself well pleased with the decision to place it before the presbyteries for discussion and to have a definite verdict delivered by December 1958. Since deliberation at this level offered the active ordinary churchgoer considerable say, the *SDE* stated that 'there can be no doubt what the answer will be'.[20]

By early 1959 the presbyteries had overwhelmingly rejected the introduction of episcopacy. This verdict was in line with the findings of a special committee on inter-church relations whose report of November 1958 declared that the supreme authority of the GA,

'one of the essentials of Presbyterianism', would have been undermined if the 1957 report, which had stated that 'decisions on
doctrinal and constitutional matters might well have to require the
consent of Bishops in the General assembly', had been imple-
mented.[21] The conclusion it arrived at proved cold comfort for the
advocates of unity:

> The idea of Bishops-in-Presbytery fails to do justice to the
> historic Presbyterian Doctrine of the Church, the Ministry,
> and the Eldership, that if put into operation [they] would
> prevent the Church of Scotland from making her specific
> contribution ... to the wholeness of the Church and that, if
> pursued, they would divide our Church and seriously retard
> rather than further the ecumenical movement.[22]

Grassroots feelings having thus been monitored, the 1959 GA
rejected the Bishops Report. On receiving the news Beaverbrook
sent word to his editor: 'you have your headline – JEHOVAH 'HAS
TRIUMPHED AND THE PEOPLE ARE SET FREE'.[23] As for
the impact of the *SDE* campaign on the outcome of this religious
debate, it is difficult to be categorical (as with any press initiative of
this kind) but, in 1966, Dr Oliver Tompkins, the Anglican Bishop of
Bristol and then a key figure in inter-church dialogue, was in no
doubt about what had led to the dashing of earlier ecumenical
hopes: 'This was largely because the situation was further confused
by the way in which the Scottish edition of a popular daily newspaper
vitiated all discussion, and still does, by shrill vituperation and gross
distortion.'[24]

Beaverbrook's *Express* obituarist reckons that the unity moves of
the 1950s merely confirmed his long-held suspicion that the Church
of Scotland was 'not strong enough in support for the faith of its
fathers'.[25] His appointment of Ian McColl as *SDE* editor in 1961
may have reflected a desire for more vigilance over an errant kirk as
well as being a reward for the successful prosecution of
Beaverbrook's first full-scale press campaign since the early 1940s.

McColl has described himself as 'the keeper of Lord Beaverbrook's Presbyterian conscience'.[26] A phone call from Beaverbrook
around 1 p.m. on Sunday was a regular occurrence, the contents of
the church sermon McColl had listened to, and whether the true
word had been preached, invariably being the chief topics raised.
McColl stood very high in the press baron's estimation as a surviving
letter makes clear:

> You re making a wonderful paper of the *Scottish Daily Express*.
> It is the proudest arrow in the quiver as far as I am concerned.
> Many years ago when I started the paper there – what disap-

pointments and struggles lay ahead – what miscalculations and follies ... If only I had Ian McColl with me in the first place, I would have been helped over all the hurdles.[27]

With editor and proprietor in one mind about Scottish ecclesiastical concerns, it is hardly surprising that an inquisitive eye continued to be trained on the kirk establishment. Thus in May 1964 an article provocatively entitled 'a true Kirk or a Tower of Babel' slammed a Church of Scotland in which 'there is no bold proclamation of the gospel ... never a word about sin or eternal damnation ... and nothing is said from the pulpit ... that might possibly cause offence'.[28]

Neither was the paper unaware that conversations between the established churches had continued for six years despite the setbacks of the late 1950s. Bishops may have been unacceptable to the Presbyterian majority but only a minority were opposed to continuing dialogue which had been sanctioned at the 1959 Assembly.

The culmination of these talks was a three-day conference on steps towards Christian unity which opened at Holland House, an Edinburgh University hall of residence on 5 January 1966. More than 120 delegates from the Kirk, the Presbyterian Church in England, the Church of England and the Scottish Episcopalian Church met to discuss what the *SDE* described in banner headlines as 'a top-secret bombshell' plan which, if finally approved, 'could mean the destruction of the Presbyterian Church of Scotland'.[29] Although the conference was private, the *SDE* had become aware of the main agenda through Professor Ian Henderson, a Glasgow University theologian and close ally in the subsequent controversy.[30] Having received from him a paper containing the main agenda, McColl felt able to inform his readers that 'a renewed attempt to plant bishops in the kirk' was intended.[31] A Covenant of Union was to be proposed whereby 'the Church of Scotland will be united under bishops with the Scottish Episcopalians ... and that the decision, having been agreed by the General Assembly, shall be irrevocable'.[32] Later the *SDE* published an extract from the document in order to depict it in the minds of its readers as 'a blueprint for a takeover of the Kirk ... by the tiny but vocal Episcopalian Church in Scotland – backed by Big Brother, the Church of England': 'The covenant must not be merely a pious expression of good will. It must express the passing of the point of no return for both Churches: we are committed and committed irrevocably.'[33]

During the Holland House deliberations, the *SDE* kept up a barrage of criticism and, at their close, its readers were informed that the original plan to agree to a covenant of union and put it forward

to the next GA had been 'destroyed' by the action of the paper in
leaking details of the document.[34] The paper quoted a leading (but
unnamed) Glasgow minister as saying that 'this week's vigilant
campaign by the ... *Express* has clearly shaken the Ecumenical party
inside the Church of Scotland', and 'kirk circles' were referred to as
acknowledging the centrality of the role that the paper had played in
recent days. As evidence for the effectiveness of the *SDE's* campaign, these unattributed comments hardly constitute clinching
evidence; more significant by far may have been the reactions of two
leading Anglican churchmen who delivered attacks on the *SDE* at
the convocation of Canterbury in May 1966. Dr Tompkins, the
Bishop of Bristol, having blamed the intervention of 'the Scottish
edition of a popular daily newspaper' for the failure of the first round
of unity talks in 1959, went on to say that: 'An Englishman can only
express the hope that the Church of Scotland, which has a proud
history of resisting the invasion of the Church by sovereignty, will
itself know how to deal with the tyrannous pretensions of this
strident spokesman of the Fourth Estate.'[35]

Unlike Dr Tompkins, Canon Hugh Montefiore of Cambridge
University (later to be appointed Bishop of Birmingham) mentioned
the *SDE* by name and, having observed that its influence on the
Church of Scotland 'seems to be very great indeed', charged that
'under cover of religious conviction, it appears to play on some of the
less pleasing aspects of national sentiment'.[36] The *SDE* viewed such
criticism as proof that its vigilance had paid off. Possibly, the paper's
Anglican critics may have been driven to speak out with such
unusual candour because of the eruption of a fresh controversy
which, from their perspective, endangered the future of unity talks
and in which the *SDE* had once again played a full part.

This was the so-called Tirrell affair which arose early in 1966 after
Dr Harry Whitley, the Presbyterian minister of St Giles' Church in
Edinburgh appointed John Tirrell, a young American then studying
for the Episcopalian priesthood, as his assistant. As this involved an
Episcopalian administering the sacrament of communion to Presbyterians, it caused great unease among Anglicans as well as within
the ecumenical kirk party, not least because agreement on
intercommunion had not proved possible in more than a decade of
inter-church discussions. As for the *SDE* it preferred to view
'Whitley's great step' as one 'improving inter-church relations at a
practical level' and the resultant furore was merely evidence that 'the
Episcopalians and our home-grown ecumaniacs[37] are much more
interested in the politics of Christian unity than in its practical
manifestation'.[38] Kenneth Carey, the Episcopalian Bishop of Ed-

inburgh, banned Tirrell from activities in all the churches in his diocese, for having taken this unilateral course. Meanwhile, the Presbytery of Edinburgh, in one of its most crowded meetings for years, split 106 – 106 over whether Tirrell could continue as a curate at St Giles' and the question was referred to the GA for a judgement. A letter was then sent by Dr Michael Ramsay, Archbishop of Canterbury, to the Moderator of the GA expressing the hope that the Tirrell affair would not come between better Anglican – Presbyterian relations. The fact that the letter was written to the Moderator – not sent to the GA itself – became a mini *cause-célèbre*. Dr Andrew Herron, a future Moderator and leading opponent of church union, felt that this breach of protocol was a revealing example of Anglican insensitivity:

> this silly mistake indicates that our Anglican friends ... though they have been studying our Presbyterian system for more than ten years, have not yet reached the elementary stage of understanding the basic principles of our government ... As they see it we must have somebody corresponding to the Archbishop of Canterbury and, if not, we jolly well should have ... Scotland is not Presbyterian by accident. But as a result of a long history of bitter struggle. Our system is native to our land and suited to the genius of our people ... The Englishman, it is said, has a genius for controversy. As the Anglican system gives opportunity for the exercise of the one, so Presbyterianism provides scope for the enjoyment of the other.[39]

What Canon Montefiore regarded as 'playing on some of the less pleasing aspects of national sentiment' was to Herron 'a sturdy insistence on the excellence of our Presbyterian system ... which has to be reckoned with by those who would seek alliance with us'.[40] Herron, as convenor of the kirk's publicity and publication department, was an important ally for the *SDE* to be able to call upon. After the 1966 GA he was to reject criticism of the press 'as though the press is our enemy': 'let us be very grateful that people are still interested in publicising the Kirk and reading about it.'[41]

Although the *SDE* had claimed that its publication of the Holland House conference had led to the proposed covenant of union being shelved, its columns were full of warnings about the need for GA commissioners to exercise particular caution in considering the report on Anglican – Presbyterian relations. On the eve of the vote to be taken on 30 May 1966 about whether to continue with unity talks, a page one leader entitled 'Decision Day For The Soul of The Kirk' insisted that 'in more than sixty years of solid conversations the Anglicans have neither given nor retreated one inch'. Further talks should be shelved in favour of pursuing 'closer relations at the congregational level' without any requirement for doctrinal changes: 'Let them meet and mingle. Let them preach in one another's churches in the cause of love and understanding, as for example in the case of John Tirrell ... Invite them to share communion in the Kirk.' 'The Kirk does not treat Anglicans as second-class Christians as Anglicans look at Kirk members. The Church of Scotland offers fellowship to all.'[42]

The GA, comprising 1 803 commissioners, decided by the small majority of twenty-three to continue exploratory talks with the Episcopalian Church. However, only 447 commissioners were present, hundreds having left the Assembly hall for lunch or to make an early start for the royal garden party at Holyrood Palace. Such an attendance suggests that a controversy which had rumbled on spasmodically for almost a decade was not as gripping for the legislators of the kirk as for the *SDE* – at least on this occasion. The *SDE* was confident that the wafer-thin majority was 'a red light flashing to Canterbury' but it asked: 'Why are crucial debates always held on Garden Party Monday? And if they must go on, why isn't an automatic closure enforced at 1 o'clock or earlier?[43]

Such revelations about GA procedures may not have increased the prestige of what was regarded in many quarters as the nearest equivalent Scotland had to a functioning parliament. Its refusal to deliver a verdict on the Tirrell case, even though it was entitled to do so as the highest court of the church, also reveals a quietist attitude. The matter was sent back to the Edinburgh Presbytery (arguably more mindful of Anglican sensibilities than any other in Scotland) which, later in 1966, refused to give John Tirrell leave to exercise a religious function at the high kirk of St Giles.

The *SDE* did not relax its guard after the conclusion of a GA whose outcome afforded it satisfaction, if not complete reassurance, about the state of the kirk. The charge levelled at the ecumenicals as 'the one body in the church remotely resembling a party ... who have a habit of capturing convenorships and gaining a majority on committees' was frequently repeated.[44] Ian McColl felt that the body of the kirk was too trusting when confronted not only with 'Anglicans well-versed in subtle aggression, possessed of a vast prelatical authority', and 'bent on extending their ecclesiastical empire', but with local supporters 'carried into blind folly in their anxiety to please'.[45] These were the words of Charles Graham who, despite being an agnostic, had the unerring ability to break down the complex doctrinal and organisational kirk debates and controversies into vivid prose for the *SDE* readership without losing sight of the essential issues at stake. McColl remembers him as 'a valued aide-de-camp in all these battles', someone whose facility with words and awareness of the popular mood helped the editor to depict the *SDE* as the guardian of the kirk's integrity.[46]

At the outset of the Holland House controversy the *SDE* had proclaimed its role as being one of 'keeping a vigilant eye on behalf of the Kirk's 1,268,000 members'[47] Then and later, McColl enjoyed complete autonomy from London headquarters of Express Newspapers even although his campaign was bound to have alienated many, not just in the religious, but in the wider Scottish establishment. In the midst of the Tirrell affair, private lobbying by several leading Episcopalians, who included Sir Alec Douglas-Home, directed at halting further attacks on the Bishop of Edinburgh on account of the damage being done to his health, met with failure. Sir Max Aitken, who had replaced Lord Beaverbrook as proprietor on the latter's death in June 1964, shared his father's basic Presbyterian ethos, according to McColl; the editor was greatly encouraged to receive a telegram from Aitken which made it clear that pressure from on high would not gag the *Express*: 'THE FIGHT CONTINUES UNDER YOUR LEADERSHIP WITH THE FULL APPROVAL OF THE MINISTER'S GRANDSON'.[48]

However deeply the new owner's Presbyterian heritage extended, he was bound to have been impressed by the circulation figures of his Scottish daily at a time when the circulation battles between rival popular dailies were becoming even more intense. The circulation of the *SDE* rose in successive years throughout the 1960s until it reached a peak in August 1969 when 670,000 copies were sold, nearly 140,000 ahead of its nearest rival *The Daily Record*.[49] Religious controversy as regular front-page news had not proved unappealing to Scottish readers in the 1960s. By contrast, the circulation of the *SDE*'s London-based counterpart was going down during the same period which strengthened McColl's freedom of action. In 1964 he managed to run a campaign opposing drastic rail cuts at a time when the London paper was praising their architect, Lord Beeching, whom the *SDE* dubbed 'Butcher Beeching'; Sir Edward Pickering, the London editor, assumed wrongly that where such a disagreement existed the Scottish paper would have to defer to its London counterpart.

McColl's ability to defend his editorial autonomy and maintain the distinctive Scottishness of a paper, ultimate control over which resided in London, runs counter to the post-war trend whereby the autonomy of successive institutions fails to withstand pressures emanating from the South. His career did not yield grievances which

might have predisposed him towards favouring the rising force of
Scottish nationalism; nevertheless, his paper played an important
role in orchestrating support for the first real Nationalist breakthrough at the 1967 Hamilton by-election. The political career of
Winifred Ewing, the SNP's Hamilton victor, was actively promoted
by the paper which provided her with a regular column and depicted
her attempts to carve out a role in the male-dominated club atmosphere of Westminster in almost heroic terms. Similar backing
extended to her party in 1968, the year in which it enjoyed startling
success in local elections. Much of the party's identifiable electoral
support matched the readership profile of the *SDE*, upper-working-
class Scots, churchgoing and socially conservative in their tastes,
being core elements of both.

It is not the purpose of this chapter to discuss the extent to which
Scotland's best-selling paper in the 1960s was responsible for
fuelling the Nationalist take-off, but the paper stressed grievances
which it knew many of its readers felt strongly about – such as central
government disregard for Scottish economic interests, the inability
of the two major parties adequately to reflect Scottish popular
concerns, and the threat to distinctive Scottish traditions, be it
illustrious regiments or indeed the integrity of the kirk – which a
party whose populist outlook was not unlike that of the *Express*'s
own, was bound to find advantageous.

Although a unionist rather than a nationalist in his own political
outlook, McColl chose the week before the 1967 GA to serialise a
book which depicted the ecumenical movement as 'Anglican imperialism' intent on subverting 'one of the few institutions left to the
Scots to feel really passionate about'.[50] *Power Without Glory*, by
Professor Ian Henderson, sold an estimated 5000 copies[51] following
its week-long serialisation in the *SDE*, possibly an indication of the
impact church controversy was having in Scotland at that time. The
author may have held a chair in Glasgow University's Divinity
Department, but the book was written in a polemical manner,
implacable criticism being reserved for the Anglican diplomats who
'in negotiating with another Church … make no concessions and so
spare their Church any dissension', and who 'rely on their fifth
column in the other church to win the civil war'.[52] For the Church of
Scotland to 'recover from its intolerable state of inner discord'
Henderson called for a cessation of all conversations for at least
twenty-five years, to 'give time for real thought which up till now has
had to take second place to ecclesiastical politics'.[53]

A majority of those who voted at the 1967 GA was unimpressed
by the closing recommendation of Professor Henderson's book.

Talks with the Episcopalians were allowed to continue 'after a searching and sometimes stormy debate' and the Assembly threw out an attempt to 'stiffen' the committee dealing with inter-church relations by including another eight members critical of unity advances.[54] However, in a speech to the GS, the convenor of the committee, the Very Revd Dr Nevile Davidson, still felt it necessary to criticise the *SDE* for 'waging a sustained and bitter campaign ... against those engaged in working for unity'.[55] Next day the *SDE* riposted in a long article on its leader page:

> Potential merger talks between the two churches can never be a matter for the private conversations of Gentlemen. This is a matter of public interest, and material for public debate and if needs be for public opposition. Dr Davidson and his friends should have learnt by this time that the silence of the *Scottish Daily Express* ... is one enterprise in which they shall never succeed.[56]

The war of attrition which the *SDE* waged against the ecumenical party within the kirk may not have stopped it in its tracks but certainly produced a strained atmosphere in which it was difficult for its proposals to be viewed dispassionately. In 1968 Dr Davidson publicly admitted that 'Scotland's ecumenical ship is in the doldrums with little wind following in its sails'.[57] No passionate debate about church unity made headlines for that year's Assembly and, in fact, thereafter the issue slipped into the background. Instead the *SDE* was concentrating on a different Scottish institution which it had discovered to have feet of clay, the Scottish Conservative party's affairs being subject to much critical scrutiny in mid-1968 over the party's failure to respond enthusiastically to Edward Heath's conversion to the cause of home rule for Scotland.

There was no other word to describe the *SDE*'s rejection of the agenda proposed by the ecumenical party other than 'dogmatic', but its reaction to other potentially far-reaching changes in Church of Scotland practice was not characterised by the same degree of inflexibility. The 1966 GA's approval of women elders was followed two years later by the approval of women ministers, important changes that were greeted with relatively little editorial comment. It could not have escaped the editor's attention that the inclusion of women in the ministry placed a fresh obstacle in the path of church unity since opposition to a similar move in the Church of England was entrenched and would remain so for many years to come.

The SDE's advocacy of closer understanding between the Presbyterian and Roman Catholic churches in Scotland may also be surprising, especially in light of the fact that many readers, alarmed by many attempts to erode the Presbyterian character of their own church, are likely to have harboured abiding suspicions about the role and intentions of the Roman Catholic Church in Scotland. During the years of ecumenical controversy the *SDE* refrained from adopting a populist line on certain aspects of Scottish Roman Catholicism which to many Protestants, churchgoing and non-churchgoing, were a source of mistrust or active resentment, the main ones being the Church's refusal to sanction a marriage between a Catholic and a non-Catholic except on its own terms as well as its right, under law, to have Catholic primary and secondary schools financed by the state.

In the *Express* Ian Henderson was given a platform for the view that co-operation with the Catholics could bring about a result far more socially valuable than anything to be achieved by negotiations with the Episcopalians: 'if the Catholic Church of Scotland ... and the Church of Scotland could reach an agreed statement on Christian ethics, such a step would be at least one salutary measure against the lawlessness which is far too prevalent in some parts of Scotland today.'[58]

At the height of a controversy about gang warfare then raging in Glasgow, the *SDE* favourably contrasted the advocacy by the city's Catholic archbishop of 'corporal punishment for delinquent boys' and his belief in 'the state's right to inflict capital punishment for grave offences like murder' with the much milder stance of the Church of Scotland on both questions.[59]

During the 1968 GA, the paper dissociated itself from Dr Whitley, normally a beneficiary of *Express* approval on a wide range of issues, when he declared that 'ecumenism would play into the hands of the Roman Church which had been quietly wanting to cash in on the Kirk's dismemberment'.[60] Perhaps most remarkably of all, under the headline 'Can religion cost you a job? Intolerance must not tarnish Scotland's name', it published a long article by Jack Webster in February 1968 critical of religious discrimination in jobs and sport, hitherto a firm taboo subject in the columns of the Scottish daily press.[61]

At a time when the *SDE* projected itself as speaking up for Scotland, this self-image would have been difficult to sustain if it had failed to encompass a religious minority which made up around one quarter of the conurbation of Scotland's largest city from which the *Express* was produced. The paper was always prepared to offer a platform to figures who reflected the view that in a time of bewildering and often unsettling change, with Scotland's basic interests at risk from denationalising forces from within and without, it was all the more necessary for her identity not only to be safeguarded but to be reaffirmed. But among those in the kirk ministry there were very few whom the *SDE* could draw upon who were able to inform important contemporary issues with a strong religious perspective. Of course, ministers with their sights set on the major offices of the church may have been unwilling to identify too closely with a newspaper that had been no stranger to partisan religious controversy. Even Andrew Herron, Moderator in 1971 and an upholder of Presbyterian orthodoxy, whilst prepared to defend the *SDE*'s right to speak out, was careful to distance himself from some of its more embattled positions.

But there was one minister whose outlook on church affairs and wider issues was sufficiently in tune with that of the *SDE* for him to be given a regular platform in the newspaper throughout the 1960s. This was Dr Harry Whitley, minister of St Giles' Church in Edinburgh whom *The Times* described in its obituary of him as 'a doughty controversialist not given to pulling his punches on any of the major issues that excited his interest'.[62] Whitley's identification with the concerns of hard-pressed working-class communities in Port Glasgow and the Govan and Partick divisions of Glasgow where he spent much of his early career, turned him into 'a militant Christian who found it difficult to live with the kirk's peace-loving Establishment'.[63] After his appointment to the ministry of Edinburgh's St Giles', a prestigious church patronised by the Edinburgh establishment, his battles with many in a kirk session drawn heavily from the top ranks of the legal profession in a bid to end the practice of seat-renting (which had hung on at St Giles' long after being discontinued elsewhere) provided the *SDE* with much lively copy, as did a long-running dispute with his predecessor, Dr Charles L. Warr who for a number of years refused to vacate the ministry and sought to delay Whitley's succeeding to honorific deaneries that went with the position.

Warr was in turn pilloried by the *SDE* 'for being the darling of the aristocracy and the establishment' and was urged to join the Church of England since his attachment to the office of Dean of the Thistle (involving royal duties upon which he set great store) revealed his 'devotion to the purple'. This unedifying dispute enabled the *SDE* to repeat its charge that the ecumenicals were more interested in ecclesiastical politics[64] than genuine Christian togetherness and the *SDE* castigated the bulk of the Edinburgh establishment for cold-shouldering the Whitleys and, in the words of Ian Henderson, for subjecting them to 'a social death of a thousand pinpricks'.[65]

In a more positive light Whitley was presented with a platform

upon which to speak out on issues ranging from the need for housing
planners to find a place for science, morals and aesthetics 'as you
create man's environment', to the desire for Scotland to assume
more direct responsibility for her own affairs.[66] He warned the GA in
1969 that if it did not come out strongly 'in favour of Scottish
autonomy ... the chance to influence the future of Scotland would
have moved from the Kirk and its pronouncements would count for
nothing'.[67]. A reading of his last volume of memoirs would suggest
that the Bishops controversy and his failure to persuade the Post
Office to commemorate either the 400th anniversary of the Scottish
Reformation in 1961 or that of John Knox's death in 1971, had
caused both he and his wife to conclude that the union had long
ceased to be beneficial for Scotland.[68] Elizabeth Whitley stood for
the SNP against Sir Alex Douglas-Home in the 1970 general
election and, in a regular *SDE* column in earlier years, she was
critical of mounting English interference in Scotland and of the
abject role of Scottish institutions in the face of such encroachments.
The author of a commemorative study of Knox, she and her
husband were notable for insisting on his relevance for the latter-day
church, but Dr Whitely was unable to persuade the kirk to lay on 'a
real celebration' for his hero in 1971, the alleged reason being that
it would be viewed as 'arousing sectarianism'.[69]

In response, Whitely made no secret of his dissatisfaction with
church procedures which is perhaps the best answer to the *SDE*'s
own question, 'why did Dr Whitley never become Moderator – a
post for which he was a clear front-runner?'[70] Thus, in his memoirs,
he claims that:

> The Kirk has in recent years had its own curia. The conclave
> of ex-Moderators, most of them decent little men, one or two
> of them astute and clever, a very few great and gifted
> Churchmen, wields the invisible power of Church politics.
> They come up every year as members of the General Assem-
> bly, while the ordinary parish minister only becomes a Com-
> missioner once in every four years. They know the rights and
> niceties of procedure, and so what ought to be a free assembly
> of ministers and elders has become a manipulated distortion of
> church government.[71]

By 1976, the date of this memoir's posthumous appearance, the
SDE was no longer being produced from within Scotland. In 1974
publication had moved to Manchester whereupon 'its expressions of
Scottishness intensified' until, on being taken over by Trafalgar
House some years later, it switched to a militant anti-devolution
line.[72] Meanwhile Ian McColl had assumed the editorship of the

London *Express* in 1971, only to find that opportunities to raise issues with a strong religious dimension were few and far between because of sheer lack of interest among the paper's English readership.

Here the concern has been with the *Scottish Daily Express*'s coverage of a long-running religious controversy within the Church of Scotland rather than with the specifics of a particular issue. Accordingly, no attempt has been made to provide a balanced or comprehensive assessment of the positions adopted by the various parties involved in the 'Bishops in Presbytery' controversy. Instead, the aim in writing this chapter has been to determine the extent to which the *SDE* was able to carry off the role, between 1958 and 1969, of presenting itself as the custodian of Protestant popular culture in Scotland in the face of what were seen as attempts to alter the doctrine and structure of the Church of Scotland in a number of fundamental respects.

It has been shown that the *SDE*, with mounting boldness, was prepared to wage a populist campaign in order to frustrate ecumenical initiatives and register its displeasure over the kirk's stance on controversial issues where it felt traditional social values needed to be reaffirmed. This involved giving a platform to outspoken church figures where they shared its perspective on issues ranging from capital punishment to commemorating John Knox, as well as seeking to influence the judgement of Presbyterians at grassroots level when proposed major changes were up for discussion at the GA. The editor of the *SDE* for most of this period was well-placed to comment on religious matters given his own involvement in the life of the kirk; moreover, the readership of the paper had, for a long period, been drawn disproportionately from the Protestant churchgoing element in the Scottish population in contrast to its nearest rival, the *Daily Record*.

It is impossible to determine, at least with any precision, the degree to which the paper influenced the outcome of the disputes in which it intervened (or indeed sometimes generated). It is not easy to turn to any vote taken at a GA and then say that the result was determined by the editorial stance of the campaigning drive of the *SDE*. Indeed it is easier to point to incidences where the *SDE*'s advice was not taken, as with the 1967 decision to continue talks with the Episcopalians. Nevertheless, it is clear that the high profile which the paper adopted in highly sensitive religious matters was a source of acute irritation to leading clergymen: two senior ecclesiastics, the Bishop of Bristol and a future Bishop of Birmingham, took the unusual step of going on public record in 1966 to express their dismay at the influence which the *SDE* had been shown to have during the 'Bishops in Presbytery' row of the late 1950s and the Holland House controversy in the first months of 1966.

The *SED*'s ability to increase its circulation while targetting, in populist fashion, pillars of the church and state in Scotland that it felt to be deficient in safeguarding the Scottish national interest, gave it a powerful voice in Scotland during the later 1960s. Those who interpreted ecumenism in the broadest sense and were prepared to enter into union with the Church of England found the paper to be a vexatious foe and the loss of momentum which this branch of ecumenism experienced after 1968 cannot be separated from the ability of the paper to explode a popular storm over their heads. But the *SED*'s ability to intimidate those who were engaged in modernisation at the expense of Scotland's traditional identity was weakened by the irresolution of Scottish Conservatism and the absense of a populist charismatic tradition within the Kirk. Without natural allies it found itself operating in a vacuum, the party that most closely shared its standpoint on the condition of Scotland being the Scottish National party, whose separtist aspirations it was ultimately distrustful of.

The willingness of secular or agnostic figures like the novelist George Blake or the journalist Charles Graham to support the maintenance of Presbyterian traditions or practices (in face of calls for their further relaxation) by deploying the argument that these were integral aspects of Scotland's national heritage whose retention, in the midst of previous struggles, had helped to ensure the distinctiveness of Scottish life, was another noteworthy feature of the debate. It is not without irony that the *Scottish Daily Express* eventually succumbed to the denationalising trends which it had been on its guard against in other institutions while the kirk, since the 1970s, has shown increasing boldness in defending, along with other churches, the Scottish approach to major public policy questions when it has been at odds with the new orthodoxy emanating from the seat of power in London.

NOTES

1.. William Ferguson, *Scotland, 1689 to the present* (Edinburgh, 1978), p. 410.
2.. *Relations between Anglican and Presbyterian Churches* (Edinburgh, 1957).
3.. Lambeth Declaration, 1958, quoted in the *Scottish Daily Express* (hereafter *SDE*), 30 May 1966.
4. *Church Unity, Questions and Answers on the Conversations* (Edinburgh

1957).

5. Interview with Ian McColl, 14 February 1989.
6. Interview with Ian McColl.
7. *Ibid.*
8. Charles Graham, 'Steadfast in the faith of his forebearers' (Obituary of Lord Beaverbrook), *SDE*, 10 June 1964.
9. A. J. P. Taylor, *Beaverbrook* (Harmondsworth, 1974).
10. Taylor, *Beaverbrook*, p. 819.
11. John McCormick, *The Flag In The Wind* (London, 1955), pp. 58-63.
12. *SDE*, 7 May 1958
13. Interview with Ian McColl.
14. Interview with Ian McColl.
15. Interview with Ian McColl.
16. Ian Henderson, *Power Without Glory* (London, 1967), p. 117. By the late 1960s 'U' and 'non-U' had entered into popular currency as terms denoting the difference between good and bad taste as determined by those in the cultural and social 'establishment' who set standards in such matters.
17. *SDE*, 21 May 1958, 27 May 1958.
18. *SDE*, 27 May 1958.
19. *SDE*, 27 May 1958.
20. *SDE*, 28 May 1958.
21. *Report of the Special Committee on Inter-Church Relations*, submitted to the Presbytery of Glasgow, 25 November 1958.
22. *Ibid.*
23. Interview with Ian McColl.
24. Bishop Tompkins, speaking at the Convocation of Canterbury, 11 May 1966, quoted in the *SDE*, 12 May 1966.
25. *SDE* obituary, 10 June 1964.
26. Interview with Ian McColl.
27. Lord Beaverbrook to Ian McColl, letter dated 19 December 1963.
28. *SDE*, 19 May 1964.
29. *SDE*, 5 January 1966.
30. Interview with Ian McColl.
31. *SDE*, 8 January 1966.
32. *SDE*, 5 January 1966.
33. *SDE*, 30 May 1966 (originally underlined according to *SDE*).
34. *SDE*, 8 January 1966.
35. *SDE*, 12 May 1966.
36. *SDE*, 12 May 1966.
37. A derogatory term which the *SDE* and others sometimes used for 'ecumenics'.
38. *SDE*, 1 June 1966.
39. *SDE*, 13 May 1966.
40. *SDE*, 13 May 1966.
41. *SDE*, 2 June 1966.
42. *SDE*, 31 May 1966.
43. *SDE*, 31 May 1966.
44. A. D. Sloan ,'This hard pitiless creed', *SDE*, 7 January 1966 (possibly a pseudonym for Ian Henderson who, days earlier, had leaked the Holland House programme to the *SDE*).
45. Interview with Ian McColl; *SDE*, 8 January 1966.
46. Interview with Ian McColl.
47. *SDE*, 1 January 1966.
48. Interview with Ian McColl. Max Aitken's grandfather had been a

Presbyterian minister in West Lothian who emigrated to Canada in the nineteenth century.
49. Interview with Ian McColl.
50. Henderson, *Power Without Glory*, p. 118.
51. Interview with Ian McColl.
52. Henderson, *Power Without Glory*, p. 176.
53. Henderson, p. 180.
54. *SDE*, 25 May 1967.
55. *SDE*, 25 May 1967.
56. *SDE*, 26 May 1967.
57. *SDE*, 24 May 1968.
58. Henderson, *Power Without Glory*, p. 179.
59. *SDE*, 3 April 1968.
60. *SDE*, 20 May 1969.
61. *SDE*, 16 February 1968.
62. *The Times*, 11 May 1976.
63. Charles Graham, 'Harry: a voice of the kirk and a man of the people', *SDE*, 11 May 1976.
64. *SDE*, 7 January 1966. On 17 June 1969, shortly after Warr's death, the paper even branded him ' an old goat' suffering from 'an old man's animosities', exceptional language to be used in the press against a minister living or dead.
65. *SDE*, 20 May 1967.
66. *SDE*, 14 May 1968.
67. *Glasgow Herald*, 19 May 1969.
68. H. Whitley, *Thorns and Thistles* (Edinburgh, 1976).
69. Whitley, *Thorns and Thistles*, p. 4.
70. *SDE*, 11 May 1976.
71. Whitley, *Thorns and Thistles*, p. 66.
72. Michael Brown, 'The Scottish Morning Press and the Devolution Referendum of 1979', *Scottish Government Yearbook 1980* (Edinburgh, 1980), p. 65.

Research for this chapter was made possible thanks to a grant from the British Academy.

11
Protestantism and gender

KAY CARMICHAEL

As a child, growing up in the east end of Glasgow in the first half of this century, the community in which I lived demonstrated significant differences between Protestant and Catholic families. It was the Protestant women who transmitted awareness of the differences. Protestant men and Catholic men living up the same close might not mix socially but there was rarely any overt difference expressed between them. Indeed there was often a silent, mutual understanding that the community life of the women should be left to the women and they should not get dragged into gossip or disputes.

The gossip among Protestant women was in the main judgmental. It focused on other women, their ability to handle their husbands and their money, how clean and well-dressed they kept their children, their ability to feed their family well and thriftily, their moral standards and what we would now call their credit rating. Disputes centred round the issues of day-to-day living such as the use and cleaning of common passages and shared lavatories on the landings, the rotas for the common wash house in the back court, the appearance of windows and how they were curtained, the noise and activities allowed to children living in the close and up the stairs.

In all of these matters the standards were normally set by the Protestant women. For reasons I as a child did not understand, their houses were better furnished, tidier, their brasses shone more brightly, even their washing seemed to hang out on the line in more organised ways. In their persons they were better dressed, the aprons they wore to do their housework never seemed to get dirty, their hair was always neat and tidy, their husband's dinner always ready on the table when he came home from work. Most important, they never, ever,seemed to get into debt.

I didn't realise that I was watching the Protestant ethic, about which I was later to read, alive and well and functioning. Nor did I realise that there were other parts of the city where the Protestants

were the 'poor whites', locked into poverty and the bitterness of
Ulster politics that they had brought with them when seeking work
as immigrants from Northern Ireland. In my experience Scottish
Protestant women saw themselves as in every way superior to
Catholic women whose religious roots lay in the Roman Catholic
areas of southern Ireland.

One did not have to look far for the reasons their husbands had
better jobs, they had more money than Catholic women and seemed
more in control of their lives. They certainly had fewer children and
were loudspoken in their contempt for Catholic families who produced prolifically. They were more ambitious for their children,
more confident that they would get apprenticeships, get a job in an
office or even, in a few cases, stay on at school and reach the pinnacle
of success by becoming a teacher.

I also sensed that they didn't have as much fun. They took their
responsibilities more seriously, were quick to reprimand and slow to
praise, their gossip tended to be less cheerful, their laughter more
restrained, than that of the Catholic women. In every situation they
were more conscious of what other people thought of them. Many
Catholic women admired their style and saw them as role models in
the struggle for respectability that was such a central part of working-
class life in Scotland, but at parties or at funerals those Catholic
women would revert to the more relaxed and libidinal styles they had
brought with them, usually from the pre-industrial world across the
Irish sea.

In Scotland the Industrial Revolution had forced people off the
land, broken up communities and torn families apart. Middle-class
women who had enjoyed some status working with their husbands in
small businesses found themselves confined to their homes, because
of the new forms of production, with completely new sets of rules for
behaviour. Respectable working-class women, wives of tradesmen
or clerks or the skilled workers needed in industry, followed the same
pattern. By the time of Victoria these women found they were
servants to a concept of the family which subjected them to an
oppressive regime which repressed their behaviour and their sexuality in ways that would have gained the full approval of St Augustine,
a fifth-century theologian who saw all spontaneous expression of
human feeling as a mark of original sin.

The Church of Rome, which at that time accepted Augustine's
view, had in doing so brought to an end a period of human history
in which the feminine principle had played an important part in
human perception of divine power. Augustine had linked his arguments with those of Paul which increased their legitimacy and by the

twelfth century anti-feminist ideas had been so absorbed into church doctrine that it could be stated as part of church law that: 'The image of God is in man, and it is one. Women were drawn from man, who has God's jurisdiction as if he were God's vicar because he has the image of the one God. Therefore, woman is not made in God's image.' The penis had triumphed.

Societies create the images of divinity that make sense to them and up to about 10,000 BC the primary power of creation had been seen to reside, not in the male, but in the female. In communities which depended for survival on the abundance of animals and the fruitfulness of the earth, female fertility was seen as the source of the greatest power and mystery. The divine was symbolised by a pregnant woman.

As styles of agriculture changed, as organisation and storage of crops went hand in hand with fertility, as men swept across the land in tides of exploration and conquest, the divinity of women began to be shared with male gods and in time became dominated by them. Demeter and Ceres might still be invoked for fertility but in the last resort power resided in Zeus or Jupiter. The power of his seed was recognised, to spill where he chose.

But rather than one god with absolute power, there were many representing a wide variety of human experience... Some were beautiful, some were ugly, some were mischievous, some were physically handicapped. There were equal numbers of male and female and always someone with whom each person in the community could identify. It was the jealous God of the Jews who came out of the desert who tried to end all that. He, and only He, was to be worshipped.

As the troops of the Roman Empire spread across the known world, acknowledging and absorbing local deities into the Olympic pantheon, a one world began to need a one God. Judaism offered the one God and Christ offered a new message of freedom and salvation. Women, in particular, responded and the first centuries after the death of Christ saw among them a great flowering of religious power. But in 313 AD the Roman Emperor Constantine was converted and thereby captured Christianity for the state. The religion which grew out of that conversion was systematically to degrade the position of women over the next 1600 years.

From then until the Reformation, women were honoured only if they denied their sexuality. Augustine and the Church Fathers taught that they were dirty and dangerous, a threat and a source of temptation. The only exception was Mary, the Mother of God and yet a virgin. She was the role image for women, very different from

the Venus or Juno of the Roman myths. But because the needs of
women are more powerful than the rules men may impose on them,
the Virgin Mary, in the private prayers of women, became the
ancient Mother Goddess invoked for fertility, for solace in grief and
thanksgiving in joy.

For both men and women celibacy was offered as the greatest
good and throughout the Middle Ages monasteries and convents
were continually being founded. The convents offered women,
particularly able and well-educated women, opportunities for developing their talents. But as the numbers expanded many of the men
and women found themselves unable to maintain the ideals of
poverty, obedience and chastity on which they had been founded,
and both monasteries and convents became the subject of ribald
scandal. They came to be seen as refuges for the lazy, the corrupt and
the unproductive, not to be tolerated in the new age which was
dawning.

In every revolution the corrective pendulum swings widely and
with the Reformation celibacy was identified as a false doctrine
which had to be replaced with an emphasis on the sanctity and
importance of marriage. Preached in particular by Martin Luther,
this became a familiar theme taken up theme in popular propaganda. The Gude and Godly Ballads illustrate this.

> God send everie Preist ane wyfe,
> And everie nun ane man,
> That thay micht leve that haly lyfe,
> As first the Kirk began.

> Sancte Peter, quhome nane can repruve,
> His lyfe in mariage led:
> All gude preistis quhome God did lufe,
> Thair maryit wyfis had.

From now on Protestantism was to romanticise family life and in the
process constrict the intellectual and spiritual lives of women
throughout Scotland.

In the Scotland of the fifteenth century Christianity was spread
very thin. It was an urban religion and Scotland was a peasant
country, the population spread out in hamlets rather more even than
villages. For the peasant, magic, healing springs, good and bad
spirits were the sources of their comfort and and their fear. It was
among these people that John Knox and his followers undertook the
task of establishing a Godly State and a religious ideology. As is so
often the case, correct behaviour was defined by setting the limits of
what was not to be tolerated, so the first task for the new authority

was to define the nature of sin. The next task was to find ways of reinforcing that message.

It was taught that human nature was essentially sinful and that a permanent state of guilt was a proper mode of relating to the authority of God. This guilt was to be the driving force of the Protestant ethic. Redemption for sin could be found through obedience to God's laws as defined by the church. The major sins were defined by the General Assembly of the new church and embodied in legislation: they were fornication, adultery, witchcraft, bestiality and mass-mongering. In times of change those claiming authority have to show their power of social control and this is most commonly linked to suppression of all forms of spontaneous or libidinal behaviour. Sexuality is an obvious target: it embodies the most powerful of human drives, it transforms people and forms bonds between them capable of resisting external authority of every kind, it seeks privacy and freedom of expression, it is highly individualistic, it is difficult to control. Protestantism set about laying the foundation for its prurient reputation for sexual policing of the population.

So the most powerful sanctions were reserved against the act of fornication. Inevitably women suffer most severely from such control since they become pregnant and their 'sin' is discovered. They were forced to name their partners just as was the case in Social Security offices until the mid-sixties of this century ... When the sin of fornication was uncovered, either as a result of a pregnancy or information offered, both partners were brought to kneel on the stool in the kirk to confess their sins, to offer repentance and to seek forgiveness. This practice has been retained by the Free Church of Scotland until the present day, although increasingly resented and rejected by young people. If the couple should fail to make repentance before the congregation, they are excluded from the community of the church and the sacrament of baptism will be refused their children.

At least both men and women were equally involved in the act of discipline. This was not the case with the witch hunts which the Protestant church pursued throughout the sixteenth and seventeenth centuries where 80 per cent of those tried were women and the other 20 per cent were men who seemed to have had a close association with women. I have wondered if these men may have been homosexual though there is no evidence to support that thought. It has been suggested, however, that the intensive searching out of fornicators did lead to an increase in homosexual practices.

Witch hunts seem to have served a variety of purposes for the young Protestantism. In the traditional way they offered an external

218

enemy, a scapegoat, on whom many of the ills that afflicted both individuals and the state could focus. For this first religious political ideology, with a need to demonstrate law and order, witches represented the most deviant group. They were female and they were normally single women living alone. To destroy them was to make both a religious and a political statement: 'The land that was purged of witches was purged of evil.' It is also argued that this persecution served the interests of the emergent male medical profession in wresting from women their role and status as healers and midwives. Perhaps most important, in killing, at a modest estimate, about a thousand women in Scotland, the witch hunt destroyed the skills of an animistic culture with its intimate knowledge of the herbs and minerals of the natural world woven into a magical web of spells and incantations. Superstition was pushed back, ritual desacralised, in preparation for the objective, 'rational' world which Protestantism presaged.

Education was seen as important so that as many people as possible should be able to read the Bible. Protestantism was indeed 'the religion of the Book'. In Scotland every parish was to have a school and literacy was linked with salvation. In this sense it offered equal opportunities to men and women but the message to women extracted from the Bible and given to them by the minister was very different from that offered to men. Woman was offered salvation through subservience and obedience to her husband in expiation for the sinfulness of Eve in the Garden of Eden; man was offered the right to rule over his wife. The Bible, with its strong emphasis on the Old Testament, was used as a weapon of social control. The New Testament, with its emphasis on love, tenderness and forgiveness, was largely ignored, as were the prophetic denunciations of the oppression of the poor which illuminate the Old Testament.

Northern Europe was not ready for New Testament Christianity and Scotland less than most countries. Sometimes it seems still not to be ready. Emerging capitalism was going to make stricter demands on human capacities for endurance and self-discipline than the looser structures of the pre-industrial society which existed in Scotland. Love and forgiveness must have seemed irrelevant in the face of the social changes beginning to be discerned. The medium through which this social transformation was to be mediated could only be the family with a stern father, just like God, a subservient, unquestioning mother and obedient children.

There was no place offered in Protestantism at this time for the unmarried woman or even the widow as there had been in earlier forms of Christianity. What we now call illegitimate births, that is births outside a formal relationship sanctioned by the church and state, were seen as deeply sinful. It is a reflection of the capacity of folk wisdom to resist the power of the state that common law marriages survived in Scotland until the middle of this century. Not only were convents closed but the aftermath of the witch hunts made it impossible for any woman to develop skills which might be misconstrued. Since the Bible placed man in authority over her, she could not compete with him. Once the universities took over the training of doctors, women were specifically excluded from the healing profession. An Act of Parliament, passed in Edinburgh in 1641, threatened women under the Witchcraft Act if they continued to practice.

More important still, Protestantism set about depriving women of any divine female figure, either Christian or animistic, with whom they could identify. In its attack on Mariolatry, Protestantism had forbidden to women the Virgin Mary and all those other women who had attained sanctity and to whom they could appeal in distress.

From the point of view of a balanced and civilised society the loss of a divine female figure should also be recognised as a loss to men. Under the previous regime, almost as under the Greeks and the Romans, there had been a range of emotional symbols with which men too could identify and to which they could turn for spiritual succour when beset by difficulties. The tenderness, which is a mark of the relationship between a mother and her children of both sexes and which is such an important component of any society, could be kept alive for men in a relationship with the Mother of God. In Protestantism, this image of an ideal mother had to go underground in favour of a single divine image of God the Father. The perception of what it meant to be a man and what it meant to be a woman were drifting even farther apart and this was to have dire consequences for relationships between men and women.

By the eighteenth century significant changes were taking place in the intellectual life of Scotland. Persecution against witches had officially ceased although the folklore was still strong. The idea of establishing a Kingdom of God was being replaced by a new set of ideas which focused more on the quality of life as it was lived. Secular alternatives abounded for the educated and privileged classes: belief in science, the pursuit of liberty, the defence of property and enlightened patriotism. These educated classes were not to be found on the repentance stool, and brothels flourished in Edinburgh and Glasgow. But Robert Burns's poems resonated in the lives of ordinary people when he wrote about witches and the power of the church over the lives of sexually active men and women in the Ayrshire farming community.

By the next century the Industrial Revolution was in full flood, forcing people off the land, breaking up communities, tearing families apart in spite of the lip service paid to the sanctity of the family. Capitalism totally denied the values of pity and tenderness in the coal mines and the factories where men, women and children slaved together. Equally, in the hurriedly thrown up tenements built to house the immigrants pouring into the industrial areas like Glasgow from the Highlands and from Ireland, values of decency of human behaviour were constantly threatened as human beings were forced to live without proper sanitation or privacy. The proliferation of pubs and prostitution provided an outlet for those who sought to anaesthetise the pain of their existence.

It was out of these conditions that the figure of the strong Scottish woman was born and what gave her strength was frequently the Protestant ethic which in other ways was so harmful to her. Those women who had incorporated the messages of endurance, of thrift, of self-denial and of independence and the importance of education – so much a part of the Knoxian heritage – were the ones who were able to fight their way out of the poverty and the socially degrading conditions in which they found themselves. Sexual repression, along with an emphasis on personal cleanliness, had its uses in over-crowded rooms and beds lacking all privacy. Dirt and immorality were shared enemies for women. Endurance and thrift made it possible to see a way out of the trap of poverty, and goals of independence made it possible for young people to seek a life and career in a different milieu to that occupied by their parents.

Those who had come straight from more relaxed, less demanding rural values were more likely to go under unless they learned quickly. Among these were many Roman Catholic families from Ireland whose value system was non-competitive, interdependent, libidinal and linked to rhythms of nature rather than to factory hooters and punctual time-keeping. Many of them were innumerate and illiterate and, unlike the Protestants, had no tradition of seeing education as part of a religious virtue. In addition the Catholic families had to cope with the inherited suspicion of all things connected with the Pope and with Rome. It was difficult for Catholic men to get into skilled jobs, or for their sons to get apprenticeships, and Catholic women had to face their Protestant women neighbours from this ground of social inferiority. Many of these women did indeed learn quickly and became Protestantised Roman Catholics in every way except for the guilt they suffered in restricting the size of their families. It took exceptional ability to compete with Protestant standards of living if you were coping with a pregnancy every year.

The Book of Genesis was again in full flood from pulpits to justify sexual oppression. The nineteenth century discovery of chloroform in childbirth was thundered against because God had punished Eve for her sin by saying, 'I will greatly magnify your pain in childbearing; in pain you shall bring forth children ...'. Yet women had to be available at all times to be impregnated because God had gone on, 'yet your desire shall be for your husband, and he shall rule over you'. By teaching everyone to read the Bible, Protestantism had played into the hands of every man and deprived every woman of an argument against him. Yet Protestant women were able to turn some of the teaching against men and use it to foster social achievement which could be more readily achieved by restricting the number of children one had. A major weapon was that sex was inherently sinful and should be disciplined even in marriage. By the early part of the twentieth century the fall in the number of children of Scottish Protestant families was another factor which differentiated them from Catholic families.

The Industrial Revolution brought with it an intensification of the Protestant view of the world at many levels. Nineteenth-century Protestantism faced powerful disputes about relations between church and state which led to the Disruption of 1843. The State Church section which emerged did so primarily as the representative of the landlord and the factory owner. The virtues of hard work, self-denial, endurance and obedience to employers were preached from every pulpit, these very virtues which had enabled women to survive and hold their families together through terrible times. But working men at the point of production saw it differently. As secular passions developed and with them ideas of trade-unionism and political parties which represented the interests of working people, male attendance at church began to decline. In most cases this withdrawal did not involve an active rejection of the church, religion or the idea of God. The fear and respect in which religion had previously been held was replaced by disinterest. Maintaining a church connection became the responsibility of the woman of the family.

Other than in Christian feminist groups, little attention has been paid to the significance of religion for women and the ways in which it differs from the significance of religion for men. Scottish Protestantism had ruthlessly weeded out all symbols of feminine religious power even to the extent of destroying the images in stained glass or in stone which represented the Virgin Mary and female saints which had acted as guides to prayer for illiterate church attenders. What was left was divine power vested in a male God who was both Judge and King. Reading the hymn book of the Church of Scotland is like reading a description of a macho, masculine deity.

> *The Lord is King! who then shall dare*
> *Resist his will, distrust his care,*
> *Or murmur at his wise decrees,*
> *Or doubt his royal promises.*

These are not images with which women find it easy to identify. The separation between 'feelings' and practical life which had been another result of the institutionalisation of the Christian church and its links with the state had left women with the responsibility which they still carry for maintaining qualities of intimacy and tenderness. Deprived of a female figure their only outlet left for tenderness was the figure of Jesus, the Son of God. Victorian times saw an outpouring of what the insensitive describe as mawkish sentiment over the Christ figure. For those who needed it, and it was not only women, Jesus became the symbol of loving, tender care as an alternative to the cold, harsh, unforgiving image of God being presented in the pulpit on Sundays, week after week.

The prayers of women are more intimate than the prayers of men. They pray, not for victory but for understanding. In an unloving world they seek a presence who will always be there for them, to whom they can turn inside their heads for comfort. They are concerned with the basic issues and the life and death of Jesus Christ spoke to their condition. 'This is my body, This is my blood' has a familiar ring to women whose bodies bleed every month. 'Take ye and eat' makes sense to women who suckle their children.

The only roles offered to women in the Protestant Church were the traditional ones of being the custodians of tenderness and caring. They took on the tasks, which they still do today, of decorating the churches with flowers as priestesses have done in their temples since time immemorial, but unlike priestesses they had no power over the sacred ceremonies. They prepared the buildings for services and made special efforts for the great rituals of the Church: the weddings, the baptisms, the funerals. When needed they prepared food and drink for the congregation, raised funds to keep the church, the manse and the parish functioning. And frequently they did this in a state of submission to emotionally and spiritually illiterate ministers who, while using them, totally failed to appreciate the power of the gifts they brought. Their contribution was not only undervalued, but seen as peripheral to the real concerns of the Christian community. What is even sadder is that the women themselves accepted the value which ministers and other men in the church put on their contribution.

A major change came at the end of the eighteenth century with the new role that opened up for women in the foreign mission field. It has been described by the Women in Scotland Bibliography Group as one of the few areas where women could serve alongside men on an almost equal footing. Women took full advantage of the opportunities and by the end of the nineteenth century there were probably more women than men serving the Presbyterian Missions. Apart from the many remarkable women who married missionaries and suffered all the problems of climate and a hostile environment while caring for their husbands, teaching, nursing and having their babies, many single women teachers and doctors served in the field.

In the 1830s church women had formed the Edinburgh Association of Ladies for the Advancement of Female Education in India and the Glasgow Ladies' Association for Promoting Female Education in Kaffraria (Southern Africa). The Power of the Book was still alive. The Edinburgh group sent out their first missionary, Miss Reid, to Bombay in 1838. Teachers went first but were followed in the 1880s by women doctors. By now the church was, indirectly, an important force in encouraging higher education for women. Women who were missionaries in their own right had first gone to India in the expectation that, being women, they had a specific role to play in gaining access to women in purdah where access by men was forbidden. In fact, by the end of the nineteenth century they were travelling widely and working also in Africa and China. Travellers in these countries can still be disconcerted on occasion to hear Scottish songs which were taught in schools by women missionaries.

That their contribution had been significant could not be discounted. This led to a slow, general recognition of some of the qualities women had to offer the church and by 1886 the General Assembly approved the setting up of the Woman's Guild and the Order of Deaconesses. The aim was to have a comprehensive structure of ministry by women as Guild members, Guild leaders and Deaconesses. But the contribution expected of women was still one of secondary status. The power of the central mystery conferred by ordination was firmly retained by men. Nevertheless, a steady sharing of organisational power evolved. In 1843, long before women gained the right to vote in parliamentary elections, the newly-formed Free Church of Scotland gave women the vote in the election of ministers and in the following century there was to be a constant stream of proposals pressing for a share of both political and spiritual power.

By the middle of the twentieth century there was a decline in all forms of church attendance and by the end of the 1980s, what Stewart Lamont, that most rigorous of Scottish religious commentators, described as 'the tide of secularism' was eroding the Protestant Church. He identified apathy, indifference and the resulting financial problems for the churches as evidence of this erosion. By 1986 only 20 per cent of Scots were attending the churches to which they claimed to owe allegiance and a steady collapse in kirk membership had meant a 1.5 per cent per annum fall during the previous decade.

In spite of vigorous representations to the General Assembly throughout the first half of the twentieth century, notably the famous 1943 'Commission for the Interpretation of God's Will in the Present Crisis' chaired by Professor John Baillie, it was not until 1966 that resistance to involving women in the organisation and policy-making councils of the Church of Scotland as elders of the Kirk Session cracked. Baillie's Commission had argued, on the basis of principles derived ultimately from the church's own message, the case for the admission of women both to the eldership and to the ministry. The decision to share lay power was followed quickly in 1968 by an agreement to ordain women ministers. This was to a significant extent the result of a long personal campaign by a pioneering woman, Mary Lusk, who was herself seeking ordination. With strength and dignity she pressed the issue throughout the church. She finally succeeded in presenting a petition to the assembly but at that stage failed to have it accepted.

Throughout Europe the 1960s had seen a radical reappraisal of religious authority along with a rise in feminist consciousness. Scottish women church members have always maintained strong international links and their determination to achieve change was supported by these contacts. Another factor in the ordination of women was the drop in 'suitable' male candidates. The rates of pay for the ministry were declining in relation to the rates offered by the fast-growing competing occupations – teaching, social work, business management, financial services, all recruiting graduates. Some of these, as well as offering more attractive financial rewards, were capable of absorbing the altruism and sense of service that had previously been funnelled into the church.

Previously too, many ministers and their parishes had relied on the devoted unpaid assistance of the minister's wife. By the 1960s, as opportunities for women improved, particularly in the caring professions, ministers' wives increasingly carved out careers for themselves which left them neither the time nor the inclination to run the Women's Guild and perform the variety of nurturing services many parishes require. This female leadership vacuum was filled by women members of the congregation who in turn began to develop a more realistic perception of their own contribution, and became consequently more open to the idea of women in positions of spiritual authority.

It could also be said that the power of the mystery which is at the heart of the priesthood was only shared with women at a point in the history of the church when it was beginning to lose significance as a force in the community. As it happens, those women who have been ordained have been shunted into the sidelines of whatever power structures exist. Their voices are rarely heard in the Assembly, not because women are unwilling to speak but because there are still only a few women who are inducted into a church, given full status and thereby eligible to take part. The decline in church attendance has meant that union between neighbouring churches is often pending and women ministers are caught in this waiting world. Often too, the parishes into which they are elected are the non-prestigious parishes that the more ambitious male ministers do not want. Women ministers are, in the main, concentrated in the poorly resourced parishes where they are engaged in traditional feminine roles of caring for the poor, the disadvantaged and women in distress. The 'manse', which may be a council house, serves not only as a family home but as a refuge for battered wives or abused children.

Although there had been forms of Protestantism in other countries which have made this decision earlier, the ability of the traditionally male-dominated Scottish Church to accept women has baffled many commentators who watch curiously from the sidelines of the Church of England where the Synod is locked in a life-and-death struggle on this issue. A significant factor has been the conviction, dating from the Reformation, that Protestants have a religious duty to emphasise the rational nature of the human relationship with God and to resist all forms of superstition. The superstition which has been most responsible for excluding women from participation in religious ceremonial has been that associated with the monthly shedding of blood. Menstruating women in many societies have been seen as unclean; in Judaism elaborate rituals were established to protect men from the 'dangerous' flux. Many primitive societies have similar rituals.

Protestantism is the only form of Christianity which has, as part of its perception of the uncompromising nature of religion, rejected this along with the many other superstitions which it saw as its duty to attack. Woman, like man, can stand face to face with God and claim salvation. This personal autonomy also made it possible for women to take responsibility for their own reproductive destiny and use contraception, and the General Assembly has in the past supported the right of women to have abortions, even though only in limited circumstances. For Roman and Anglo Catholicism, the issue is not primarily that woman does not have a penis, although that is a powerful factor. It arises from a fundamental rejection of the possibility that a menstruating woman can be permitted to pollute the sanctuary. In the Russian Orthodox Church women still learn from their mothers not to take communion while their blood flows.

The Protestant church has acted as the most powerful protagonist of patriarchy as a justification of authority. Those Old Testament images of a fierce, punitive, unforgiving and judgmental God bit deep into the Scottish psyche both in personal relationships and in institutions. Social and economic factors interacted with the church's emphasis on the woman's role as being one of subservience. When men had to work hard in industries such as the shipyards, it was essential for the economy of the family that the husband's health be protected, that he get the most nourishing food, that he be not disturbed when he needed to sleep. While not all men succumbed to this very seductive role, the majority could not help but see themselves as powerful. Many embraced the role of the tyrant with eagerness.

The emphasis on an exclusively male deity may also have helped to create the idealised image among men of a man who is all man, who is not concerned with domestic affairs or with the care of children, whose primary concerns are with work and whose leisure interests involve him in male activities like hard drinking or football. More 'feminine' interests were seen as irrelevant and any man showing any feminine traits would be jeered at as a cissy. The existence of male homosexuality in Scotland was totally denied until the late 1960s as a terrible slur on the national identity. Homosexuals had to take refuge in London.

The most dangerous combination for women and children is to live in economic dependency with a man who is both trained in patriarchal values and trapped in a sense of powerlessness or frustration. Women and children, particularly girl children, then become the scapegoats for aggressive – sometimes sexual behaviour which is justified by the male 'need' to behave in the way he does or else a 'need' to establish his authority over them. As so often happens, women and children are not only held down by fear but also by a collusion with their oppressor whose views are reinforced wherever they turn. They have been taught by the church that they should submit to male images whether they be of man or God. This has resulted in claims that 25 per cent of all reported crime in the cities of Edinburgh and Strathclyde are connected with wife assault. It is the second most common form of violence reported to the police and we know from research that it is grossly under-reported as are crimes of rape and sexual assaults on children.

Our institutions and our professions are still heavily permeated by patriarchal values. In Britain the most obvious is perhaps the Westminster parliament which starts every day with prayers of a traditional type and which runs its business in a way suitable to men who have no domestic responsibilities of any kind and forces its minority of women members to behave as if they too were men.

Universities, local authorities, hospitals and prisons are among the institutions which are dominated by male hierarchical patterns and styles. So too are the professions of teaching, law and medicine as well as the ministry. Women, to be successful in gaining a share of power by getting promotion, have in most cases to go along with established patterns of competitive, driven, achieving styles of work which are fundamentally different from the co-operative, trusting and interdependent styles which come more naturally to them, based as they are in the idea of mutuality of relationships rather than in ideas of dominance.

The General Assembly, which is the closest institution we have in Scotland to a parliament, is totally male-dominated both in style and membership. It has proved particularly resistant to any suggestion that the deity might have any attributes that were not totally masculine. In 1982, a remarkable Scottish woman, Anne Hepburn, while offering up the prayer at the annual meeting of the Women's Guild of the Church of Scotland, used the phrase, 'God, our Mother'. It was widely reported and the church erupted in discord. In order to handle the hubbub, the General Assembly, 'amid bubbling controversy, and lively media interest' set up a study group to examine 'the theological implications of the concept of the Motherhood of God'. The 1984 Assembly, this time 'amid volcanic controversy and feverish media interest', made the extraordinary decision not even to discuss the report it had commissioned.

For theologians, both male and female, the sex and gender of God cannot be a real question. The deity they envisage transcends all these characteristics. But the average Protestant is not a theologian and has been shaped by the man-made language of the Bible and of male preachers over the centuries to accept an image of God as exclusively male. The issue is not, however, closed. It is kept alive by women theologians and groups of women who meet inside and outside the official venues of the church to express their deep conviction that the God to whom they pray is one who has characteristics with which they can identify. So hurtful is this exclusively male language to some women, they have felt compelled to leave those parishes which in their language, rituals and beliefs are so insensitive to their deepest needs.

Meanwhile, for most men and women in Scotland, increasing secularism means that such discussions seem irrelevant. They may continue to get married in a church, they may take their babies for baptism, they may ask a minister to officiate at the funeral of a parent or elderly relative, but these are the rituals of a folk religion rather than of an ideology that governs the intimate behaviour of their lives.

As the industrial revolution recedes into history, the Protestant emphasis on hard work, endurance, thrift and independence is seen as less necessary, sometimes irrelevant, sometimes even unsuitable for a society based on the new technologies, new styles of living. New values and symbols are evolving. Concern is increasingly expressed for the quality of life in this world rather than in the next. Groups which are trying to give both men and women some sense of their relationship with the cycles of birth, life and death would not primarily describe themselves as religious. There may be individuals among them who have a religious orientation but they deal with private matters. The emphasis of these groups is often not on the individual's relationship with a male God, but on a female principle, Gaia, which represents the planet on which human beings have their home. Men are seen as sharers in that female principle and currently throughout Scotland groups of men are meeting together to explore their capacities for tenderness and other qualities which have been seen as exclusively female. More and more women are trying to change structures, to escape the trap of being forced to renounce their femininity in order to succeed in what is still a male-dominated world.

The planet is increasingly perceived as an intricate system of interdependent entities, of whom human beings are only one. All living things, indeed what we in our ignorance may see as non-living things as well, are to be honoured. The Book of Genesis is rejected with its notions of male domination. The superstition which the Protestant church saw as its duty to repel is being reviewed as a repository of folk wisdom couched in the only symbolic language which was available to those whose knowledge it reflected. Women are recreating the lost knowledge of plants, herbs and healing. In health care the old notions of omnipotent authority are being replaced by complementary relationships between patient and doctor and complementary and alternative medicine. Other professions are slowly yielding to the new trends. In some parts of the world, particularly in Africa and some parts of South America, the role of the minister or priest is more and more being devolved to lay helpers and the local community, particularly women.

Most important, the concepts of sin and guilt which were so much a part of the power of the ministry over women are being challenged by a new theology in which the emphasis on the primary sinfulness of the human race is being replaced by a celebration of the miracle of creation. Women, and their role in creation, are being seen as equal partners with men in that celebration.

Protestantism in both Europe and America is facing its own crisis as its cautious attempts to change and open up to these new, vibrant forces are stimulating a counter-revolution of patriarchal fundamentalism. As some sections of the church hover indecisively about making a commitment to the future, the training colleges for the ministry are filling up with students whose faces are turned firmly to the past and what they see as the certainties of the Old Testament, where men are men and women are women and God is now and always will be totally male.

If they succeed in grasping power in Protestant structures it will turn to dust in their hands. Congregations will continue to diminish as more and more women enter the work force and the pool of labour available to do the church chores and raise funds will be maintained – as indeed it is already in some churches – only by the retired and the elderly. It may be that the Protestant reformation has served its historical purposes, one of which was to hold women in the role of carer and support to the men who were in turn servants of the machinery of production.

The machines in Scotland have gone and other important changes have taken place. Women have a right to retain the family home if they are left caring for children after a family break-up. They can claim social security not previously available to them, to enable them to do that. And they can get divorced thanks to the legal aid scheme. Thus they no longer need to have the tea on the table the minute the man comes in the door from work. Nor do they need to tend him as if he were a child who must be looked after and propitiated because if he's off sick, dies or leaves, the family will have no money. Nor do they need to listen to a man preaching to them from the pulpit messages that are irrelevant to their lives. We are facing the task of seeking new ways of relating to each other as men and women who are concerned with the fundamental mysteries of the human experience.

As the walls come down over Europe, so too the walls are coming down between the various denominations of Christianity. The establishment in Scotland and in Europe of offices of the Justice, Peace and Integrity of Creation movement is only one symbol of this, but a very important one. It is an organisation which honours women as partners in the search for a spiritual wholeness that is firmly rooted in taking responsibility for the way all human beings live and work together. Women, because of the way they live their lives, are more attuned to ideas of wholeness than men who have so often divided their lives rigidly between home and work, having different styles of behaviour for each. If there is a future for any form of religion in Scotland it will have to grow from many roots in our history, pre- as well as post-Reformation. But it will have no validity unless it acknowledges and allows itself to grow out of and learn from the pain and humiliation that women have endured under the banner of a male Protestant God.

REFERENCES

BURLEIGH, J. H. S. (1960) *A Church History of Scotland*, London: Oxford University Press.

CHITTISTER, J. (1983) *Women, Ministry and the Church*, New York: Paulist Press.

FLEMING, J. R. (1933) *A History of the Church in Scotland 1875-1929*, Edinburgh: T. and T. Clark.

FOX, M. (1983) *Original Blessings*, Santa Fe, New Mexico: Bear and Co.

FOX KELLER, E, (1985) *Reflections on Gender and Science*, New Haven and London: Yale University Press.

HEALEY, E. (1986) *Wives of Fame*, London: Sidgwick and Jackson.

HEPBURN, A (1989) 'Wounded Daughters', *Newsletter of the Presbyterian Health, Education and Welfare Association*.

HEWAT, E. G. K. (1960) *Vision and Achievement 1796-1956: A History of the Foreign missions of the Churches in the Church of Scotland*, Edinburgh: Nelson.

HURCOMBE, L. (1987) *Sex and God*, London: Routledge and Kegan Paul.

LAMONT, S. (1989) *Church and State*, London: The Bodley Head.

LARNER, C. (1981) *Enemies of God*, London: Chatto and Windus.

LARNER, C. (1984) *Witchcraft and Religion*, Oxford: Basil Blackwell.

MacCUNN, F. A. (1895) *John Knox*, London: Methuen

MARTIN, M. E. (1975) *Protestantism*, London: Weidenfeld and Nicholson.

PAGELS, E. (1988) *Adam, Eve and the Serpent*, London: Weidenfeld and Nicholson.

ROSS, I. (ed.) (1939) *The Gude and Godly Ballads*, Edinburgh: The Saltire Society.

SMOUT, T. C ., (1986) *A Century of the Scottish People 1830-1950*, London: Collins.

STRACHAN, E and S. (1985) *Freeing the Feminine*, Dunbar: Labarum Publications Ltd.

TAWNEY, R. H. (1926) *Religion and the Rise of Capitalism*, London: John Murray.

Women in Scotland: an Annotated Bibliography, Edinburgh: The Open University.

Violence Against Women, *Women's National Commission Report*.

Community of Men and Women, (1986) *Report of the General Assembly Board of World Mission and Unity*

12
The Ulster Connection

STEVE BRUCE

INTRODUCTION

There are two good reasons why any consideration of Scottish popular culture must consider the 'Ulster connection'. First, the external ties between Scotland and Ulster have had considerable impact on the histories of both places. Second, the external relationship resonates so strongly with tensions within Scotland. Although I will argue that the claim that Scotland is as sectarian as Ulster (or that it easily might so become) is hysterical nonsense produced by journalists looking for a story in the run-up to the Twelfth of July Orange Walk, elements of Ulster's bitter rivalry between Protestants and Catholics are to be found in 'north Britain' and this essay will consider them.

It is difficult to write about such large issues over such a long time scale without falling into banal and inaccurate generalisations about the Scottish 'mind'. Some social scientists may object to us drawing general conclusions about the values, beliefs and sentiments of very large populations from the actions of a small number of individuals and organisations, but in the absence of modern techniques of opinion polling we have little alternative. Anyway, there are good grounds for arguing that it is only from the careers of events, individuals and organisations that one can reasonably make inferences about popular opinion and culture (a view cogently argued by Blumer, 1954). On both practical and analytical grounds then, this chapter will concern itself with a small number of critical moments in recent Scottish history and from these offer generalisations about the impact of Ulster on Scottish popular culture.

PRE-HISTORY AND HISTORY

The Scoti who first settled what is now Argyll under Fergus Mac Erc in the fifth century came from Ulster. The common origins of the two people allowed early Scots historians such as Boece and

Buchanan to pad out a fictitiously ancient history by borrowing stories from Latin historians who used 'Scoti' to refer to the inhabitants of Ireland. In a landscape where until very recently travel by sea was considerably easier and faster than travel by land, it was inevitable that there would be constant movement of population between the north-east of Ireland and the west coast of Scotland. In the seventh century, lowland Scots formed a major part of the population which was 'planted' in Ulster. Perhaps some 70,000 Scots (of a total Ulster population of about 250,000) migrated (Macafee and Morgan, 1981, 47). And the ties were not exhausted by permanent settlement; even without the 'push' factors of famine and political unrest in Ireland, there was regular seasonal movement, with large numbers of Ulster people working in Scottish lowlands agriculture. After the middle of the eighteenth century, patterns changed, with a larger number of the Irish settling permanently in Scotland. The causes of this migration can be readily listed. Wages in Scotland were higher and the growth in the industry of the western and central lowlands meant a demand for labour, either in the new factories or in filling the gaps left in the agricultural labour force by the movement of Scots into the new industries. The failure of the 1798 rebellion in Ireland was one 'push' factor, as were the famines of the early nineteenth century.

By then Scotland was a thoroughly Presbyterian country. The Reformation had initially affected only the lowlands and Caithness in the north, but the evangelical revivals of the late eighteenth and early nineteenth century had seen most of the Highlands converted to Calvinist Presbyterianism. Although there were remnants of old Catholicism in parts of the western highlands and in Banff and Buchan, the vast majority of Catholics in Scotland were Irish immigrants, and were concentrated in the western and central lowlands. In the co-existence of two populations competing for scarce resources and radically divided by religion, one has the basis for enduring conflict. A catalyst was provided by the fact that many of the 'Irish' who moved to Scotland were Ulster Protestants, already possessed of an active tradition of Orange rivalry with Catholics. Ireland in the eighteenth century was littered with secret societies and informal militias. These were largely agrarian movements. Protestant and Catholic small farmers and peasants banded together in defence against each other in movements such as the Defenders and the Peep O'Day Boys. The Orange Order (named, naturally enough, after the Dutch princedom of King William) was founded after a skirmish at the Diamond in County Armagh in 1795 which saw at least twenty-five dead (Senior, 1966). Initially the gentry were ambivalent toward the Orangemen. They had the right religion but they might develop their activities from destroying and expropriating Catholic property to stealing from their betters. It was only when the United Irishmen, with their French Revolution rhetoric, seemed a more present danger that the gentry entered the Order. In the relatively peaceful period of the first two decades of the nineteenth century, the Order waned, but with the arrival of Daniel O'Connell the Orangemen began to march again. There was then a further waning, but the 1886 Home Rule bill gave Protestants a new reason to band together. The Order had initially been a rural movement of peasants and some gentry and hence it was largely Church of Ireland. For a while in the eighteenth century Ulster Presbyterians flirted with the idea of an alliance with Catholics against their common Church of Ireland oppressors but, persuaded by conservative ministers such as Henry Cooke and frightened by the Home Rule movement, Presbyterians joined the Orange Order in large numbers and made it the popular voice of Ulster Protestantism.

Orangeism was brought to Scotland by soldiers of the Scottish Fencibles sent to Ireland in 1798 to help quell the rebellion. It fairly quickly spread through the western and central industrial lowlands where it offered an expression for anti-Catholicism and a fraternal organisation in which men who lived a hard and unrewarding life, often new to the impersonality of the town and the factory, could develop their sense of self-worth and self-confidence. Like many such fraternities, it allowed a form of 'ethnic closure' to be practised. To work in certain jobs and in certain factories you had to be in the Orange. That the Irish immigrants were poorer, less well-educated, and less well-acquainted with the circumstances of industrialisation meant that they began at the bottom of the economic heap. Some Protestant workers benefited from them staying there and used the local lodge as a vehicle for exclusion. Some employers, like Baird and Co., ironmasters, of Coatbridge 'used patronage of the Orange Lodge as a form of company paternalism with which to create Protestant worker identification with management and thus undermine trades-union organization' (Brown, 1987, 164).

It was not just at the level of popular religion that Scotland and Ulster were linked. The formal church lives of the two countries were also inexorably intertwined. Irish Presbyterianism had its origins in the work of Scots Presbyterians (Holmes, 1985, 1-53) and it was only in 1840 that the Irish Presbyterians established their own General Assembly. All the schisms in the Scottish church had their corresponding divisions in Ulster, even when, as in the case of the division between anti-burghers and burghers over whether they

could take the Burgess Oath, the cause of schism was not present in
Ulster. Even after 1840 ties between the two churches remained very
close with many Ulster probationers studying for the ministry in
Glasgow and Edinburgh and ministers on each side of the water
being called to charges on the other.

ANTI-CATHOLICISM

It would have been surprising if there had not been a hostile nativist
reaction to the Irish in Scotland, who were seen as an economic and
social threat, as well as a challenge to the truth of the Reformed
religion. The middle of the nineteenth century, with the controversy
over the government grant for St Patrick's College at Maynooth, saw
considerable 'anti-popery' agitation, especially from Free Church
clergy. Not surprising, given that the vast majority of Catholics were
Irish, anti-popery was also anti-Irish. Looking back now, the heated
anti-Catholicism of the Scottish Reformation Society's *Bulwark* or
The Witness, edited by leading lay Free Churchman Hugh Miller,
seems understandable. These magazines were produced by men
who took their religion very seriously and they believed that Roman
Catholicism was very much the wrong religion. What stands out
more stunningly is the common everyday abuse of the Irish by such
papers as the *North British Daily Mail*, which peppered news reports
with condemnation by adjective: 'Yesterday at the Central Police
Court, an ape-faced, small-headed Irishman ... A middle-aged,
malicious-looking Irishman. ... Two surly-looking sons of the Em-
erald Isle ... Pat O'Shannan, a startled-looking Irish tailor, with a
cruel Tipperary visage ...' (in Handley, 1947, 108). Implicit racism
took a long time to disappear. But what did diminish rapidly in the
second half of the nineteenth century was aggressive combative anti-
popery. In the lowlands the Free Church rapidly became more
theologically liberal. In the kirk, anti-Catholicism became quaint
and even a little despised. This can be clearly seen in the career of the
last Scottish Presbyterian clergyman to make a career out of ex-
posing the evils of Rome. Jacob Primmer acquired his training in 'the
popish controversy' in the 'anti-popery' classes funded and organised by Edinburgh lawyer John Hope. After theological training he
devoted his life to fighting 'Popery, Ritualism and Rationalism'. He
did these things aggressively enough to become nationally known
and to ensure that no Church of Scotland parish would call him to
a charge. All his working life he was kept in the financially precarious
position of missioner and the Home Mission Committee often
engaged in petty harassment by withholding parts of his salary. Year
after year he had to petition the General Assembly to be paid in full,

which does not suggest overwhelming support for his work.

The first home rule crisis of the 1880s had considerable impact on the political life of western Scotland, as it had on Liverpool and Lancashire, with many 'Irish' Scots being active in Irish political organisations. A number of Scots were actually elected to Westminster as home rulers by Irish constituencies (Gallagher, 1987b, 42-84).

The same quarrels in the second decade of this century had far less impact, perhaps because, as Gallagher argues, while the first crisis coincided with economic depression in Scotland and raised local fears about an the influx of poor Irishmen which would follow the collapse of the Irish economy, the second coincided with a period of relative prosperity on the Clyde and in the mining valleys of Ayrshire and Lanarkshire. It also coincided with a very small but symbolically interesting injection of Orangeism with the establishment in Govan of a Glasgow yard of Harland and Wolff, the great Belfast shipbuilder, whose workforce was almost entirely Protestant. Harland and Wolff's reputation was such that the historian of Celtic football club blames the sectarian rivalry of the 'Old Firm' on its workforce's support for Rangers but, as Bill Murray argues, the antagonistic relationship between Rangers and Celtic was well-established before 1912.

But there was considerable support in Scotland for the Unionist cause. The Glasgow Presbytery of the Church of Scotland unanimously sent a motion to the Belfast Presbytery supporting their opposition to Home Rule (*Scottish Protestant Review*, 28 August 1912). In his address commending the motion, Revd Dr Brown referred to the parallels between the Scottish Solemn League and Covenant and the Covenant which it was proposed should be signed by the Ulster people. In answer to those who might belittle such efforts, he quoted Burns:

> *The Solemn League and Covenant*
> *Now brings a smile, now brings a tear;*
> *But sacred freedom, too, was theirs;*
> *If thou'rt a slave, indulge thy sneer.*
> (*Scottish Protestant Review*, September 1912, 134.)

When Sir Edward Carson came to speak in Glasgow, only 8000 turned out to hear him. In contrast, Liverpool managed to produce over 150,000 people at 7.00 a.m. on a Sunday morning (Gallagher, 1987b, 72). Although the Church of Scotland's Glasgow Presbytery

displayed solidarity with the *sentiments* of its sister church across the
water, more direct action was not promoted and it was left to an
independent evangelical minister – the Revd James Brisby – to
organise clerical legitimation for the Scottish branches of the Ulster
Volunteer Force (UVF). Brisby was an Ulster emigré with an
independent ministry based initially in Bridgeton. When his services
became too popular for his church, he moved to holding Sunday
services in the City Halls in Candleriggs. He had been elected to the
Glasgow School Board in 1911 with 84,200 votes but he was beaten
by the liberal United Free Church minister and future Labour MP,
James Barr. The *Glasgow Weekly News* said: 'Rev. Mr Brisby, who
seems to have taken the place so long held by Harry Alfred Long as
Protestant champion, came very close.' Once elected he was impo-
tent. On the grounds that the Protestants had no representatives on
the Voluntary Schools Committee (which was concerned with
Catholic and Episcopal schools), Brisby proposed that no representative of voluntary schools be permitted to act as Convenor or
Vice-Convenor on any of 'our committees'. The motion could not
even find a seconder.

As they were in Ulster, the Scottish UVF units were organised as
'athletic clubs' attached to Orange Lodges. There were seven in all,
claiming one thousand trained men and as many again in training.
On 28 March, between four and five hundred Volunteers were
presented with colours which had been consecrated by Revd James
Cooper, Professor of Church History at Glasgow University (who,
ironically, was often a target for Jacob Primmer's criticisms for
ritualistic tendencies). The Marquis of Graham addressed the meeting. In the course of a rousing denunciation of 'some brutes in
parliament' who would put Ulster out of the Union, he announced
confidently:

> Not only were there thousands of men in Ulster but there were
> thousands of men outside Ulster who would have nothing
> whatever to do with that obnoxious thing called Home Rule ...
> When they in Scotland remembered what their own country
> had passed through for the sake of religious freedom their
> hearts warmed to those Ulstermen. What were these volun-
> teers for? They were out to back up the Ulstermen in their
> fight. They were men of the right stuff. (*Scottish Protestant
> Review*, April 1914, 69.)

The Marquis, and more enthusiastically Brisby who spoke after him,
thus began what became a firmly established tradition of Scottish
unionists and Orangemen offering martial bluster.

The question of church support for the Covenant can serve as a convenient index of the different degree of feeling about home rule in Ulster and Scotland. In Ulster the massive popularity of the Covenant can be seen in the considerable involvement of the Presbyterian Church and the Church of Ireland in organising and promoting the signing. In Glasgow, solidaristic support had to be organised by an independent evangelical Ulster emigré.

The onset of the Great War turned attention away from Ireland. The opportunism of the 1916 Easter Rising brought a minor revival of anti-Irish sentiment, ably expressed by Andrew Amos, the disillusioned Border radical in John Buchan's *Mr Standfast*, whose description of Ulster perfectly captures the grudging sense of Presbyterian common identity.

> Glasgow's stinkin' nowadays with two things, money and Irish. I mind the day when I followed Mr Gladstone's Home Rule policy, and used to threep about the noble, generous, warm-hearted sister nation held in a foreign bondage. My Goad! I'm not speakin' about Ulster, which is a dour, ill-natured den, but our own folk all the same. But the men that will not do a hand's turn to help the war and take the chance of our necessities to set up a bawbee rebellion are hateful to Goad and man.

The aftermath of 1916 also brought an increase in 'Irish' political activity with a large number of Sinn Fein branches being founded and a lot of money being raised for the nationalist cause. But the partition of Ireland and the consolidation of the Free State and Ulster governments allowed the Irish question to slide from the front pages. The (as it turned out temporary) solution to the Ulster problem meant that when relationships between Protestants and Catholics once again became fraught in Scotland, there was no additional amplifying resonance from the instability of Ulster.

ANTI-CATHOLICISM IN THE THIRTIES

The 1930s were a time of political unrest throughout Europe, and in Scotland there was a very minor upsurge of militant Protestant politics, largely through the Scottish Protestant League led by Alexander Ratcliffe in Glasgow and Protestant Action led by John Cormack in Edinburgh. For a very brief period both parties won seats in local council elections before collapsing in internal factionalism and defections.

The decline of both movements has been dealt with at length elsewhere (Gallagher, 1987a; 1987b, 150-69; Bruce, 1985). The cause can be summarised as the interaction between a lack of a coherent programme and the lack of an appreciative audience. 'Kicking the

Pope' was fine, but given the very small amount of council business
which had religious elements this did not provide much of a guide to
action, and both movements were unsure of their political direction.
Partly because his concerns were heavily weighted to the religious
failings of Catholicism and partly because of his desire for respectability, Ratcliffe never managed to build a strong base in proletarian
Bridgeton and Dalmar-nock, areas of strong Orange sentiment.
Both he and Cormack were too independent to be welcomed by the
Orange Order and neither managed to develop support in Ulster.

There were actually relatively few Catholics in Scotland and –
unlike the Ulster situation – they were not trying to alter Scotland's
sovereignty. Outside of the western lowlands concentration, they
were thus a little difficult to construe as a 'threat' to the Scots. They
were concentrated in one part of Scotland while, importantly, the
Free Church and the Church of Scotland were national organisations with parish structures which had not yet moved with population distribution. This had the important effect of reducing the
salience of anti-Catholicism in the courts of both churches. Any
orthodox Presbyterian would be 'anti-popery' in theory but only
some ministers were in parishes where actual social relations with
Catholics were an issue. In contrast, the conflict between the Free
Church and the Kirk which rumbled through the third quarter of the
nineteenth century was something which concerned *all* Presbyterians. A similar observation can be made about the geographical
division of Scotland. The highlands of Scotland were conservative in
their theology and quite ready to believe that the Pope was the anti-
Christ. But there were very few Irish Catholics in the highlands (and
the native ones were almost Protestant). The absence of actual
competition (hence the complete failure of Orangeism to recruit
north of Dundee) meant that anti-Catholicism remained an idea
unconnected to any social reality. The lowlands of Scotland had lots
of Irish Catholics. But they did not have the religion. The middle
classes were fairly liberal in theology and, despite the best efforts of
such evangelicals as Thomas Chalmers (Brown, 1987), the 'Protestant' working classes were largely irreligious.

The potential for conflict was also reduced by the failure of
political and ethnic lines of division to match and reinforce each
other. The evangelicals in the Free Church tended to be Liberals, as
for quite different reasons, did the Irish. The formation of the
Liberal Unionists offered the possibility of a tidying-up and a clear
confrontation but the Irish did not play their part. Against the advice
of such men as Hugh Murnin, the Stirlingshire miners' leader and
later Labour MP, to form a separate Catholic Christian Democratic

party, the Irish and their descendants, once the home rule issue was resolved, threw themselves into secular labour movement politics.

In one of its last displays of hostility to the 'Irish' (which by now meant the Scottish grandsons and granddaughters of the Irish) the Church of Scotland General Assembly in 1923 heard a report entitled *The Menace of the Irish Race to our Scottish Nationality* (Handley, 1964, 358). The authors had no complaint about 'the presence of an Orange population in Scotland. They are of the same race as ourselves and of the same Faith, and are readily assimilated to the Scottish race'. But Irish Catholics 'cannot be assimilated and absorbed into the Scottish race. They remain a people by themselves, segregated by reasons of their race, their customs, their traditions, and, above all, by their loyalty to their Church, and are gradually and inevitably dividing Scotland racially, socially and ecclesiastically.' (Handley, 1964, 358.) This was, actually, not the case. Race turned out to be a far less enduring property than was thought in the 1920s. Their 'customs' turned out to be those of socio-economic circumstance, and changed rapidly with increased standard of living. For example, despite the church's position on contraception, the Catholic birth rate declined to the mean (Kendrick *et al.*, 1984). Which left only loyalty to their church and even this was less than ironclad. Although the Catholic Church hierarchy was widely seen to have 'won' when the 1918 Education Act had consolidated the separation of state and Catholic schooling and provided state funding for Catholic schools while leaving the church in control of hiring, especially after 1946, an increasing number of middle-class Catholic parents sent their children to state schools. The problems of definition and identification make statistical certainty difficult but we know that the rate of 'lapsing' from the church was high: one estimate suggests that 16 per cent of the total population of Scots Catholics 'fell away' between 1951 and 1976 (Bruce, 1985, 222).

An important part of the decline of anti-Catholicism in Scotland was Scottish impotence. Even if most Protestant Scots had shared the sentiments of a Cormack or a Ratcliffe, they would have been able to do little about it because the British political system is heavily centralised and the centre lies outside Scotland. Unlike the Stormont administration in Ulster, there was no power base in Scotland which could be used to reward Orange Scots. The voters who elected John Cormack to the council but voted for a Labour man for Westminster knew the futility of sending one or even twenty Protestant Action members to Westminster. A similar lack of autonomy was beginning to affect Scottish capital. Sectarianism was

most successfully reproduced where, as in the once strongly Orange
Vale of Leven, factory owners lived locally, were elders of the kirk,
patronised local football teams and sports associations, and shared
the same values and prejudices as their skilled Orange workforce
which acted to close out the initially unskilled immigrants. In the last
half of the nineteenth century four firms in the Vale, all in the
printing, dyeing and bleaching business, employed 6000 workers
(Gallacher, 1982). By 1952 only 1700 people (two-thirds of them
women) worked in the textile industry. About 2000 out of a local
working population of about 12,000 worked on the Strathleven
industrial estate, three-quarters of them employed by just two
American firms. And this pattern was repeated all over central and
lowland Scotland. As small companies became absorbed by increasingly distant companies, the communal ties which linked masters
and men broke down. Scottish industry became increasingly subject
to the universalistic values of multinational corporate capitalism. An
English manager answerable to an American board was not interested in the religion of his workforce.

THE ULSTER TROUBLES AND SCOTLAND

The outbreak of the recent period of civil unrest in Belfast and Derry
in 1968 was as much a surprise to Scots as it was to the English. This
section will consider the responses to the Troubles of the Orange
Order, the Churches, and the mass media.

Orangeism and paramilitaries

The modern Ulster Volunteer Force (UVF) actually predates the
Troubles and was a response to what some working-class Protestants *anticipated* would be the consequences of Prime Minister
Terence O'Neill's liberal reforming unionism rather than to the civil
rights movement and the later resurgence of the IRA. Initially slight,
recruitment increased rapidly in the early 1970s. Whereas the UVF
was small, secretive and from the first openly willing to use terror in
its 'armed struggle' against republicanism, the Ulster Defence Association (UDA) was a large federation of popular vigilante groups
which sprung up in areas of Belfast in 1972 in response to communal
violence.

At first many Scottish Orangemen were keen to join in the
defence of their 'own people'. In 1971, Scottish Grand Secretary
John Adam toured Orange halls and enrolled ex-servicemen and
men with National Service or Territorial Army experience who were
willing to go to Ulster to fight. Reports vary of the numbers who
signed up but it was common for west coast lodges to produce 15,

20, and 25 volunteers. If repeated throughout the Order this would have meant some 3000 volunteers. Those I have interviewed insist that they were in earnest and that it was only because the UVF said that it did not yet need them (the UDA had not yet emerged as a powerful and coherent force) that they did not go. Already there was a division between the leadership and some of the rank-and-file members. The latter thought they were being asked to ready themselves to fight alongside the UVF. The leadership believed they were compiling a register of people willing to aid the 'constitutional authority'.

Generally speaking it was those working-class Protestants with the closest family and friendship ties to Ulster who were most active in support of the UDA and UVF. Initially many of those who joined Scottish support cells of the two organisations confined their activities to fund-raising. However welcome such help was, some argued that 'giving them fucking tinned food was nae bloody use. The IRA was using guns and bombs. Were our people supposed to throw fucking Spam at 'em?'

Some weapons were collected and shipped to Ulster but they were often of very poor quality. The main purchase of one UVF cell, which led to them all being imprisoned, was of a fifty-year old rusted-up revolver which had been found on the beach at Dysart. The only time a Scottish group is known to have got a large consignment of arms – when a young gunshop assistant murdered his manager and sold some seventeen rifles and handguns to the 'Supreme Commander' of the UDA in Scotland – they never made it to Belfast. Instead they were transported ineptly around Scotland, sometimes by couriers who had to be coerced, before coming to lie in a damp cellar where they stayed for sixteen months until all the handlers were lifted by the police. In all some thirty men were convicted for their part in a series of crimes which were of no assistance at all to the UDA in Ulster.

What was of more use was the steady trickle of mining gelignite which found its way to Ulster. The typical career was of a UDA or UVF cell coming across a miner who either volunteered or was persuaded to steal four or five sticks at a time from the coal face. This would be accumulated and shipped as a decent load to Belfast (in one interception, the police found 263 sticks of gelignite and 275 lbs. of sodium chlorate, the basis for home-made explosives), where it was used with fatal consequences by loyalist paramilitaries. In addition, Scots formed an important link in a chain of small arms being sent from Canada to Ulster via Liverpool or Glasgow.

Generally speaking the greater the public support for an activity, the larger the numbers involved, the more selective an organisation can be, and the higher the degree of commitment it gets from its members. The lack of Scottish support for paramilitary activity can be seen in the weakness of many UDA and UVF cells. Around a nucleus of two or three highly committed men there was usually a penumbra of associates who felt some sympathy for Ulster Protestants and were attracted by the military trappings but who had little depth of commitment. The shift from fund-raising into gun-running and acts of political violence in Scotland itself was enough to cause such people to re-evaluate their involvement. The lack of intense commitment explains the willingness of many low-level UDA and UVF men to co-operate enthusiastically with the police. In 1979 some ninety or so people connected with the UDA in Paisley and Dumfries were arrested by the police; only two of them did not make a statement. With one or two notable exceptions, even most *leaders* of UDA and UVF cells proved only too willing to co-operate with the police.

And it was not only after arrest that such co-operation was common. Although my records are not exhaustive, I have details of 24 major cases relating to paramilitary activity (almost all of them under the Prevention of Terrorism Acts) and every one of them either originated with, or was facilitated by, volunteered evidence. Although the circumstance of having to justify 'grassing' people who were previously one's comrades encourages people to find honourable reasons for their betrayal, I think we can take as genuine the professed reluctance to bring Ulster's troubles to Scotland and I offer the following as an illustration. On 10 March 1973 an explosion ripped a hole in the roof of the Apprentice Boys' Hall in Landressy Street, Bridgeton, in Glasgow. A few hours after the blast the following letter was sent to the *Daily Record*:

> Sir, I am writing to you because I feel that the troubles which have taken place in Northern Ireland over the last few years could be inflicted on us in Glasgow. I am sorry but I must remain anonymous – I would be killed if it was known I was informing against the Protestant cause. My main reason for doing so is that I have young children and have fears for their safety should the outrages which are happening in Belfast happen in Glasgow. I foned [sic] 999 about one o'clock this morning and told them that big Bill Campbell and another man, George – I don't know his second name – had taken explosives into the hall in Landressy Street. I know for a fact that yesterday afternoon the same two men collected about 20 sticks of gelly from a butcher's shop in Bridgeton.[1]

According to the writer, the explosives had been destined for the

Catholic chapel in Clyde Street. But they never made it: the gelignite was unstable and exploded while Campbell and Martin were at a meeting in the hall. When, six years later, the same UVF group bombed two Glasgow pubs frequented by Catholics, the police were again much aided by advance information about the group.

Scottish opinion leaders united to condemn the pub bombings. In justifying what he described as exemplary sentences, Lord Ross said the trial had:

> revealed an appalling picture of a gang of thugs intent on obtaining arms and explosives to be sent to Northern Ireland to assist other violent men engaged there in illegal and dreadful sectarian fights. That is bad enough. But in addition explosives had not only been accumulated in Scotland but used here. To all decent minded people here, the activities of the accused are seen for what they are – wicked, brutal and senseless. The accused have really chosen to wage war against society and society must be protected. This court always takes a most serious view of crimes involving arms and explosives and those involved can expect no mercy ... Others who may be tempted to continue evil work of this kind should realise that they will be liable to similar or even greater sentences. (*Scotsman*, 23 June 1979.)

Orange Lodge Grand Secretary David Bryce agreed: 'The sentences will be a warning to other people who think there is something romantic about obtaining arms. We in the Orange Order certainly do not condone violence nor do we condone the gathering of arms. There is no place in our organisation for people like those convicted or for anyone involved in paramilitary organisations. (*Glasgow Herald*, 17 June 1979.) That the legal establishment shared Lord Ross's view is clear from the subsequent pattern of sentencing which has reached some sort of record with the sentences for the Perth UDA group found guilty of making ammunition. The supposed ring-leader and instigator, a man with no previous record, was given sixteen years for conspiracy to further the aims of an illegal organisation.

We should be clear about the extent of support for these activities. Roddy MacDonald's claim in 1976 of thousands of UDA members was an exaggeration even then. Today there are at most a few hundred people who are involved in some minor way in actively supporting the Ulster Protestant paramilitaries and most of them confine themselves to fund-raising.

The initial response of the Orange Order leadership to the civil rights movement was to endorse the conservative Ulster unionist view that the unrest was simply old republicanism in new clothes

and to make loudly supportive noises. John Adam's enrolling of
potential volunteers has already been mentioned. There was a
considerable increase in the number of Orangemen crossing to
Ulster for the 12th of July marches. In 1970 the chartered MV
Manxman took over a thousand Scots Orangemen from Ardrossan
to Belfast and the *Scottish Daily Express*'s Jack Webster claims that
there were 4000 Scots at Finaghy field.

In 1969 and 1970 thirty-eight people were killed in the Ulster
Troubles. 1971 and 1972 saw a rapid increase with 174 people dying
in 1971 and a further 186 dying in the first six months of 1972
(Flackes and Elliott, 1989, 411-12). In that year, the *Scottish Daily
Express* headlined its Twelfth issue; 'Scots in Belfast Frontline': 'Ten
thousand Scots Orangemen flooded into Belfast yesterday to join in
the flag celebrations'. In a militant rejection of appeals for the
demonstrations to be called off, Scottish Grandmaster Thomas Orr
said before sailing: 'We will march on Wednesday no matter what
happens. If it does erupt into civil war then I'm sure that many Scots
will want to remain. (*Scottish Daily Express*, 11 July 1972.) In an
emotional speech of support at the Finaghy field, Orr echoed the
Marquis of Graham in repeating his assertion of support: 'We shall
support you in any way and in every way we possibly can ... I assure
you, friends, our offer of help is no empty promise.' (*Scottish Daily
Express*, 13 July 1972.) That help took a number of forms. Partly to
counter the propaganda value of Catholic families being evacuated
to the Republic, the Order organised some small-scale 'evacuations'
of Ulster Protestants. During the 1974 Ulster Workers' Council
Strike, the Order sent food to Belfast. A number of west coast lodges
offered a social service of 'rest and recreation' for loyalists from
particularly troubled areas. The murder of four Orangemen in
Tullyvallen Orange Hall in Newtownhamilton, South Armagh in
September 1975 produced another brief bout of enthusiasm for
aiding Ulster Protestants. There was excited talk about evacuating
the Protestants of South Armagh and one district lodge bankrupted
itself buying camp beds and other emergency supplies for the
evacuation. Grand Lodge sent a delegation to Belfast which had
talks with a group of paramilitaries (*Irish Times*, 9 December 1975).
The Glasgow County Grand Lodge established an Ulster Relief
Fund (which still exists) which paid for some Protestants to be
brought to Scotland for holidays but did little more (it is maintained
now in case civil war breaks out in Ulster and mass relief is needed).

But as the conflict went on, and as more became known about
the activities of loyalist paramilitaries, the Order worked to distance
itself from the UDA and UVF. In the autumn of 1976 Roddy

MacDonald declared in a television interview that he would be happy to buy arms and ship them to Ulster. Leading lodge officials tried to expel MacDonald but the 300 delegates to a special disciplinary hearing of Grand Lodge refused to agree that he had brought the Order into disrepute. Clearly their sympathy for what MacDonald was doing persuading them to 'believe' his claim to have been manipulated and misrepresented by the media. The five most senior officials – including Grand Master Orr who had previously promised to do 'anything' to help Ulster Protestants – threatened to resign unless the annual general meeting a week later supported a motion 'which utterly rejected all support, be it active or tacit, of terrorist organizations, whose actions contravene the law of the land'. Grand Lodge supported the motion overwhelmingly. MacDonald refused to do the honourable thing and resign and his membership of the Order again became a public issue when he led a party of Scots to Belfast to help the UDA in the 1977 loyalist strike.

By now the Orange leadership was committed to distancing itself from its more militant members. What the hierarchy wanted was to make the Order's reality accord with its professed self-image. While recognising that most members were working class, David Bryce, Grand Secretary, offered the following observations about the Order:

> We require our members to be not only Christians but church members. We bar anyone with a criminal record. Hooligans are the last kind of people we want ... We are devoted to the Reformed Church and the Protestant succession. We are pledged to uphold the Constitution but not without change. Believing as we do in the principles of freedom and liberty, we have thrown our weight behind a Scottish Assembly. We have made representations on the abortion laws and demanded better medical treatment for women in the West of Scotland. We have made representations to Spain and Russia on questions of individual freedom. On upholding the law and the good of society, it is foolish to think we are simply an anti-Catholic organization. We do want to sustain the Protestant religion in its purest form. We do want an end to segregated schools. But remember too that we oppose all disruptive and destructive organizations ... We are against all terrorist groups and armed men who seek to usurp the rule of law, regardless of their motivation. (Graham, 1978.)

The ethos of the Order was called into question again by the formation in 1980 of the Scottish Loyalists, a group of mostly young impatient Orangemen and Apprentice Boys of Derry who had become frustrated with the police's willingness to allow Troops Out marches in Scotland. Their response was to organise counter-demonstrations and do everything possible to stop the marches. The street set-pieces became more frequent when, as a response to the 1981 hunger strike and the death of Bobby Sands and nine other republicans, a number of republican flute bands were started in Govan, Coatbridge and Dumbarton, among other places (Freeman, 1986). One short-lived band from New Stevenson, Ayrshire demonstrated its allegiance to the Irish Republican Socialist Party by calling itself the Noel Little/Ronnie Bunting Flute Band but most supported the IRA. While the Order condemned such parades they also condemned the counter-demonstrations.

A second source of tension within the Order was the response to the planned papal visit in May 1982. To many Orangemen it seemed not enough to organise petitions and well-behaved demonstrations. They wanted to make sure that if the visit did go ahead it was heavily disrupted. A vice-chairman of the Scottish Loyalists said: 'We have plans to smash the Mass and wreck the Papal visit to Scotland. If the police try to stop us we will fight them. If the police want blood or the streets, they will get it.' Generally speaking the Orangemen who support the paramilitaries are those least interested in the religious aspects of Orangeism and prefer to see their activity as 'political' (the Young Cowdenbeath Volunteers Flute Band, for example, has Catholic members). But they were still disappointed with the Order's reluctance to engage in active 'struggle' against the papal visit. And, however unjustly, they blamed the Orange leadership for the visit passing off almost untouched by demonstrations.

The Order's response to the 1986 accord between the British and Dublin governments was also perceived by many rank-and-file Orangemen as weak. Traditionally the Order has refrained from initiating its own politics and has supported the 'unionist' (i.e. Conservative) candidates in elections. David Bryce, who was instrumental in trying to purge the Order of paramilitary elements, broke with this tradition and launched the Scottish Unionist Party which threatened spoiling election campaigns. First pronouncements talked of maximising publicity by fielding anti-Accord candidates in English constituencies. Four months later the SUP threatened to field only nine candidates, all in Scottish seats. Then it threatened to field no candidates but to advise supporters to vote for the candidate most likely to defeat the Conservative. In fact, very few of those involved ever had any intention of standing. The idea was a publicity stunt and it was fortunate that the near eradication of Tories from Scotland gave the Scottish media such a powerful story that the futility of the SUP plan was never highlighted.

The most recent form in which the argument within the Order has been cast concerns uniforms. Partly inspired by the politicisation of young Catholics through republican flute bands, some young men in Fife in September 1987 formed the Young Cowdenbeath Volunteers flute band and took as their uniforms and banners replicas of those of the 1914 14th battalion of the Royal Irish Rifles. At first hearing this sounds like the sort of celebration of British martial tradition that the Order should very much favour. But the uniforms presented a perfect ambiguity. The 14th battalion is what the 1914 Young Citizens Volunteers (which was part of Sir Edward Carson's Ulster Volunteer Force) became when it was incorporated in the regular army and the Cowdenbeath band had chosen their own name so that their initials were also 'YCV'. Thus what superficially appeared as an act of military remembrance could also be seen as a sign of support for the present-day and illegal UVF.

On the 1st July Orange parade in Broxburn, West Lothian, the YCV band was ordered off the parade by Grand Master Magnus Bain, but despite the police becoming involved, the band insisted on marching. A number of bandsmen who had already played through came back to line their way and applaud them onto the field. They halted in front of the saluting platform and played the Wild Colonial Boy – the anthem of the original YCV. Clearly infuriated, Bain at one point turned his back on the band and scuffles broke out. A number of collarettes were taken off and thrown at the platform. There appeared to be considerable rank-and-file support for the YCV band.

A further and current instance of the rift between the leadership and some of the rank-and-file is the recent attempt to discipline JG MacLean for bringing the Order into disrepute. Since 1971 when he stood for the council in John Cormack's old seat of Leith, MacLean has been the leader of loyalism in Edinburgh. He was vice-president of Cormack's Protestant Action and is District Master of the Edinburgh District of the Orange Order. There were a number of charges concerning giving unauthorised statements to the media and not punishing Orangemen for allowing a paramilitary display and fundraising for loyalist prisoners at a dance but, to quote from the Grand Lodge minutes, his main offence was that he was the:

> spokesman for the Edinburgh Loyalist Coalition which resulted in the Orange Order in Lothian Region being defined as 'sectarian' in the Chief Constable's report of 29 August 1988. Also that because he 'could not give any form of guarantee that there would be no violence should Republican parades be permitted' as spokesman of the Edinburgh Loyalist Coalition

and the known District Master/Organiser of Orange parades in
Edinburgh which resulted in the Regional Council on 4 October 1988 approving recommendations from the Chief Constable imposing new conditions on [Orange] sectarian parades.
Despite the slightly awry grammar, the nature of the argument is
clear. MacLean was willing to organise counter-demonstrations to
republican parades even if that meant restrictions on Orange demonstrations and gave liberal critics another stick with which to beat
the Order; the Order's national leadership was not. MacLean could not
be disciplined through his private lodge, District lodge or County
lodge because he had too much support. So the case was taken at a
full meeting of the 300 or so members of the national Grand Lodge
and the vote went in MacLean's favour. A clear majority decided he
had not brought the Order into disrepute by his actions.

These disputes all point to a major division in the Order. The
national leadership, supported by some of the older members, wish
to make the Order what its documents claim it to be: an organisation
of church-going respectable temperant Christians. Given that
church membership is no longer popular – in the lowlands basically
only the middle classes are church-going – and given that the
Protestant churches have become more liberal and ecumenical, this
was always going to be difficult. An anecdote illustrates the problem.
Law 3, Section II of the 1986 *Laws and Constitutions of the Loyal
Orange Institution of Scotland* states that 'Before a candidate is admitted, the Lodge must be satisfied that he is of the Protestant faith,
[and] is not married to a Roman Catholic'. An Orangeman's private
lodge questioned his marriage to an ex-Roman Catholic. He insisted
that she regularly attended the local Church of Scotland. The lodge
asked for a letter from the woman's minister to establish her *bona
fides*. When asked, the minister refused, because he did not see that
it was any of the lodge's business. The Orangeman suggested that
members of the lodge attend the kirk themselves where they would
see his wife worshipping. A few months later when the matter was
again raised, it turned out that none of his accusers had attended
services at the local kirk! The matter was allowed to drop.

The tension between the middle-class kirk elders such as Bryce
and Bain and the working-class members is amplified by the Order's
response to the Northern Ireland conflict. Middle- and working-
class Protestants in Ulster differ in their attitudes to violence, not
least because the working class bears the brunt of IRA activity.
Those furthest from day-to-day conflict are least likely to think it
appropriate to engage in paramilitary activity. Scots contacts with,
and responses to, Ulster work sideways – middle class to middle

class and working class to working class – and thus repeat the Ulster tensions in Scottish Orangeism. The Orange leadership wants to confine its acti-vities to making representations to government, holding demonstrations, and – as in the Scottish Unionist Party idea – attempting to win publicity for the unionist cause. Parts of the working-class membership (and large parts, if the votes in the MacDonald and MacLean trials are any guide) are more sympathetic to the paramilitaries, more determined to attack manifestations in Scotland of Irish republicanism, and angry that the leadership is so unresponsive.

The churches

The rapid decline in the popularity of anti-Catholicism in the Church of Scotland from the end of the last century has already been mentioned. Ratcliffe and Cormack were almost without clerical support; what little they had came from eccentrics and independent evangelicals. The difficult life of Jacob Primmer has been described. The kirk's response to the recent unrest in Northern Ireland has been to become even more deliberately ecumenical, a process which can be very clearly seen in the improvement of relationships with the Catholic Church hierarchy. The deliberate cultivation of ties with the Vatican reached its climax in May 1982 when Pope John Paul II visited Scotland and was invited to New College (the Church of Scotland's main theological faculty) where, under the gaze of John Knox's statue, he was greeted as a brother in Christ by the Moderator of the General Assembly and other church leaders.

In the nineteenth century, many Presbyterian ministers were Orange chaplains. Although it was the independent Brisby who organised the UVF colour parade, there were two kirk ministers on the platform and the colours were dedicated by a Professor of Church History. In the 1950s, the Grand Master was a Church of Scotland minister – Alan D. Hasson. Now there are only a handful of ministers in the Order and the most prominent – Arnold Fletcher – is in his seventies. It has become increasingly common for church bodies to question the legitimacy of the Order. In 1979 the Jedburgh Presbytery reacted to the formation of a new lodge in the Borders by asking its members to 'earnestly consider whether the mainly "anti" emphasis which appears in Orange activities is the best way of upholding New Testament Christianity' (*Glasgow Herald*, 26 April 1979).

The Scottish newspapers

A long and close reading of Scottish newspapers since 1968 suggests

two things: the absence of any special sympathy for Ulster Protestants and a deliberate censorship of news about Scottish sectarianism. Taking the second point first, there has been a deliberate
playing down of stories of Orange and Republican demonstrations
and of routine small-scale sectarian violence in such towns as
Coatbridge, Airdrie and Motherwell. When I was doing the research
for *No Pope of Rome*, a well-known Scottish journalist, who was also
a Christian, asked me why I wanted to write about such matters:
'You'll just give them credibility and stir it up!' In 1981 and 1982
there were a number of vicious sectarian attacks in Coatbridge and
Dumbarton and it is widely reported by well-informed sources that
senior Strathclyde police officers called a meeting of editors and
asked them to play down reports of these incidents for fear of
provoking further responses.

The Ulster coverage of the major Scottish papers does not appear
to have been markedly different to that of the English papers. The
Scottish Daily Express and the *Glasgow Herald* did not give obviously
more room to Ulster than did English papers aimed at comparable
readerships: at first the coverage was extensive, but by the middle
1970s only the most appalling outrages merited the front page. For
example, in November 1972 the *Scottish Daily Express* gave more
space to its spurious discovery of Nazi Martin Bormann in Latin
America than it did to Ulster.

One can find particular parochial interests. The *Scottish Daily
Express* (23 August 1969) ran the story of the establishment of a
three-man commission under the chairmanship of Sir John Hunt to
consider the conduct of policing in Northern Ireland as a personality
feature about one of the three, Glasgow's Chief Constable Sir James
Robertson. When interviewed about his task, Sir John managed
completely to miss the political importance of what was seen by
unionists as a threat to a loyal and hard-pressed force of brave men,
and by nationalists as long-overdue examination of a sectarian
militia: 'I know Belfast well and have been in the city many times.
Football matches are frequently arranged between the RUC and
Glasgow forces. In fact, a police bowling team came over only a
month ago to play in the annual contest. They are a friendly lot.' The
murder of Scottish soldiers might be given a lot of space (noticeably
less so as the years passed) but this is because they are Scots rather
than because Scots feel close to Ulstermen. Editorially the *Scottish
Daily Express* has maintained an 'even-handed' moderate unionist
position on Northern Ireland. At the beginning, there was some
sympathy for the civil rights movement, and until it was suspended
in 1972, there was considerable criticism of the intransigence of

Stormont. Although some reports of rioting might have made it a little clearer that a lot of it was done by *Protestants*, that the paper was unionist and Scottish does not seem to have produced a deliberate attempt to blame everything on republicans. Coverage of Ian Paisley, for example, was every bit as hostile as in the English press, and on 21 October 1972 a *Scottish Daily Express* editorial commented on William Craig's 'shoot to kill' call by suggesting that 'Mr Whitelaw ought to consider seriously whether Mr Craig should be interned for incitement'.

In terms of insight and understanding, the *Scottish Daily Express*'s perceptions were no more acute than those of English papers. Violence was attributed to 'A small band of evil or crazed individuals [which] is trying to destroy civilised life in Northern Ireland' (9 February 1971) and the offered solution was more 'Christian common sense'. The leader writer's response to the UDA's confrontations with the army was to be equally critical of all parties in Ulster: 'It should be brought home to the Irish people that if they are intent on national suicide the British Army cannot and will not be involved' (18 October 1972). It was clear that, for the *Express*, Ulster Protestants were part of the 'Irish people' and as much part of the problem as militant republicans.

When not avoiding Scottish sectarianism, the *Scottish Daily Express*'s approach was to accentuate the positive. For example, in 1969 when Derry was burning, the leader writer took as his third topic the story of a Catholic priest organising a collection to help pay for the repair of Bargeddie, Lanarkshire, Orange Hall which had been defaced by vandals, and commented 'So by good men and good will are the hooligans defeated' (13 August 1969).

ULSTER AND THE DECLINE OF SCOTTISH SECTARIANISM

I am suggesting that the main consequence for Scottish Protestants of the Ulster conflict has been polarisation. A very small minority of mainly working-class Protestants in the Lowland urban belt, generally those with strong personal ties to Ulster, have become active in the cause of Ulster loyalism, some to the extent of illegality. But the majority of Scottish Protestants have gone in the other direction. Their main response has been to distance themselves from those who were once 'our own people'. In so far as they think about Ulster, they see it as a salutary lesson of what happens when one allows religion and politics to mix. Those with influence in the churches and in the media have deliberately promoted liberal and ecumenical positions. Even in the Orange Order, the leadership has moved a long way from the martial rhetoric of the early 1970s. The increasingly hostile attitude of many Scots to anything which smacks of 'sectarianism' has increased pressure on the Orange Order. Although the Orange hierarchy still petitions and marches on behalf of Protestant principles, in order to counter its increasingly negative image it has to act even more aggressively against those of its own membership who wish to be active in support of Ulster loyalists.

This goes on against a background of the disappearance of sectarianism in Scotland itself. The social, political, and economic conditions which eroded religio-ethnic divisions have already been mentioned, but the overall picture can be suggested by pointing simply to the extent to which the 'Irish' and Scottish Catholics have become assimilated. There are many indices of assimilation, but the two main ones are improving socio-economic status and intermarriage. Like many immigrant communities of industrialising societies, the Irish came into Scotland at the bottom and for a number of generations formed the lowest layers of the class structure. This has now changed so that Catholics, most of whom are the descendants of the Irish, have a socio-economic profile very similar to that of Protestants (Bruce, 1988).

Enduring discrimination requires that one be able to distinguish those against whom one wishes to discriminate. Here intermarriage rates become significant. A survey of 'mixed marriages' in Ulster regarded it as news that the rate had increased from 2.9 per cent of all marriages contracted between 1953 and 1957, and 5 per cent between 1968 and 1972, to nearly 10 per cent of all marriages between 1978 and 1982. Comparable figures are not available for all Scottish marriages but we know that by the 1970s almost half of all marriages contracted by Scottish Catholics were with non-Catholics (McRoberts, 1979, 237). Compare this to the closed nature of Catholic society in the mid-nineteenth century: in Greenock in 1851, some 80 per cent of Irish men and women married within their own number (Gallagher, 1987b, 49). Even in the circles from which the Scottish paramilitaries are recruited, mixed marriages are common.

Writing in the late 1940s, Handley was struck by the extent to which the descendants of the Irish still formed closed ghetto-like communities. This is no longer the case today. Catholics have spread out and have become absorbed with a very large number no longer being identifiable even as 'lapsed' Catholics (Piggott, 1979, 220-3).

Had Ulster not erupted one might have expected the slow process of assimilation and the attenuation of differences to have continued evenly. What the Ulster crisis has done is to accelerate the process.

In small pockets there has been an increase in support for Irish republicanism and for Irish cultural activities: in clubs in Garngad, Paisley, and Coatbridge, money is raised for the IRA with 'buy a bullet' dances. There has been a matching increase in support for Protestant paramilitary activity. But these are the responses of very small minorities. Generally we can accept Gallagher's conclusion that:

> While residual sympathies were revived by post-1968 events the great bulk of the Scottish population showed no desire to make the Ulster quarrel its own ... Those who wished to make it a pressing local issue were thoroughly isolated from the bulk of public opinion. Scots who might have half-tolerated religious or pro-Irish zealots because there did not seem to be any harm in doing so or because they suddenly remembered their own Catholic Irish ancestry or Calvinist childhood, emphatically refused to give them houseroom once the toll of death and destruction mounted just sixty miles from the Scottish coast. (1987, 294.)

Even for those Scottish Protestants who are involved in fund-raising for loyalist prisoners or less legal forms of displays of solidarity with Ulster, their involvement with Ulster is only loosely connected with anti-Catholicism within Scotland. A leading Scottish UDA man, in talking about the future of Ulster, found nothing odd in drawing on Protestant-Catholic relations in Scotland as an example of the way forward: 'Like we do here, [Ulster loyalists] have got to accept that the Taigs are there. They're not going to go away. They've got to give them a bit more, give them a say in things and get on with it. It can never go back to the way it was.'

ACKNOWLEDGEMENTS

In addition to the editors, I would like to thank David Bryce, 'James Costello', and 'Doctor Death' for their comments on drafts of this essay. Harry Reid and the *Glasgow Herald* very kindly gave me access to their cuttings library, much of the original research was funded by the Economic and Social Research Council, and The Queen's University of Belfast has been generous with study leave; I would like to thank all three institutions.

NOTE

1 When I first used this illustration in *No Pope of Rome* I did not notice some inconsistencies of prose style and spelling which now seem glaring. The author combines being unable to spell 'phone' with being able to correctly use the future conditional. It may well be that this is a result of journalistic tampering, either to tidy it up or to make

something which was very articulate read more authentically working class. I could not find the original, which was given to the police, but the journalist who reported the story believed it to be genuine and recalls that the police took it to be authentic. That the facts in the letter are correct can give us reasons to accept the sentiment as genuine.

REFERENCES

BLUMER, H. (1954) Public Opinion and Public Opinion Polling. In D. Katz, D. Cartwright, S. Eldersveld and A. M. Lee (eds.), *Public Opinion and Propaganda: a Book of Readings*, New York: Holt, Rinehart and Winston, 70-8.

BROWN, C. (1987) *A Social History of Religion in Scotland*, London: Methuen.

BRUCE, S. (1985) *No Pope of Rome: Militant Protestantism in Modern Scotland*, Edinburgh: Mainstream.

BRUCE, S. (1988) Sectarianism in Scotland: a contemporary assessment and explanation, *Scottish Government Yearbook*, pp. 150-66.

CAMPBELL, A. B. (1979) *The Lanarkshire Miners- a Social History of their Trade Unions, 1775-1874*, Edinburgh: John Donald.

FLACKES, W. and ELLIOTT, S. (1989) *Northern Ireland: a Political Directory*, Belfast: The Blackstaff Press.

FREEMAN, J. (1986) Republicans Marching to the Scottish Beat, *Glasgow Herald*, 15 September.

GALLACHER, R. (1982) The Vale of Leven 1914-75: changes in working class organization and action. In T. Dickson (ed.), *Capital and Class in Scotland*, Edinburgh: John Donald, 210-32.

GALLAGHER, T. (1987a) *Edinburgh Divided: John Cormack and No Popery in the 1930s*, Edinburgh: Polygon.

GALLAGHER, T. (1987b) *Glasgow: the Uneasy Peace*, Manchester: Manchester University Press.

GALLAGHER, T. (1989) Bearing of the green, *Observer Scotland*, 9 April, 12-13.

GRAHAM, C. (1978) Now is the time to get things back in Order, *Scottish Daily Express*, 8 December.

HANDLEY, J. (1938) *The Irish in Modern Scotland*, Cork: Cork University Press.

HANDLEY, J. (1964) *The Irish in Scotland*, Glasgow: James Burns.

HOLMES, R. F. (1985) *Our Presbyterian Heritage*, Belfast: Presbyterian Church in Ireland.

JOHNSTON, T. (1920) *The History of the Working Classes in Scotland*, Glasgow: Forward Publishing.

KENDRICK, S., BECHOFER, F., MCCRONE, D. (1984) Recent trends in fertility differentials in Scotland. In H. Jones (ed.) *Population Change in Contemporary Scotland*, Norwich, Geo Books, 33-52.

MACAFEE, W. and MORGAN, V. (1981) Population in Ulster 1660-1760. In P. Roebuck (ed.), *Plantation to Partition*, Belfast: The Blackstaff Press, 46-63.

McROBERTS, D. (1979) *Modern Scottish Catholicism 1878-1978*, Glasgow: Burns.

MURRAY, B. (1984) *The Old Firm: Sectarianism, Sport and Society in Scotland*, Edinburgh: John Donald.

PIGGOTT, C. A. (1979) A Geography of Religion in Scotland. Ph.D. thesis, Edinburgh University.

PRIMMER, J. (1916) *Life of Pastor Jacob Primmer*, Edinburgh: Wm Bishop.

RATCLIFFE, A. and Mrs (1933) *My Week in Gaol*, Glasgow: Scottish
   Protestant League.
SENIOR, H. (1966) *Orangeism in Ireland and Britain 1795-1835*, London:
   Routledge and Kegan Paul.
SUTHERLAND, I. (1981) Doing the Orange Walk, *New Society*, 9 July,
   49-50.
SMART, A. (1988) *Villages of Glasgow, vol.l*, Edinburgh: John Donald.
WOODS, I. Irish immigrants and Scottish radicalism, 1880-1906. In I.
   MacDougall (ed.), *Essays in Scottish Labour History*, Edinburgh: John
   Donald, 65-89.

Index